REAL BIRTH

Women Share
Their Stories

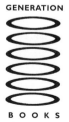

ROBIN GREENE

GENERATION

BOOKS

Published by Generation Books,
an imprint of Windows on History Press
604 Brookwood Drive
Durham, NC

Copyright © 2000 by Robin Greene

Design, editing, and production by Invisible Ink, NC
Printed in the United States of America

Library of Congress Cataloging-in-Publication data applied for

ISBN 0–9654499–3–9

REAL BIRTH

for
Michael, who cleared the path,
and for
Dan and Ben, whose journeys into this world
transformed my own journey through it

ACKNOWLEDGMENTS

I WANT TO OFFER MY heartfelt gratitude to the more than two hundred women with whom I spoke and to the seventy-six women I interviewed. Their time, honesty, and trust were generously given, and without their help this book could not have been written.

I also want to extend my profound thanks to Dr. Rick Randolph, whose gifts of patience, medical expertise, and friendship guided and encouraged me throughout this project.

I would also like to gratefully acknowledge the following individuals: Ruth Kravitz, for her close friendship, unflinching faith, and positive attitude; Julie Tetel, for her integrity, intelligence, and gift of partnership; Emily Colin, for her sharpness of eye and excellent critical sense; Pat Roberts, for all her encouragement over the many years of our friendship; Ethel and Burton Greene, for their unconditional love; Nancy and Joe Colonnese, for their constant love and support; Virginia Bell, for her enthusiasm and excellent feedback at critical moments; Frances Dowell, for the gift of her well-crafted words; Jen McCreary, for her transcription and listening skills; Maura High, for her concern for details; staff and board members at the North Carolina Writers' Network, for their support and friendship; Judas Riley Martinez for her encouragement and love; Carol White, for her constant smile, professionalism, and photocopying expertise; and to all my Methodist College colleagues and students who expressed their interest and good wishes.

CONTENTS

FOREWORD

Ariel Gore

ÕØ

WE TELL OUR BIRTHING STORIES to make sense out of the intrinsically irrational. And we listen to other mothers' stories because, more than any other rite of passage in our lives, giving birth shows each of us to be completely human beings. Take, for example, the thirty-six stories in this book. In each one, the voice of a whole woman sounds out loud and clear. Our birthing stories are stories about our children and about what really happens in childbirth, yes. But even more, they are stories about ourselves, stories about becoming ourselves.

I had my daughter when I was nineteen years old, broke, single. I was living in a converted wine cellar at the time and in a foreign country where, when it came down to it, I didn't even know the word for "push." I gave birth in a hospital surrounded by well-meaning fools, but refused their pain-killers.

And yet—whether you are married or single, an accomplished career woman or a wandering teenager, preparing to give birth in a hospital or at home, a mother-to-be or a mother of many—you can, I think, relate to my story. As I can to yours. We tell our birthing stories to remember. And we listen to other mothers' stories because we imagine their experiences can do something to prepare us, learning from women like Mary (who gave birth in an army hospital), Valerie (who had a good doula), Stacy (who sees birthing as a rite of passage), Christina (whose marriage fell apart after she got pregnant), Elli (whose child died after birth), Millie (who had triplets), and all the other mothers in this book.

When I was in labor, I still believed the popular myth that when it was all over, a "strange amnesia" would set in and I would forget the pain. I never did forget, but fearing that amnesia, I scrawled a panicked note to myself during transition: "NEVER DO THIS AGAIN." In *The American Way of Birth,* Jessica Mitford wrote that she was reassured to discover "the word 'travel' is derived from 'travail,' denoting the pains of childbirth. There is in truth a similarity between the two conditions." And she was right. The only other time I had scrawled those four words, I was on a thirty-six-hour bus trip down a half-paved Tibetan highway: "NEVER DO THIS AGAIN." Nine years later, and against my own wise warning, I hope for nothing more than to do it again someday. That's the funny thing about panicked notes—we never do seem to follow our own best advice.

When I had my daughter, the goddess smiled on us and gave me a short labor—I felt the first tightening at midnight and was a mother by morning. Had I the courage and resources for a home birth, it would have been uncomplicated, but because the nurses and doctors at the hospital had just gotten a bunch of new gadgets they wanted to try out, I was subjected to a fair amount of torture.

The Italian hospital staff left me alone through most of my early labor, and I did a good job scaring them away during transition by cursing in English when they tried to come near me with their needles. They laughed and called me "the Gypsy from the North." But just when I'd had enough of the natural hell of labor and I was crouched in the corner of the bathroom plotting my own suicide and several murders—my little hospital gown and out-of-control hair making me the picture-perfect lobotomy candidate—one of the nurses found me and, apparently sensing my vulnerability, started screaming at me in Italian. As I stood up, my water broke and the nurse shoved me into a wheelchair and pushed me into the dreaded delivery room. There, the torture crew lifted me out of the wheelchair, dropped me onto a metal table, clamped my ankles into restraints and started chanting "spingere" (push).

My sister and my baby's dad, who had gotten into the room somehow, screamed, "No drugs!" and held back a blond nurse with a giant needle in her hand. Meanwhile, apparently because I was not pushing hard enough, a second nurse held my jaw shut while a third produced a wide leather strap from beneath the table and pulled it down tight over my belly in a bizarre attempt to push the baby out herself. While I tried to push and keep track of all the insanity, a guy I'd never seen before (my OB was on vacation) stared between my legs, and then, shouting something, suddenly sliced into my perineum.

As he was reaching for the forceps he wouldn't need, my daughter popped out. A split second later, a nurse threw all the doctor's tools into a deep metal sink and they crashed, metal on metal, welcoming my daughter to this harsh, harsh world.

"NEVER DO THIS AGAIN," I had told myself. But when I think back on it now, I wouldn't trade that night for anything. I'd make better plans, yes. I'd remember to remember the word for "push." I'd stay home with a midwife. But I know better than to imagine that I'd have much more control over the whole fiasco. The Hindus were right, after all, when they attributed birth to Kali, the goddess of chaos. She smiles on us when we are giving birth—but she also makes us scream. And she never lets us forget that when we give birth to our children, we are also giving birth to ourselves as fully human beings.

PREFACE

ॐ

THE NARRATIVES IN THIS COLLECTION emerged from interviews with women who had recently given birth. To find those willing to speak candidly about their birthing experiences, I placed an advertisement in a national publication directed at new mothers. I received over two hundred responses, conducted seventy-six interviews, and selected thirty-six stories. I chose the stories of women from a range of socioeconomic circumstances and cultural backgrounds. There are stories from women who are well-off financially and from those who struggle to make ends meet. Some women are young, others are older. There are narratives from white women and from women of color. Some describe a first birth, others a second or third birth. Some women bring a strong religious faith to their stories, others do not. And while not all fifty states are represented, most geographic regions are.

Nearly all of the women interviewed for this book spoke to me by telephone. There were only a few I could meet and interview in person. Nevertheless, each of the interviews began as a formal, tape-recorded dialogue with a stranger, and ended as an intimate conversation with a friend. During most of the period that I worked on this project, I taught evening classes at a local college. Ordinarily, I'd arrive home around eight P.M., eat a quick dinner, get my young son Ben to sleep for the night, and conduct interviews from nine P.M. to midnight.

Usually, I sat on the floor in my half-darkened bedroom, listening to the strong voices of these women. I'd have the same list of prepared questions for all my interviews, but more often than not, I didn't ask them. I quickly learned never to fill a silence with a word of my own; the women I interviewed inevitably had a word more poignant, more accurate than any I could offer. When I relaxed and allowed my natural sympathies to guide me, the women I spoke with seemed encouraged toward greater openness, and I was encouraged toward more authentic listening. Later, these conversations were transcribed, condensed to eliminate redundancy, and my own voice as interviewer was edited out. I wanted no intrusions into the stories, no editorial voice to interfere.

Frequently, the women I interviewed asked that I correct their grammar; they didn't want to "sound bad" and were often afraid that worrying about correct speech would be distracting. And so, in the end, I did correct some grammar, occasionally adding missing words or rearranging paragraphs to forge necessary connections or to include vital information. But I have stayed true to the diction and speech patterns of the women whose stories are included here. Each narrative is prefaced by a brief biography, but I've omitted information on race, ethnicity, and religious identity to allow each woman's story to unfold naturally. When race or ethnicity becomes central to the narrative, it enters the narrative; when it is not central, that information goes unstated. Some names, locations, and identifying details have been altered at the request of the interviewees who wished to ensure their anonymity, but I have tried to preserve essential information so that the stories are consistent with each woman's recollections.

Often, while I was writing the book, curious well-wishers would question me about the veracity of the stories. They'd ask, "How do you know these women are telling the truth?" or "How can you be certain that they're remembering correctly?" My response was always the same. These women speak emotionally and credibly; they recollect details and specifics through the filters of their own psyches—but who doesn't? What we perceive to be true and what we remember as true becomes our truth. Our ongoing sense of reality depends on it.

The narratives that unfold in the following pages present the personal realities of thirty-six women as they remember their birthing experiences. Dr. Rick Randolph, a family physician who has delivered many babies over the years, reviewed the narratives and glossary to make certain that the medical information is accurate and correct. I'm grateful to Dr. Randolph for his help with this project, and I want to thank all the women I interviewed over the years for sharing their stories and making this book possible.

One

HOSPITAL BIRTHS

THE MAJORITY OF AMERICAN women choose a hospital as the place where they'd like to give birth. Frequently this decision is based on the long-held and widespread belief that a hospital provides the safest place for both mother and baby, but often it simply reflects the fact that a hospital offers the only choice available for those women who want a strong medical care component to their birthing experiences. In many areas of the country it is assumed that a woman will want to deliver in the local hospital; to consider alternatives is to challenge orthodox views of obstetrical care and to offend loving family members who only want "the best" for mother and baby. Many women have excellent hospital delivery experiences and feel quite satisfied with both the facility and the care they've received. But for other women, the institutional policies of the hospital don't allow them the birthing experience they had imagined or desired. As a result, issues of control, personal responsibility, and the lack of institutional flexibility sometimes enter into these women's stories.

Although each birth is unique, the first four stories presented here follow the most usual scenario—a vaginal birth without complications. Statistically, most women do deliver vaginally and most do so without medical problems. The fifth story in this section presents the account of a woman who had an emergency C-section with her first son. With her second pregnancy she is able to find a physician willing to allow her to try for a "vaginal birth after cesarean," or V-BAC, which she feels will allow her to have the birthing experience that she had "missed."

There are many medical risk factors that can indicate that a vaginal birth may not be in the best interest of either mother or child. And, for one mother in this section who chooses to have her children by cesarean, this form of delivery seems a preferable alternative to vaginal delivery. Nonetheless, for most expectant mothers, cesarean deliveries are a surprise and have the potential to leave the new mother feeling dissatisfied or disappointed. On the other hand, some women who have had C-sections feel satisfied and grateful to have received the expert medical attention they needed.

ॐ

Shoshana and her husband, Bruce, are both psychiatrists. They live outside New York City with their two boys, Gregory and Matthew, ages five and four years.

Doctors Make the Best Patients

I graduated with a BS in nursing in 1977, and the first job I got was at this little hospital in a very ethnic neighborhood. I worked primarily as a nurse in the labor and delivery suite. It wasn't a teaching hospital, and they had no interns or residents there, which meant that we had to be the ones to contact the clinic doctor on call when a woman got ready to deliver. I certainly learned a lot there. In fact, after a year of working full-time, I'd delivered so many babies and managed so many emergencies that I decided to go to medical school myself. I had to go back to college for two years to fulfill premedical requirements because my nursing background didn't fill the necessary prerequisites. I worked part-time for those two years and really blossomed—I enjoyed being a student.

I was living at home while I attended college. I remember one day my mom called the hospital while I was working. She said a letter just came from medical school. I told her, "Ma, I don't want you to open it, but if you hold it up to the light, can you read anything?" And she said, "Well, the first word is 'congratulations.'" I had been in the operating room, assisting a C-section. When I got this news, I walked right back in and said to the obstetrician, "Look, I'm really sorry, I can't help you with this anymore. I just got accepted into medical school, and I have to sit down for a few minutes." The patient was under general anesthesia, so I wasn't talking in front of her.

I went to medical school. Somewhere during that time, I got very captivated by psychiatry. I was getting older and a little tired. I hadn't met anyone yet, but I knew that I wanted to get married and have a family and that psychiatry would allow me to have both a professional and personal life.

After medical school, I took training in psychiatry. And that's where I met my husband—he was in his last year of training in the same program. We met in the psychiatric emergency room, which they call the Crisis Center. So I always say that ours was a romance begun in crisis.

When I graduated, I became medical director of the same Crisis Center where we had met. I was very ambitious and totally into it. After my second year there, we started to try to get pregnant, and lo and behold, we had trouble! We tried for about three years, then turned to a fertility clinic at the local medical center. In the first cycle, I got pregnant. It was classic! I mean, classic infertility! You get totally consumed by trying to get pregnant—crying when your period comes, regulating your love life. The whole nine yards. It can really devastate a marriage.

My husband and I were thrilled when I tested positive. I continued to work, but the whole nine months I had trouble concentrating on my job. I started to get really tuned in to my body. After having so much trouble getting pregnant, and being an older, first-time parent, everything else in my life paled in comparison to this pregnancy. I had been very ambitious, but now it just trickled away.

I was going to a group of fairly conservative doctors. Here I was, a physician myself, the wife of a physician, and the daughter-in-law of an obstetrician. The group had their own Lamaze training, and I remember going to that and being very turned off.

My husband came with me, but he was a little less passionate about how it was all going to happen. He wanted a healthy baby, and that was it. The group was clearly preparing patients for this group's particular way of practicing. The very first session dealt with subjects like "if you need a cesarean," and information about IVs, and blah, blah, blah. The instructor wasn't giving us choices. And I couldn't tolerate that. I went only a couple of times, then switched to a Bradley instructor at around six months.

My husband agreed and came with me to all the sessions. He learned how to help me relax. I was really terrified. I had been an OB nurse and had seen first-hand real complications. Back in 1977, they used a medicine commonly called Twilight Sleep. They put it into a vein, and, to use a technical term, the woman would go "crackers." She'd be messed up and in horrible pain—say and do strange things, and then not remember! There'd be women who'd stand up in their beds, trying to rip out the IVs, screaming things like, "Get this basketball off my leg!" They'd be out of their minds. It wasn't the way it was supposed to work. After witnessing a few of these, I would draw up the syringe, and squirt it down the sink. This is illegal, but I just couldn't give it to these women. I remember, one doctor had the nerve to say that he never had any problem with "his women" on this drug—but the truth is that none of the nurses were actually injecting it!

Anyway, I was terrified. I remember talking to my obstetrician and telling him what I didn't want. And he would hedge. He'd say, "Well, we don't shave anymore, and unless you need one, we don't give you an enema." They wanted to put in a Heplock in case they needed immediate access to a vein. I could understand that, but I didn't want to be hooked up to an IV. And they were already talking about an epidural if the pain got too bad. I was having trouble with this group and wasn't comforted by anything they said.

My due date was May 21. I quit work two weeks before because I wanted time for myself—time to think and feel, and get the baby's room ready.

I was worried that the contractions would be so overwhelming I wouldn't be able to cope. I was very anxious. I kept saying to my husband, "Bruce, make sure you tell them that I don't want this, that, and this. . . ." He's a very reasonable man and understood where I was coming from, but it was hard for him to get past his medical background. We made agreements and came to an understanding. I was expecting unendurable agony—the kind where you'd rather slit your throat than have to take another minute of the pain. That's what I was really prepared for!

May 21 was a Monday that year. All weekend long, I had terrible restlessness. The house was spotless, so the next thing I wanted to do was shop—every mall in a fifty-mile radius! I couldn't get enough. We went to two malls on that Sunday and watched the movie *The Hunt for Red October*. I kept having to get up, go to the bathroom and move my bowels. And I was having strong Braxton-Hicks contractions.

Sunday night when we turned in, nothing was really happening. Then at midnight, I woke up with contractions. I went to the bathroom and sort of hung out at the toilet. They became stronger and more regular; I began timing them. At about 1:00, I thought, *Well, I need some company,* and woke Bruce up. We went downstairs into the kitchen and timed them again. Bruce rubbed me. Then, all of a sudden, they went from twelve minutes apart to eight, then seven minutes. I was in pain, and I needed to work very actively with the contractions, but I never moaned or cried and never felt close to losing it.

I spent a lot of time on the toilet, rocking back and forth with the contractions. It felt like stomach flu, or the cramps you get with bad diarrhea. I knew that the best thing I could do was to stay home for as long as possible. Then, when the contractions became five minutes apart, I got very excited. I began pacing and singing, "It's a hap, hap, happy day!" Then, when a contraction came, I'd put my arms around Bruce's neck, and he would hold me, standing up in the middle of the kitchen. I would still sing, "It's a hap, hap, happy day" . . . and that's how I got through the contractions. "A hap, hap, happy day" . . . four minutes . . . then three minutes. . . . I looked at Bruce and said, "I think it's time to call the doctor." All the while, part of me, the clinical part, kept saying, *This woman's really cooking in labor,* and the other part is saying, *This can't possibly be, because it's so far from unendurable.* My experience wasn't jiving with the reality of what I had seen.

Bruce called the doctor, and the doctor began to explain that this was a first pregnancy and that these things usually took a bit longer . . . but Bruce cut him off—after all, he was talking to two doctors here! So we drove to the hospital, which was about fifteen minutes away. I made him drive very slowly because the bumps hurt.

It was raining. When we got there, Bruce said that he'd let me off at the door and that he'd park the car and meet me in a minute. But I told him, "Absolutely not! I can't be alone for a minute." We parked and walked together in the rain, got ourselves up to Labor and Delivery and into a room. This hospital was not the hospital where we worked; we had intentionally chosen another hospital because I didn't want a million people coming in to visit me.

The nurse checked me. I was six centimeters and my first thought was that she'd made a mistake. But then I thought, *Well, this is May. She's probably been here for a year and ought to know how to do a cervical examination.* Then, the next thing I know, this strange man walks into my room and says to me, "Hello, I'm Dr. Kent. How are you doing?" I had heard of him; he works with midwives, and they're known to be the most progressive group in the area.

He asked if I was managing the pain okay, and when I told him I was, said he'd be back to check me later. Bruce told me that the doctor on call from my group had Dr. Kent covering for him. But I could have cared less—I was busy having a baby and didn't care who was going to catch it.

We were very happy and excited still. I continued singing, "It's a hap, hap, happy day." The nurses, I guess, thought that we were managing so well, and asked if we wanted to use the birthing room. I was angry and told them, "Yes! Didn't you read my birthing plan? What, do I have to prove I can handle it before I can get in there?" We picked up our things and moved.

Somewhere around eight centimeters, when I went into transition, the contractions got pretty intense. I was standing and leaning over the side of the bed. I was doing deep breathing, but not following any Bradley technique.

A medical student came in and needed to take some information and do a quick physical exam. *I was a medical student once*, I thought. I told him that we'd have to do it in between contractions. I must have seemed so together. I heard him softly say to the nurse, "Doctors make the best patients."

I had to go to the bathroom. On the toilet, my membranes ruptured. Everything popped with an enormous pressure. I made a big mess but felt glad that it happened in the bathroom. And right after that, I started to feel the pressure of the baby's head coming down. It started to get tough. I wanted to sit Indian-style on the bed, but when I did that, it created a deceleration of the baby's heartbeat. The nurse got panicky. She said, "You can't do that! You're sitting on the baby's head." I would have been happy standing up, but they wouldn't let me. I wanted to climb off the bed—it was horrible. I still wasn't yelling or anything, but I remember calmly saying, "I'm not prepared for this!" Then she said, "Nobody is!" Funny how you remember absolutely everything.

In retrospect, I feel that she should have encouraged me at that point or helped me to find a more comfortable position. I was beginning to get frightened and feel out of control. Then she said that the baby's heart was not looking good. She slapped an oxygen mask on me and then I was scared. She called in Dr. Kent. What a lovely man! When he walked in, the tension went right out of the room.

He checked me and the heartbeat, and said, "The baby's fine. You don't need oxygen, and the baby doesn't need oxygen." All the tension just left. Some people are just meant to be around women who are having babies—it's like they have an aura. I was in transition, and his calm was a gift.

I sat up with the headrest raised. No stirrups—pretty civilized compared to what I had seen. I was pushing now, and I hated it. I would have preferred ten more hours of hard labor to this pushing!

Dr. Kent asked if I wanted an episiotomy. Later, Bruce said that I looked like the girl in *The Exorcist* when she spins her head around. "Yes! Get the baby out!" I screamed.

The sweat was pouring off my back. I just can't describe it. I remember feeling like I couldn't take it any more. It was overwhelming. My legs were trembling, and I felt out of control. I couldn't get into the pushing the way I could the contractions. I had no idea of time.

He must have cut an episiotomy from here to Michigan—and Gregory just fell out. We knew he was going to be a boy; we'd had some ultrasounds done earlier. When Gregory was born, Bruce showed him to me, and they wrapped him up and took him to the warming table. I could see him. He was red and screaming and sounded just so lusty and wonderful! Bruce and I were holding hands and kissing and crying and watching him—I couldn't wait to get him into my arms!

To this day, I can remember how he smelled. I remember the exquisite pleasure of having Bruce and I pressed together, looking down at our new son. I can see his long eyelashes, and how they lay on his cheeks. How little his ears were, and we could see Grandpa's nose. He was the cutest baby ever born.

℘

When I spoke with Mary at her home in Fayetteville, North Carolina, she was a new, first-time mother staying at home with her infant son. Mary had recently resigned from the army where she had worked as a paratrooper. She was twenty-eight years old at the time of our interview. Her husband, Jeff, was on active military duty.

Army Hospital Birth

Benjamin's almost five months now, but I still clearly remember the day that I went into labor. I'd been having very hard Braxton-Hicks contractions, and

I was three weeks overdue. But as I'd been having Braxton-Hicks almost my whole pregnancy, I didn't think anything of it. Then at about eight, Sunday night, they moved down. So I figured something was going on, and I started to time them with a stopwatch. And I just kept watching that old clock. My contractions would be five minutes apart, then fifteen, back to five, or twenty, or four—never regular. About two in the morning, I got scared because they were getting real strong. I tried to call my sister in Raleigh, and the phone rang and rang. I thought, "Oh, this is great, nobody's there and Jeff's not waking up." My husband sleeps so soundly that I couldn't get him up. Then at about six in the morning, I was frantic because the contractions were really starting to get strong. I kept on saying to him, "Hey, you got to get up, take me to the hospital." And Jeff goes, "They're not five minutes apart, they're not five minutes apart." And he goes back to sleep. Finally, at about eight, I convince him that I have to go. He's gotten a full night's sleep but is still insisting it's false labor. So I tell him, "Look, I don't care if they're not five minutes apart, I need, for my own sanity, to know if this is the real thing or not."

So he gets up. You know, he's in the army and was going to just blow it off at work that day anyway. He wasn't in any kind of hurry. I'm getting everything ready upstairs and just kind of patiently waiting when I have a very strong contraction and need to lie down on the bed. I'm waiting and waiting, and then I'm thinking, where the heck is my husband? So I walk down the steps, look across the room, and there he is, sitting on the couch eating cereal, watching TV. Talk about relaxed!

When we get to the hospital—now this is Womack [the local army hospital]—I was around three centimeters. They tell me to walk around. So we go downstairs and walk. In the meantime, I throw up in one of those dome waste cans. I was walking along eating ice chips and, all of a sudden, I feel very nauseous. I tell Jeff that I'm getting sick, so we scuttle up to the waste can and I let go, with all the mess running down the side . . . it was awful. When I went back upstairs, I was almost five, so they admitted me.

Then they got me in their little robe and put me in this little cubicle, which didn't have any windows and was very bland, kind of painted beige. At Womack, it's very primitive—a free birth, except for my meals, but kind of primitive. While we had been walking around, I went to the family practice clinic in the building and saw my doctor there and said, "Hey, Dr. Poole, you want to deliver a baby today?" And he goes, "For sure!" So he came up and was with me, on duty, the whole time—that was nice.

They hooked me up to an IV which was SOP—standard operating procedure. Very automatically then, they put two monitors on me, and I have to lie the whole time on my right side because of the equipment. My husband was, of course, there with me—by now he was doing great. And I thought I did very well because I didn't take any medication whatsoever and I never really screamed. I hadn't thought beforehand about medication much and although the pain was very bad, I didn't want the medication. What I did the whole time was watch the monitor. You know, in childbirth classes they tell you to open your eyes, and my husband would say, "Alright, going up, going up, going up." Then he'd say, "Peaking—it's peaking." And I'd begin to relax because I knew that the pain was going to go down.

Other than my husband, I labored alone in this room. I mean, it was only the size of a walk-in closet—space for a little bed, a tiny bathroom on the side and the machinery—that was it. There wasn't even sitting space.

One really bad time I had was when I couldn't use the bedpan. I just couldn't go! And then a mean old lieutenant nurse tried to get the bedpan underneath me, but it hurt too much to get off my side . . . I just couldn't move. It wasn't the monitors now, it was just the way the baby was positioned—I couldn't manage to get on my back. Then the nurse left, and suddenly I thought I could go. I tell Jeff, "Get the bedpan." But he says, "I don't know what to do!" I yell, "Just get the bedpan, the goddamn bedpan!" But he's still telling me, "Honey, I just don't know what to do. I don't know what to do!" Finally, I say, "Forget it now—the urge is gone!" When I was delivering, they had to put a catheter in me.

Another bad moment was when the baby's heartbeat went down so low the nurse told me to change sides. I remember saying to her, "I can't do it, I'm trying, but I can't do it!" Then she said, "Honey, sometimes you gotta do some things you don't wanna do just because it's for the baby's sake." Southern accent and all. It took me a full five minutes, but I got over on my other side.

It was late afternoon when the doctor came back in. He broke my water, and I remember being kind of apprehensive about that. I asked, "Is it going to hurt?" He just said, "Well," and did it anyway. It was actually kind of neat—warm and relaxing to have all this water gush out of you. It didn't hurt at all.

I was probably at about six centimeters by then, and I guess he thought breaking my water would speed labor along. And he was right. The next thing I remember was the doctor checking me and saying that I was at nine centimeters—transition. You know, I had been having contractions the whole time, but all of a sudden, WOW . . . the urge to push took over! And I mean it's just the most amazing thing I've ever felt. My body took over, and the baby like just wanted to push itself out. I had no control. I start blowing and yelling, "I have to push, I have to push!" So the doctor checked me again and said, "You're at ten centimeters, go ahead and push."

I'm still in that little room, when finally the head crowns. I hear the doctor say, "Okay, we're ready to go!" But now he tells me, "Mary, don't push until we get you all set up in the delivery room!" They wheel me out in the same bed, into the hall, and about twenty-five feet into the delivery room. But I have to push again! I'm blowing out . . . almost there, and then I get leg cramps. I'm trying not to push, and I'm trying to straighten my legs out because they're curling up. At last, I'm in the room and they say, "Okay, Mary, you're going to have to get over on the other bed now!" Here I have this baby sticking out of me, and they make me get up and over to another bed! I don't know how I did it; I just kind of scooted over! And there's my husband in this funny hat, with the mask and everything on, looking weird.

But the funniest thing is was when I get onto the table and they say, "Okay, let's put your leg in the stirrup." They put my left leg in the stirrup, and next go to put my right in, when the nurse fumbles, and I'm like, "Please hurry! Please hurry!" I'm wanting to push the baby out, but she says, "Doctor, the stirrup's broken, it won't stay up." You know, I'm like, *whew, whew*—blowing my brains out 'cause I'm ready to push this baby. And finally, the doctor comes over and tries to adjust the leg stirrup. I'm lying there, and he says to the nurse, "You're going to have to hold her leg up." So she grabs my right leg and holds it like that. Then she says to me, "Honey, you need to shave your legs!" So I say to her, "You know it's kind of hard to shave your legs when you can't see them!" Hairy legs or not, she held my right leg up for the whole delivery.

By now, I was totally detached from the baby. I was completely self-involved. I had my eyes closed the whole time I was pushing, and when the baby's head popped out and the doctor said, "Hey, Mary, I want you to take a look at your baby," I couldn't even open my eyes. I just figured if I opened my eyes the pain would rush right in. I couldn't deal with the realization of the whole thing, so I didn't see the baby until they had pulled it out and suctioned the mouth. They pulled it out, and someone immediately took it over to the cleaning-up table and did some stuff. And I was just lying there saying, "Thank you Lord, thank you for getting me through this!" I was just glad to have it over with.

Then, all of a sudden, I realized they didn't tell us what it was. We had wanted a boy so bad that when the doctor told us, "It's a little boy!" Jeff and I just looked at each other and screamed, "It's a boy!" We were so happy.

The whole birth at the hospital, from start to finish, went from about noon, when I realized I was officially admitted, to 5:23 that evening, when I delivered. Thinking back, the one thing I would do differently—not anything connected with the birth—would be the breast-feeding situation in the hospital afterwards. At the hospital they fed water bottles with 5 percent glucose solution. There was this philosophy of telling new moms to breast-feed for only two to three minutes on each breast so their nipples didn't get sore. And, of course, my colostrum was there, but I didn't have any milk, and Benjamin took right away to the water bottle instead of nursing. It was easier for him. I kept asking for breast-feeding help, but the nurses were saying, "Well, honey, I just can't help you right now." Nobody was willing to help me out. Finally, I had this specialist, a young man, who probably wasn't even married—and there he was holding my boob trying to help me out. I had no modesty because I needed help. Afterwards, I felt resentful that I had such a hard time in the hospital. When I brought Benjamin home, he just refused to nurse for twenty-four hours cause he was used to the bottle. So I called my sister who's a breast-feeding counselor in Pennsylvania, and she said to dump the water bottle—go cold turkey on it—because he wants that more than he wants the breast milk. But I got out the bottle during a weak moment and almost gave in. I had the pan out and was boiling the stuff when I realized that if I gave in at this moment I'd be resentful for the rest of my life. So I just poured it down the sink and washed out the pan. That was one of the hardest days of my life, and I cried a lot. I had postpartum blues. The baby was crying, and I thought he was starving to death. But I stuck it out and he finally caught onto nursing.

I remember my mother saying that women forget a lot of the pain of childbirth. I was the youngest of six and kept asking her while I was pregnant, "What's it like?" But all she'd say is, "I can't remember." I said to her, "How can you forget what it's like to have a baby—you've had six of us!" But she'd always say, "You just forget the pain." And I guess it's true—here I am, five months later, and I can remember the experience, but can't feel the pain.

What I do remember most is the feeling of amazement that I had had a baby. I remember thinking that first night, "I just can't believe it, I've actually had a baby!" I was such a tomboy growing up. I was a paratrooper in the army, and also worked on a farm—all these rough, tough things. And now I'm a mother. I'm still overwhelmed by the amazement and wonder of it all—and the concern, of course, of whether I can be a mother.

ം

Joey is a stay-at-home mother who lives in Norfolk, Virginia, with her husband, Tom, and son, Spencer, age twenty-one months. Here she talks about her son's birth and the many changes that pregnancy brings into married life.

First Baby

The story of my pregnancy really begins before conception. I'm a research-type person and I have to thoroughly explore an issue before I make any big decision. So it was with child-bearing. I was very much in love with my husband, Tom—we had a beautiful, sharing, passionate relationship. We both worked full-time; he was managing a mortgage company, and I was a litigation paralegal working in personal injury. Our days consisted of working, working out, eating out most of the time, and unwinding together at home before going to bed. He's ten and a half years my senior, and we'd been married for two years before we began to think about starting a family.

I was clueless about pregnancy and childbirth, so I began my research. I bought *Before You Conceive* and then *What to Expect When You're Expecting*. I devoured both books and was sure that I wanted to bring a baby into our lives. I would just look at photos or drawings of pregnant women and ache to have a big rounded tummy followed by a cooing baby in my arms—I imagined us rocking and nursing our cares away.

I went to my OB/GYN for a prepregnancy visit. He prescribed prenatal vitamins for me at my request and answered two pages of my questions. We talked about epidurals, and I remember he said, "Oh, believe me, you want one!" I look back on this now and chuckle. I didn't know yet what I wanted or how I wanted to birth. I was just trying to absorb as much information as I could from all the sources I could.

I had heard it takes the average couple six months to conceive. It took Tom and me five months—but it felt like five years! Each month when I got my period, I'd be incredibly disappointed; it was really depressing. Finally, one Wednesday during my lunch break, I bought a basal thermometer so I could start charting my temperature.

That Friday, Tom and I went out. We had a lovely dinner, went to a movie, and then had a passionate, romantic night. All through the movie, though, I remember being really nauseous and feeling like I had terrible gas. I told Tom, "Boy, this is going to be a whopper"—referring to my period, which I expected any time. On the drive home, I mentioned to him how much my breasts hurt, and how I felt kind of peculiar, almost outside of my body, looking in.

I never did get to use my basal thermometer. The next morning, I crept silently out of bed and did a pregnancy test. I had gone through five already. I couldn't believe my eyes—it was positive! I began to try to think of some clever way to tell Tom. Nothing fancy came to mind, and I just couldn't wait. So, grinning my face off, I woke him up and said, "Guess what?" He just couldn't get over it! We were like a couple of school kids—giggling and cuddling. Tom didn't want me to tell anybody until I'd seen my doctor and had confirmation. But, we couldn't resist and told all our family that day.

I saw my doctor the following Wednesday. He said I was six weeks along and gave us a November 21 due date. I quit work one week later and have been home ever since. I had a lot of projects to finish before Spencer arrived and felt like I had such a short amount of time to do them. I reupholstered our couch, refinished some furniture, made curtains, latched a rug, and sewed three quilts. It was a hot summer—in fact, I couldn't believe how hot it was. Previous summers, Tom and I would always go to the beach together—we lived for it. But now, I couldn't stand to be outside in the heat and would tell him, "Go by yourself."

The pregnancy progressed wonderfully. We did an ultrasound in June, and saw our sweet little boy kick around and suck his thumb—which interestingly, he's never done outside the womb. I was amazed at how active he was; I still hadn't felt him move.

What I could feel, though, was myself—changing emotionally and physically, evolving into the mother I was becoming. Unfortunately, all these changes didn't feel right for Tom, and our marriage went through huge transitions during this time.

I guess it began when I went to my first LaLeche League meeting. Actually, my mom encouraged me to go since I wanted to breast-feed. I was about five months pregnant. That first meeting was held at a park on a beautiful day, and there were all these toddlers nursing and running around. I must admit that I was shocked initially—it's something I was never exposed to. In fact, I'd never been exposed to little ones much at all. Now, of course, nursing my twenty-one-month-old seems the most natural and normal thing to me.

It was a confusing time for us. I started changing, and Tom must have felt like, *Who is this woman? This is not how I expected it to go.* And, in some sense, it wasn't what I expected either. This was all new to me. We'd talk about issues and disagree about some things, like the family bed. He was all for breast-feeding, but we never could agree on how long. It was all very confusing because I really didn't understand me either. I was responding to my body, trying to figure things out, and Tom and I were being pulled apart. During this time, I read *The Well Pregnancy Book*—I really enjoyed it. But Tom's not a big reader and would always refer to it as "The Book." He began to blame all my changes on it and on LaLeche League. I was his wife, and he wanted to place the blame outside of me.

But it wasn't like anybody was pushing anything on me. I'm a real cuddly, snuggly-type person, so the family bed, extended nursing, and responding to your baby's cries immediately were issues I embraced because they were natural to me. I think Tom felt left out, threatened, scared—he didn't know what was happening to me. In fact, he even referred to LaLeche League as "a cult."

My pregnancy, meanwhile, was going along pretty smoothly, except for some minor physical complaints. At first, I had morning sickness. I never actually vomited, but I'd feel queasy. When that passed, I had terrible heartburn. Some nights, I'd even lie awake and cry. Spencer was head-down, and he would raise his arms above his head and move them around—it was just excruciating, and I'd actually be angry with him! It would literally feel like a needle shooting down into my vagina. I'd be fine one moment, walking along, and then boom! One step and he'd catch me—I'd be doubled over in pain, thinking, *I love you, why are you doing this to me?* Sometimes, I'd get down on my hands and knees and rock, trying to get him to change his position.

I wanted to have a natural childbirth from the start, and Tom supported that. We went to prepared childbirth classes together, but Tom wasn't into it the way I was—it wasn't happening to his body. One time, he actually fell asleep during class. I was really disheartened. They say that the man is three months behind the woman in her pregnancy, and I felt that to be true. It wasn't as real for him as it was for me. On Mother's Day that year, I expected a card—I already felt I was a mother—but he had no intentions of giving me one! We were completely out of sync all through the pregnancy. It was one heartache after another with us. We kept bumping heads, and we were so disappointed.

During childbirth classes, I decided that I wanted to write a birthing plan. I kept finding books that would help me with decisions. I honed it down to two pages. I wanted a natural childbirth. I didn't want my water broken, didn't want a fetal monitor, an episiotomy, or any Pitocin. I didn't want any interference; I just wanted to progress naturally. I brought it in to my doctor the next visit, and we all dated and signed it. I was really disappointed in him though—I felt like I was receiving cookie-cutter care. I felt like a number. I'd go in, have my visit, and he'd say, "Everything's fine . . . blah, blah, blah." He was always very pleasant, but he was in such a hurry. It didn't feel right to me. I wish I had confronted him, but I didn't; I just didn't have the nerve. When they did the ultrasound at around seventeen and a half weeks, they gave me a new due date—December 2, a whole two weeks later—and told us it was going to be a boy. Tom had been sure it was a girl. He comes from a family of eight, and there are only two boys. But I suspected a boy! We decided to circumcise. Actually, it was Tom's idea; I didn't want to, but it was really important to him.

We bought a crib in September—and this was a big deal, because now we could start getting Spencer's room ready, though he never used it! At thirty-four weeks, we began doing perineal stretching every night. Tom wasn't happy about this—stretching me and making me uncomfortable— but I said, "Look, I would rather have this than be cut. Think of it that way. Which would you rather?"

Then, we toured the hospital—I couldn't wait! I wanted to get a feel for everything, plus the tour meant we were one step closer to birth. They had labor and delivery rooms. Then, about an hour after the birth, they took you into a postpartum room. It was beautiful, just great. My birthing plan was set; I knew what to expect at the hospital; and all major decisions were made.

One Thursday, I lost my mucus plug. I began to climb the walls—although I knew it could still be three weeks away, I had this strong feeling, *I'm going today;* I'd had so much false labor. But on that Thursday, I was sure. I had lunch with a friend in Norfolk. I figured I would come home and then go to the hospital. But it didn't happen.

The following Thursday, exactly one week later, I went to lunch with my friend Karen again. I was having really strong contractions, and when I returned home, I called Tom. He came immediately. I walked around a while, and the contractions kept coming, so we packed our last-minute things and went out to supper at one of our favorite restaurants. On my salad I had balsamic vinegar, which has been touted to bring on labor. We told everyone there, "We're going to have our baby!" I was so ready.

But then the contractions stopped. I was so very disappointed and thought, *Spency, for months I've wanted to see your face.* I couldn't wait to nurse him—I felt we were going to be perfect together. Spencer would be born, and he'd not have any reason to cry—we'd nurse and be the perfect team.

Friday came and still lots and lots of contractions, so we figured, *today.* No. Saturday came, and the contractions were one on top of the other, so strong that I did some breathing patterns. I'd sit in the rocking chair with my feet up and breathe through the contractions, but when I'd get up and move around, they'd stop. I phoned the doctor on call that morning, and she said to come over to the hospital and she'd check me. I was 80 percent effaced and one centimeter. All these contractions—for days, weeks—and still nothing! I couldn't believe it!

I thought, *Spencer, what are you doing here, buddy?* I was still having heart-burn; I was restless; I couldn't sleep; I was overweight and miserable. When I left the hospital, the doctor told me, "Well, go home, and I'll see you some time this weekend." But when I got home, I remembered that I had read that nobody knows for sure when the baby will come. That Sunday came . . . and Monday . . . and Tuesday . . . and Wednesday . . . and Thursday . . . and Friday. . . . Then Friday night—actually Saturday at 1:19 A.M.—I felt my first real labor contraction.

I stayed in bed and waited for another, then another, and said to Tom, "Honey, I'm going to take a shower, but I'm not sure this is it."

My mom was flying in on Sunday, so I'd been cleaning and cleaning with enormous energy. I'd scrubbed the floor every day for a week. It was ridiculous—I even went to a friend's and started cleaning her house!

We timed the contractions all night. I was buzzing around the house, doing stuff. I put towels on the bed for Mom, got things into place, and repacked our bags for the hospital. I didn't sleep and couldn't rest. By 8:00 A.M. , we figured I could vacuum, which I had been so anxious to do. We live in a townhouse and have people on the other side of us. The contractions had been five minutes apart for hours, then slowed to seven minutes, but were getting stronger. I still didn't trust that this was real labor because we'd had so many false alarms before.

We called the doctor and decided to leave for the hospital. We stopped at Dunkin' Donuts on the way, and Tom got coffee. At the hospital I waited in the lobby while Tom checked us in—we'd preregistered, so it didn't take him long. We were escorted to our room. Our nurse came in and put a fetal monitor on me. I had stated in my birthing plan I didn't want to be on the monitor, but when I told the nurse she said, "Well, I want you to stay on the monitor until the doctor gets here." I'm like, "Okay, I guess I can do that." Tom went and got our bags from the car.

The contractions were pretty intense. I was alone. Then the nurse came in, had her back to me and was asking all these questions. Tom was downstairs phoning everyone, and I was at the point of needing him. She was asking all these questions, and I started to lose control of my contractions. I was just gritting and bearing, trying to get through them—every muscle was doing the opposite of what I needed them to be doing.

The doctor showed up about forty-five minutes later, and the first thing he did was break my water! He came to check me and broke my water! I was in a kind of daze, and I couldn't believe it! I was only three or four centimeters along. He said, "I want you to stay on the monitor for another ten minutes, and then I want you to get up and walk around." So, here I am on the monitor, and he's broken my water against my wishes! I had asked the nurse, "Do you have a copy of my birthing plan in my folder?" I had mailed it in. It wasn't there, but, happily, we had brought an extra copy with us. When the nurses looked at it, we could hear them at the desk chuckling, like, *Ha, ha, ha—natural childbirth, right. Here comes another one! We'll see how far she makes it!*

Tom could see I was upset and said, "A few more minutes and we'll get up and walk around." But I said, "Oh, no! I'm not getting out of this bed!" It was then that I lost all control and began asking for an epidural. Thankfully, I had told Tom before, "No matter what I say, you remind me that I can get through this naturally." I had warned him that when I got to transition I'd probably ask for medication.

It was not going like I had wanted it to, but I wasn't really thinking about much at the time; I was just experiencing. My friend Karen, who we wanted at the birth, came to the hospital and fed me ice chips between contractions. Tom fed them to me initially, but kept spilling them—he was just so shaky.

They came with a syringe to draw blood, which they needed to do for the epidural. I hate needles, but at the time, it didn't affect me. I remember my doctor standing by my bed *with his back toward me* while I pleaded for medication. He was hearing me but not empathizing. He said something, like, "Okay, great . . . ." And I'm thinking to myself, *No, I want it right this second. You don't understand what I'm feeling here!*

He left, came back in a few minutes, and said, "Look, I've got a lady next door, and her baby is a member of the Mile High Club—he's just not coming down. I'm going to have to do a section on her." I was really surprised he was telling me this. Then he said, "If you want an epidural, the anesthesiologist is coming here for her, so if you want one, now is the time." He left and said he'd be back in a minute.

Tom got right in my face and told me, "Jo, you can do this!" And I was thinking, *If I don't get it now, I'll never get it. . . .* But Tom was right there blowing in my face, saying, "You don't need it!"

So, at my husband's urging, I told the doctor, "No," when he returned. I am so thankful Tom was there!

I remember asking my doctor, "Am I in transition?" And he said, "Oh yeah!" Once I knew that, I felt I was going to make it. Tom tried to change my breathing, but all I could do was pant. Karen was just beautiful. She kept saying, "You're doing great!" I had lost control of my labor, but Tom and Karen helped me get back on track.

Soon after, a nurse came in, and I said, "Look, I've got to push!" She said, "Hold on," quickly checked me, and said, "You're not ready to push yet." The thing was, *I* was ready, but *my doctor* wasn't. He was attending the woman next door, and they hadn't expected me to go this fast.

My body started pushing—I had no control. I was fighting my body, but it was no use. Finally, the doctor came in and *actually allowed me to push*—like I needed permission. When I think about that now, it really burns me up!

My first pushing contraction was a learning contraction; I was pushing with my face. Then I pushed correctly, and Spencer was born with four more contractions.

I remember Tom asking, "Is he crowning?" and the doctor saying, "Yes." I pushed again, and the doctor said, "Wait, wait!" The cord was wrapped around Spency's neck. He said, "It's got to go," and he cut the cord. I was really disappointed; I had wanted Spencer to be placed on my tummy with the cord attached. I wanted to wait until Spencer was ready—but it didn't happen that way.

They put Spency on my tummy, but the nurse took him from me before I could even look him over completely. I should have screamed at the top of my lungs, "Don't take my baby!" but I didn't.

When he was returned to me, he was all bundled up. I wish that we had been skin to skin. I had a small tear on the left side. I held Spencer while the doctor sewed me up. Tom was ecstatic. He took pictures—it was sweet. We attempted our first nursing, but Spencer wasn't interested right away. Before long, they took him off to the nursery. This was something that I accepted— I had to be away from him for four hours. Now, it makes my blood boil. I would never again allow my baby to be taken from me.

After my postpartum visit, I never returned to this doctor. I was angry with him, yet at the same time, I felt a connection to him because he was present when I birthed my baby. I left but never confronted him.

Tom and I had a difficult first year adjusting to our new roles as parents. I had very strong feelings about many things, and at various times I was like, *It's my way, or the highway.* But we were able to work through a lot of our difficulties, and our marriage is stronger now.

Looking back at the birth itself, I wish I had had better control of my labor. Even though I had a natural birth—a very positive birth—I wasn't happy about many things and would make some different choices the next time around.

Patti is a stay-at-home mom who lives with her husband, Adam, and one-year-old daugh-
ter, Haley, in New Jersey. Patti is the youngest of ten children and always wanted to be a
mother. When it came time to choose the kind of birth experience that she wished to have,
Patti chose "not to be a martyr," and to take medication to control pain. Here, she describes
her positive experience with Nubain and a successfully administered epidural.

Born for the Role

My husband, Adam, and I weren't trying to get pregnant, but we weren't avoiding it either. Adam had the attitude, *whatever will be will be,* but in my heart, I really wanted a baby very, very badly. On the day I told Adam I was late with my period, I figured he'd run off to the bathroom. He has a nervous stomach and whenever something goes wrong, he runs for the toilet. But he didn't. He was very excited, and that made me feel good.

It was the winter of '94, and we were having horrible weather up here. I took an in-home pregnancy test on the day of a blizzard, but I was only two days late and the results were inconclusive. I waited a couple more days and that's when I told Adam I was late. It was a Friday evening, and we ran out in all the snow to the drugstore for another pregnancy test. This time, the moment I peed on the stick, *boom,* it came right up! Without a doubt, the results were clear.

I had an appointment for my yearly check-up the following week, so I went to my OB/GYN and killed two birds with one stone. He's in practice by himself and has two other doctors who cover for him if he's not there.

The first part of my pregnancy was an absolute nightmare. I never in my wildest dreams thought it would be anything like that—it was horrible! I still get kind of sick if I think about it. I vomited no less than six or seven times a day, except when I was working. Then, I could somehow hold it back. I worked at a nursery/day care school from 9:30 to 5:30 and as soon as I'd walk out the door at 5:30, I'd start vomiting in the parking lot. And sometimes I'd have to pull the car over to vomit, although I carried bags with me. It was awful—and all during that miserable weather when it was tough to drive.

I was working with three-year-olds and couldn't really explain to them what was happening. I'd be nauseous all day, but starting at around 3:00, it would kick in so badly that I'd start to sweat and get dizzy. But I'd hold back because I didn't want to throw up in front of the children. And you can't leave three-year-olds alone. So I'd start vomiting at 5:30, and the only way I could stop was if I went to bed. I'd literally go to sleep at 6:15.

It was pretty brutal. The doctor, nurses, women off the street would suggest different things to take—and I tried everything—vitamin B6, ginger ale, ginger snaps, Saltines, flat Coke, bland foods, C-bands that you put on your wrist to prevent motion sickness—nothing worked. I'd wake up ravenous in the morning at 5:30, 6:00, and I'd eat like there's no tomorrow. Fortunately, when I threw up that evening, I was sure that breakfast was already digested. The baby was at least getting nutrition. I'd pop a prenatal vitamin right before I closed my eyes at night, so never once in all nine months did I ever throw up my prenatals.

Adam was extremely supportive. I mean, unbelievably so. Every time I'd kneel over the toilet, he'd rub my back. Often, I couldn't even make it to the toilet, and I'd throw up the nastiest things in the sink. Adam would clean it up; he didn't even flinch; he just did it.

The weekends were the worst. I never thought about quitting my job, because at work the children somehow gave me the strength to not throw up. I dreaded the weekends and snowdays—we had many of them that year—because I would vomit from the minute I woke up till the minute I went to bed. It was so bad that many days I actually thought, *I'm not going to live to see tomorrow.*

My mother, who had ten children, would say over and over, "I promise you, I promise you, at twelve weeks and one day it will all stop." She threw up with all ten of her pregnancies. But twelve weeks came and went, and I was still throwing up.

Finally, at around fourteen weeks, I began to feel human again. I still threw up, but it was more like twice a day. At seventeen or eighteen weeks, I stopped vomiting on a regular basis, and at twenty weeks I began to feel 100 percent. It was the first time I was able to appreciate and enjoy my pregnancy.

Adam and I attended childbirth education classes at the hospital where I was going to deliver. We thought that they taught Lamaze there and that they'd be pushing natural childbirth. But the teacher's attitude was, *whatever makes it enjoyable for you.* They no longer were preaching natural, they just preached informed. That made me feel good, because I didn't want any pressure to give birth in a certain way.

The year before I was pregnant, in August of '93, I'd been with one of my sisters when she gave birth naturally to an almost ten-pound baby. She was on Pitocin, but didn't get an epidural when she asked for one—the anesthesiologist just never showed up. I saw the agony that she went through. I never wanted to be a martyr or a hero; my plan was to go without drugs for as long as I could, but if I needed an epidural, that was fine. I'm the youngest of ten, and all my four sisters gave birth naturally. Yet everyone around me, including my sister who'd gone naturally but not by choice, said, "Do the drugs, do the drugs!" Also, I had two friends who were pregnant right along with me, and they had the same attitude: whatever will be will be.

I went into labor on the night of October 6, four days past my due date. My doctor was getting married, and the last day that he'd be available was October 6. On the 5th, I went in for a check-up, and he stripped my membranes and said, "There, that ought to put you into labor." And I said, "Yeah, but I guarantee it'll happen a couple of hours after you go off duty." Sure enough, it did. He was available up until dinner time on the 6th, and my water broke at 10:45.

The stripping of my membranes had been pretty uncomfortable, but nothing happened the rest of that day. Then, on the 6th, I lost my mucus plug. Now, looking back, I realize I was beginning to have contractions, but at the time I assumed it was just Braxton-Hicks. I'd been having them for like a week. They were not consistent—some would be long, others short. So, I thought, *Oh yeah! Big deal!*

One of my sisters was coming in from Florida that day, and so I was busy cleaning my apartment, cooking dinner. I even went to the car wash and scrubbed my car inside and out. I was having cramps all day, but only thought, *I don't have time for this!*

We had a nice dinner. My sister came with her husband and two children. After dinner we played Balderdash, and at about 10:15, I said, "Okay, I'm tired, I want to go to bed." They were tired, too, because they had traveled all day down from Boston, where they were visiting my other sister. My nephew was ten at the time, and the last thing he said to me was, "Aunt Patti, will you please have the baby tonight?" And I said back, "No, I'm not ready."

That was Thursday night, and they were going to be leaving Saturday, so I figured that after they left I could clean all day Sunday and have the baby on Monday.

We kissed goodnight and went to bed. Then, boom! My water broke! Adam and I were lying like spoons—he was cuddling me from behind—and he had his hands on my stomach when we heard this *pop!* A shudder went through my body. I thought I was the only one who heard the *pop*, but Adam asked, "What was that?" And I said, "Did you hear that, too?" Within thirty to sixty seconds, there was a sudden gush between my legs. I gasped, then ran into the bathroom. I sat on the toilet, and Adam stood over me. It sounded like I was urinating. I said to him, "I'm not peeing! I swear I'm not!" We were flabbergasted.

At 11:30, I started to get little twinges, so before it became too late, I called the doctor who was covering. I had to leave a message, and she called back and asked, "Any contractions?" I told her, "No." She said, "Okay, check into the hospital at 8:00 in the morning, but if you start to get them in the middle of the night, and they get bad, go ahead in early."

Murphy's Law. As soon as I hung up, the contractions started—they were faint but coming consistently at three minutes apart. I didn't know what to do. Adam's mother said that her contractions never got worse than period cramps, so I thought, *Oh my gosh, for all I know, I could deliver right here in my bedroom.* I hopped in the shower and got ready to go.

At 1:15 in the morning, I woke up my sister and her husband to tell them we were leaving for the hospital. She thought I was joking. There I was, fully dressed with my bag in hand, and she said, "No, you're not! You're lying!"

The drive to the hospital was only fifteen minutes. They checked me and I was only about two centimeters dilated. Normally, they would have sent me home, but because my water had broken, they allowed me to stay.

I was put in a labor-and-delivery room. I was in utter disbelief and also a bit disappointed that at three minutes apart, I was only two centimeters. So, I settled in and got on my little bathrobe and slippers, and I walked the halls like you see in the movies. We looked at the nursery and spied on the babies, but after a while, I was getting really bored, so I played Tetris on the portable Nintendo.

At 3:00 in the morning, I said, "Maybe we should rest." Adam relaxed in a reclining chair, but he was freezing and the air conditioning was very loud. After a while you didn't hear it, but initially, it was this almost deafening sound. He covered himself with my bathrobe, and I was under the blankets—we just rested.

The contractions started to get kind of bad, so at about 4:00 I was given some Nubain. I rested until 6:00, until the Nubain began to wear off. Nubain made me feel very foggy and completely relaxed, very peaceful, like I was constantly drifting off to sleep, but never *really* asleep—kind of on the cusp, in between. I remember thinking, *Oh, here comes a contraction—but who cares?*

At about a quarter to six, I told Adam to call his mother, step-dad, and sister who was living at home and was a teacher. They were going to be with us, and her sister needed to call in before 6:15 in order for the school to get a substitute. Adam called.

At 6:00, the nurse came in and asked, "Are you ready for an epidural?" And I said, "No, I'm going to try to go without." She left the room, I got one more contraction, and said to Adam, "Go get her!" Adam ran after her because I was concerned. My sister had wanted an epidural, and they had wanted her to wait until she was five or six centimeters dilated. She waited, and then when she requested it, they said that they'd send the anesthesiologist down. He didn't show up until she was nine centimeters and almost ready to push. So, in my mind, I kept going back to that and thinking, *I better not lollygag around.*

Two minutes later, this guy came in. I couldn't believe it! I thought, *Wow!* Adam had to leave the room 'cause he can't handle stuff like that. We'd seen a video of an epidural being administered, and it had freaked us out. But I thought, *What the heck!* I leaned over, he did it, and I didn't feel a blessed thing. He was so sweet—just the kindest, kindest doctor.

I felt warmth running through my body. I could just feel it. Everything was numb except for a patch, the size of a golf ball, by my inner thigh. I told the doctor that there was a blank spot, and I pointed to my thigh. He adjusted something, and bang, the spot was gone. By 7:00, the epidural was completely up and running, and I was completely comfortable. They checked me, and I was eight centimeters. I was told that the epidural would slow my labor down, but it didn't seem to.

A few minutes later, my in-laws arrived—stepfather, mother, and sister. I began to rehash the whole night's story—like I'm doing now. They were eating my graham crackers, drinking water, just all excited, and doting on me. We were all having a good time. We shot a video and took pictures, made phone calls to my family in Florida.

Then, at 8:00, the nurse came in to check me again. I was at ten centimeters, and she said it was time to push. I remember this vividly: I was so tired from talking, and so relaxed from the epidural that, at this point, I wanted to take a nap! I actually said to her, "Well, can I take a nap first?" She said, "No, honey. You have to push now."

Then I noticed that my sister-in-law, who never intended to stay for the delivery, was putting on one of those yellow hospital gowns. They all put on gowns and stayed.

I was in a "C-position." I'd recline, then to push, sit up to form a C. The only way I could tell I was pushing was if I made my face hurt—'cause I didn't feel anything. So I just made my face hurt as much as I could.

I hardly remember the covering doctor. She was a woman. I guess she must have felt a little goofy about having such a big audience. Basically, she didn't say too much. She wanted to let us do our thing. The nurse was the one who gave me support. She'd tell me, "Oh yes, there, push!" And she'd go, "One, two, three, breathe. . . ." Her name was Vicky. In literally six pushes, the baby was out. She was six pounds, eleven ounces. I didn't feel that I should have needed an episiotomy, but they gave me one. She came out after fifteen minutes of pushing. I just assumed I didn't get an episiotomy because she seemed to just slide right out. In fact, I didn't know she was born till they handed her to me. I was still pushing! They had to tell me to stop. And they're like, "Here you go! It's a girl!"

They immediately turned off the epidural, and I began to feel pressure, not pain. I watched the doctor stitch me up. She stitched me too tight, and just last month I had to return, get cut, and stretched.

When they put her on my belly, I again felt utter disbelief. You have to understand where I'm coming from. I'm the youngest of ten. I have four older sisters and I've seen them have babies my whole life. I was twelve when I became an aunt, so I've always felt like an aunt. When Haley was born, I felt like I was waiting for someone to come—one of my sisters—and take her away like she was my niece, not my daughter. It took a long time for it to sink in that this baby was truly, truly mine. My entire life I wanted a baby so badly. I wanted a child more than anything in the world. I started baby-sitting at twelve. I've always loved children. And with my job I worked with children.

So here it is, thirty years later, and I have my own. It just seems surreal. My brother and my mom, who are both up from Florida this week, just said to me the other day, "You finally got the baby you wanted." So they knew, too, how badly I wanted one. I was born for the role of mother. When I was a little girl, I wanted to be two things: a flight attendant and a mother. I was a flight attendant, and now I'm a mother. I've realized my dreams. Sometimes, when Adam is at work, I'll be home with Haley and feel incredibly at peace with my life. The rest of the world will be busy, and I'll just nurse and stare at her. I'm the most relaxed I've ever been—utterly at peace.

℘

Previously from New York, Sue lives in Charlotte, North Carolina, with her husband, Tony, and their three children: Anthony Dominic, age four; Alannah Corinne, age two; and Thomas Donald, age three weeks, whose birth is described here. Sue is a stay-at-home mother, and Tony is a dock worker and truck driver.

C-Section, Again

None of my pregnancies were planned, and none of them were unwanted. From the time Tony and I married, our system was, *when we got pregnant, we got pregnant*. I figured I was married and that we would have children until we were done.

Before I got pregnant with Thomas, I had a miscarriage at seven weeks. It was disappointing, but I quickly became pregnant four weeks later. Almost until Thomas was due, I thought I had become pregnant two months after the miscarriage, so his due date ended up being a surprise.

I had nausea on Christmas Eve and didn't know I was pregnant. I thought I'd come down with some kind of stomach flu, and I was really upset. Then I had morning sickness through my whole pregnancy, which had never happened before. Even during the last trimester, I'd feel sick on and off at different times of the day. But I wasn't actually vomiting, so I could deal with it. Other than the nausea, it wasn't an uncomfortable pregnancy.

For the other two babies, we had OB/GYNs—different doctors at different hospitals in New York: one out on Long Island, one closer to the city. Both were very bad experiences. This time we switched to a midwife, which was a nice change, and planned to give birth at home. She was a lay midwife, which is illegal in this state, and in practice by herself. I hired another midwife as a back-up, and she assisted during my labor, too.

My midwife was very relaxed, but she monitored everything I did—my diet, the exercise I was getting. Basically, her attitude with prenatal care is to take care of your overall health during pregnancy.

Everything went along fine. Then, on September 5, I went in to see the midwife and she said, "Wait, something's not right. You have to get a sonogram 'cause you're further along than you think, or else you're having twins." So I went in, and that's when we discovered my due date was wrong and that I'd been pregnant four weeks longer than I'd thought. I was like, "What, you can't tell me that!" Now, my due date was in five or six days rather than four weeks. But he came two weeks late anyway, so I did have a little bit of time.

I went into labor in the middle of a Sunday night. My daughter was sick—she had a cough. We were sleeping on the couch together, and I had her kind of sitting up. I could just tell it was labor, and I just lay there because I knew I had a long road ahead of me. Even though some of the contractions would wake me up periodically, I could still sleep through them at this point. So, I slept as much as I could until morning, when I called my midwife to let her know. Tony had been working that night, so he wasn't home. When he arrived, he went upstairs to sleep a bit. Neither of us knew how long this labor would be, and we thought he'd need the rest.

The midwife was at another delivery, but that woman, who lived a ways out in the country, wasn't progressing much. The midwife decided to drive back to Charlotte and told me to call when the contractions lasted a minute and were five minutes apart. Then she'd come over, which was okay with us—we didn't want her here too soon. She suggested that I mess around with my husband to get things going. That's what the doctor ordered, and that's what we did. My sister, who lives a few blocks away, took my kids. So that's how we spent Sunday afternoon.

That night, by midnight—which was technically Monday, my contractions were getting stronger, and I called the midwife. I was excited 'cause I really expected to have the baby at home. With my other son, they sectioned me before I ever went into labor. My daughter never dropped into the birth canal and had to be sectioned. I had labor with my daughter, and I handled the pain. I never wanted any medication. In New York, I had a labor coach who taught me to welcome the contractions and use them to deliver the baby.

So that's what I did now with my son—I welcomed my labor. When the midwife arrived, my sister was here and ready to take care of my kids if they woke up. The contractions were really strong, and I was having back labor, which is where his head was.

Mostly, I was on all fours, or else I'd squat. These were the only positions that made the contractions bearable. She checked me all during this time. I was about eight centimeters dilated when she got there, and by 3:00 or 4:00, I was completely dilated and felt like I needed to push.

I started pushing 'cause I couldn't help it—it hurt not to push. The baby's head had been engaged, and that's why I thought this baby would actually be born at home. I had hopes. But after I had been pushing a while, the midwife wanted to check me and see how far down the baby was. She checked, and he wasn't there anymore. Instead of engaging further, his head had disengaged.

I had been laboring upstairs. Now, the midwife wanted me to go downstairs and walk around to see if the baby would reengage. Tony and my sister were hungry and making pizza. When I walked toward the kitchen, Tony said, "Check the pizza, see if it's done." One whiff and I went running. I got sick and continued to get sick every half hour for some time after that.

But the vomiting actually felt good, and the midwife said that it might help labor. Sometimes women vomit and it progresses their dilation or breaks their water. But it wasn't doing anything with me—nothing was doing anything, no matter how hard I pushed. It got to be like 6:00 in the morning, and the midwife said, "Drink a glass of wine." Sometimes wine will slow contractions down long enough to allow you to get some sleep. So we did that, but I couldn't sleep. She called the back-up midwife to come over, and they both tried to figure out why the head was not engaging, why it was doing the opposite of what it should be doing. I was still real uncomfortable at this point and had to keep pushing 'cause it hurt if I didn't.

Then they tried this hip thing—where you bend over and two people, one on each side of you, hold onto your hip bones and push in. It's supposed to open up your pelvis, and a lot of times the baby will drop in because the pelvis is being pushed open. But it didn't work. In fact, he was crawling back up while they were doing this.

Meanwhile, red flags were going up for me 'cause this is what happened with my daughter at the hospital—she never engaged. With this son, he was engaged, but disengaged—which, I guess, is even worse. So red flags were going up, and I was becoming nervous that I'd have to go to the hospital. I really didn't want to, and we continued trying to engage the baby until 12:30 the next afternoon; I had been in labor for thirty-six hours.

My sister had taken my kids back to her house in the morning, and we were alone. By 1:00 the midwives discussed my situation and said to me, "You need to go to the hospital because the baby hasn't moved. He's not engaged anymore and you've been pushing for hours and hours." It was awful. I started to cry. When my daughter was born, I had had a tentative diagnosis of cephalopelvic disproportion (CPD), which means that my pelvis isn't big enough to physically pass the baby. A lot of OBs give that diagnosis to women who really don't have it, so my midwives, my husband, and I were all skeptical—although my mom has it, and it can be passed down.

My husband called ahead to the hospital and to our insurance company to let them know what was going on. My husband and I drove to the hospital alone, since the midwives were illegal. When we got there, I told them, "I'm in labor and we need to go up. I'm a walk-in." They were all asking, "Where's your OB?" And I'm like, "I don't have one."

They were all really confused, so it took a little while to get me in a wheelchair and up to a room. Meanwhile, the contractions were getting closer together and much, much stronger—so strong that I couldn't breathe. It was really scary, 'cause my body was like trying to get the baby out. I'd been in labor before, but this was very tough, and I was screaming, "Get me an epidural—now!"

When the regular staff OB came in, he told us that since I'd been in labor all these hours and he didn't know what my body was doing, we should get in touch with the midwife and have her call him. He told her that he didn't care if she was illegal, but needed to know everything that had gone on so he could take care of me as his patient.

He could have reported her but didn't. The hospital was really good about it. The midwife told him in medical terms what was going on. He said that they were going to put an internal monitor on the baby and a contraction monitor on me in order to find out how strong the contractions really were. Also, the internal monitor would break my water and that might bring the baby down. I kept telling the doctor that I couldn't handle my contractions, but he looked at me like he probably looks at a lot of women who are in labor and say that. He said that he'd monitor me for about an hour, but after just five minutes he came in and said, "Whoa!" The contractions were so strong at this point that they were actually dangerous. They had to give me a drug to stop them so that they wouldn't hurt the baby. It was like 4:30 by now. I'd been doing this in agony for three-and-a-half hours!

The baby still didn't drop. I was told, "Your baby's not coming." And at that point, I knew I was having a C- section. Actually, I knew it an hour before. Tony had kept saying, "Don't give up," but I knew that if those intense contractions weren't bringing my baby, he wasn't coming out that way. I remember feeling scared and praying.

They finally gave me an epidural because they knew I was having a section. The only thing I could think of was that two hundred years ago, we wouldn't have made it. That's what my body was still thinking; it didn't know that a C-section was coming; it was saying, *Get this baby out of here!*

The C-section happened at the forty-two-hour mark. I was awake, and my husband watched—which was good, 'cause that's what I wanted. It took this third section for him to be able to stomach it; he couldn't watch the other two.

Everyone there was very good, and I joked the whole time. This was routine for me—my third section. In fact, I was much more awake than I'd been with the other two, where I had to have spinals rather than an epidural.

We had known that the baby was a boy from the sonogram. Soon after they pulled him out, they handed him to Tony. I heard from the nurse that many women get body tremors, even after a vaginal birth, from the trauma. It's almost guaranteed to happen after a section, so they give the baby to the father because the mother's often shaking too much. I could see my husband holding him. Then, he put the baby right by my face. He was healthy and weighed seven pounds, eleven ounces.

With my first section, they told me what to do to recover, and it was awful. With my second, I did the opposite of what they told me, and my recovery was much better. This time, I was out of the hospital forty-eight hours after the section, and I was going up and down the stairs with laundry two days after I got home. Recovery would have been great, but they gave me something—it must be new—Steri-strips. They put these little tapes across my stitches, and I had an allergic reaction to them. It was horribly itchy, and they had to give me cortisone. This slowed recovery a bit, but the problem went away.

Strange as it might seem, I feel much more resolved now after this last section, because I believe I was given a full shot at a vaginal birth. With my son, they sectioned me without letting me go into labor. With my daughter,

I labored for twenty-five hours, but when they sectioned me, I felt like I didn't get a full shot at trying for a vaginal birth. This time, not only did I do everything I possibly could have, but I also got answers to my questions. These answers now help me resolve the last two sections that I felt so emotionally uncomfortable about. I kept thinking that somebody was doing something wrong and that's why I got sectioned. Now, at least, I know that there's something physically not right, that I can't deliver vaginally—it's not my fault.

And I don't feel victimized from this last experience like I had before. I'd felt like they had done this awful thing to me, that they had butchered me. Lots of women are C-sectioned for no good reason. Now I know that wasn't the case with me.

I know now that my body couldn't do it. When I labored in the hospital with those terrible contractions, my labor was not normal. It was really strange, I can't explain it. My baby even somehow knew that things weren't right because he was trying to crawl back up inside me, trying to get away from the birth canal.

The whole medical field—they don't tell you enough. They don't give you enough information—women who are C-sectioned, especially, aren't given enough.

I spoke with the OB who delivered this last baby 'cause I was thinking about a fourth child. This time it would have to be an absolutely planned C-section because of my physical problem. I have a lot of scar tissue because I've had three surgeries close together on the same spot, and he said that I'd be better off waiting about six years so my body could have time to heal. But I'm not willing to wait another six years. I'd have to have another right away or not at all—and I haven't made up my mind yet.

∞

Mesa birthed both her daughters while living in Ithaca, New York, an upstate college town. At the time, her husband, Stuart, was employed as a set designer for the theater department at Ithaca College, and Mesa was a graduate student in English and taught part-time. Kate, whose birth is described here, is now four, and Sasha, their second daughter, is three.

Opting for a C-Section

I came to parenthood late. We never made the decision to have a baby. We got pregnant accidentally. I remember one afternoon talking to a friend on the telephone and telling her I had reached that point in my life where I had to make this decision, and didn't know how. I hadn't been around babies. I didn't feel fated to have one. Yet I wasn't strong about not wanting kids either. Here I was, thirty-four—tick, tick, tick—talking to a friend about whether or not to have a baby, and little did I know, as I was speaking, the decision already had been made.

When I realized that my period was late, I bought an in-home pregnancy test. I remember looking at the result and feeling a flood of pure joy. Maybe intellectually I couldn't figure out what I wanted, but as soon as I saw that I had a baby, I felt pure unadulterated joy.

Another friend of mine was about six months pregnant at that time, and she and I began to discuss a lot of things about pregnancy. She was very certain that she wanted to have a midwife. Carefully, she was thinking through her pregnancy and birth. This was her first baby, too. And I was going along in a similar vein with her. I certainly agreed that a woman's birthing experience had become absorbed into a medical experience, and that instead of being able to have a birth and celebrate the baby, the focus was on medicine, doctors, and prevention of illness. The woman had little to do with it. She was a body on which doctors performed their professional business, and this was awful. My friend was using a midwife, and I decided to use the same practice. There was one doctor associated with two midwives.

Everything was moving along fine, but when I was about six months pregnant, I began to realize that somehow giving birth wasn't going to happen for me. I'm only five feet tall and small all over. They still use a pediatric speculum to examine me. I know that many women feel that there's no way a baby is coming out of them, but I had a lot more justification than most women. Most women are the size of normal adults. I'm the size of a twelve-year-old child.

At around this same time, my husband and I began attending Lamaze classes, and I started feeling very disjointed. I was beginning to realize that I wasn't *psychologically fitting in* with the other women. Early on, I remember we were asked to respond to the question, "How do you feel about your pregnancy?" Every one of the other women talked about the great miracle of birth, the joyful sense of the baby growing in them. And I felt terrible. I was sick in the morning and remember wishing that a woman could simply lay an egg. I'd take care of my egg if I had one! And I'd much rather take care of an egg than have this baby growing in my body. It's kind of a duality: I love the idea of having a baby, but I don't love being pregnant. I guess a lot of women feel that pregnancy is an intimacy, a bond, because the baby is a part of you. I basically didn't like it. I put up with it—I wanted my baby. But pregnancy for me is being sick, having to pee all the time, being uncomfortable, and witnessing the alarming way your body changes. It's a nightmare. All these women diet, try to keep themselves fit and, all of a sudden, there they are, growing monstrously.

Most women, I think, feel the connection with their babies on a level different from me. I always retained a sense of *my private self.* I love babies and cherish my children, but I'm also this private, separate person. And I think there are women who don't have that much separateness from their children.

I remember one mother in a playground once. Her child was in the sandbox and got sand in his mouth. The mother just leaned over and used her own tongue to get it out of his mouth. It was like he was an extension of her body. I wouldn't do that. It was as though her son was really never out of her body. I don't want to eat my kids' dirty mouths.

And then I remember that the Lamaze class instructor was planning to show a film of a woman giving birth, and I absolutely did not want to see this film. It wasn't fear, it was an issue of privacy. I have a strong sense that the genitals are very private. And I guess that's odd because I'm not a particularly modest person. I go to nude beaches and I've been a nude model. But the idea of watching something as intimate and personal as giving birth was not appealing. I know a lot of people like watching; for instance, they like watching people making love in movies. But it's not where the experience is for me. There's a *wrongness* in watching. When you're making love, you should be inside the experience, not outside and watching in this voyeuristic way. And for me, it's the same thing having to watch a woman give birth. It's too intimate, personal, private—somehow a violation.

And as I was being gripped by all these feelings, I came to realize that I didn't want to give birth in a hospital with a midwife. Or a doctor. Or anybody, for that matter. If someone could tell me that everything would come out alright, I would have preferred to have had my baby *at home by myself*. But I knew that that wasn't going to happen. At about six months pregnant, I told my midwife that I wanted to have a C-section. She referred me to the doctor, which ended up being rather ironic. The doctor, you see, was the head of a task force in charge of reducing the cesarean rate in the county. This doctor was Korean and didn't speak very good English. He struck me as a very technocratic doctor and made comments on numerous occasions about how the midwives' lack of sterility was actually rather disgusting to him. He was an ill-suited man to be working with these midwives. And I think, given his preference, he always would have gone for cesareans. He seemed to like the idea of surgically removing a baby from a woman. But here he was involved in this effort to lower the rate of cesarean births, and here I come, having gone to a midwife first, and now coming back to request a cesarean, for no other reason than I didn't want to give birth. He was in a quandary, and he wanted me to talk to a psychologist and then to confer with another doctor.

Although, at bottom, I felt that there would be a medical reason for my needing a C-section—because I'm so small—I didn't believe that I could present them with a real medical analysis. After all, *they* weren't saying, "You look too small to pass a baby." And they should know; they were poking up there all the time. And that was another thing that was going on—I was becoming, unlike most people, more and more *uncomfortable* with vaginal examinations. As I've gotten older, I've gotten more emotionally vulnerable, and instead of becoming more callous towards medical exams, they have become less and less bearable to me. I've also developed a lot of resentment toward the medical community. Every time you're in a medical situation, you're in a deeply bureaucratic situation. No one responds to you as an individual. They have a rule to cover everything. Protocol takes precedence over individuality. I'm someone who absolutely cannot abide bureaucracies of any sort.

When I went to the psychologist, I found myself face to face with a woman who had deeply wanted to give birth vaginally herself, but had to have C-sections. She always regretted this and felt deprived of having a real birthing experience. The two of us, I think, looked at each other across a vast gulf. At that point, I was realizing that I didn't want a birth and didn't want a labor, *a public labor*—and that was how it seemed to me. Giving birth for me is as private and intimate as having sex, and thinking about doing either in front of an audience of strangers made my flesh crawl.

And again, remember, I'm five feet tall. Both my girls were eight-pound babies. My first was twenty inches long—about one third of my height. And I think I had a realistic sense that I couldn't have birthed my babies vaginally anyway. If I could have been assured of a perfect vaginal delivery at home alone, perhaps I would have gone that way. But, of course, I couldn't. That's why, given what I felt, I needed to explore other options.

I wanted to keep the medical staff away—excuse me for being blunt—away from my cunt. That was my desire. I wanted birth to be quick, and to get the doctors away from me and my private body—but I wanted my baby.

I also felt very strongly that the experience wasn't something really important to me. What was really important was the baby. *I wanted that baby.* I was writing letters to my unborn baby and really looking forward to this child. I didn't have the connection to the experience of giving birth that most women seem to have. Birth only seemed to be a necessary evil.

And yet I really respect the sense that some women have of birth as a powerful transformational experience—that it's a labor of love and has great spiritual effects in women's lives. I respect that. But I can't help that I don't feel it. I believe that symbolism is a powerful force in our lives. I believe the symbolic act of getting married to your lover is very important and it's not the same as living together. I think symbolic events really have great psychological weight. But birth didn't carry anything symbolic for me.

After speaking with the psychologist, who must have filed some report back to my doctor, I went to see another doctor, a woman doctor, who was Indian, and also didn't speak good English. By this time I took a more medical approach. I told her that I was small and that I was quite sure that I'd end up having a C-section anyway. I told her that I didn't want to go through labor and wanted to just plan a cesarean. She wasn't very involved and didn't seem to care. It was all okay with her. I went back to the Korean doctor, and he was the one who ultimately did the C-section.

And despite all these hoops I jumped through, I'm not sure that I successfully managed to avoid all the stuff I wanted to avoid by having a C-section. They had to catheterize me and I found that experience horrifying. This female nurse had to scrub away at my vagina and insert a tube. It was absolutely unbearable to me. And she did it in front of the collective staff of the operating room. The procedure contained everything I was trying to avoid.

I remember a few days before the scheduled C-section, my husband and I went out yardsaleing. I can remember that brooding grayness of a typical Ithaca spring day. And I remember a song came on the car radio. It was some funny folk song about a farmer who plants an enormous turnip which he can't get out, so he begins to sing: "Come on, turnip, come out, come on, turnip, come on out!" But would that stubborn turnip come out? No. So his wife has to come out, and she pulls and sings, and then the dog comes out, and he pulls and sings. And on and on with this succession of creatures all pulling the stubborn turnip. On the day of the cesarean, we planned to play a tape I had asked my husband, Stuart, to make of Erik Satie's music. He's a French composer, and his music has very simple, haunting, contemplative kinds of tunes. There's a sadness mixed into a kind of happiness. I was trying to create the right emotional atmosphere to the surgery. But unfortunately, Stuart recorded the wrong side. Men! It was the louder, more brassy side, and I was disappointed. But even that mistake seemed somehow like life itself—with all its stupidity and complications.

I had spinal anesthesia that numbed me from the waist down, but allowed me to be conscious. And to get this, I had to crawl over on my side into a fetal position while some guy poked away back there. The room was cool, and I was shivering uncontrollably. I had to remain very still so that he didn't poke the wrong thing. I was just very nervous and cold. They had to come and cover me with warm towels. After the anesthesia was in me, they put up a tent so I couldn't see them cut. And that was fine. The fiction that I'm solid flesh through and through, I think is a healthy one. I don't like thinking of all the inner workings of my body, which means, of course, mortality. So they put up the tent and the baby was very high. In fact, the midwife who I had seen that morning told me that she felt the baby would have been a cesarean anyway. The baby was just very high and wasn't showing any signs of coming down. And so, when the doctor made the incision, which I couldn't feel at all, neither he nor the assisting doctor could get the baby. They had to physically push her down from the outside. And so I started singing, "Come on, turnip, come on out, come on, turnip, come on out." And I remember many little eyes flashing over to me—it was all I could see of these masked people. I think they wondered if I had gotten punch-drunk from the anesthesia. But it seemed quite clear to me—here was my stubborn turnip.

And then suddenly, everybody yelled, "There it is!" Then they all yelled again in unison, "It's a girl!" And out came this little squalling thing. I felt an enormous thrill of acceptance and joy. A girl! I didn't realize until that moment that what I wanted was a girl. And I think I would have felt the same way had it been a boy. They took her away and did their hospital thing. I had asked to be put out afterwards so they could stitch me up. Then, I was in a recovery room. When I woke, I immediately wanted my baby. But first, they wheeled me into my room. Then they brought me Kate. I remember all that I wanted to do was to look at her. I was mesmerized. There were these expressions that flitted across her face in succession. I think this happens to all babies. She'd have this angelic little smile, and suddenly there'd be the axe murderer's fury. And then there'd be kind of a bored look. Every kind of emotion that was possible in human experience was going on in this little newborn's face. I was astounded. I remember thinking in all seriousness, why don't we just have a television channel where we could put a camera on the faces of newborns so that we could watch them all day!

$$\infty$$

Lisa lives near Memphis, Tennessee, and runs a halfway house for people transitioning from prison. She lives with her husband, Richard, who teaches eighth-grade history, son Robert, age seven, and daughter Anna, age fifteen months. Lisa's first pregnancy was an emergency C-section, and her second pregnancy resulted in a stillbirth at six months' gestation. Here Lisa briefly discusses her first two birthing experiences and then describes her third, which was complicated by health problems and resulted in the decision to have a planned C-section.

It's the End Result

I had an emergency C-section for my first child, Robert. We'd planned for a natural birth and had taken classes, practiced breathing, and felt completely prepared. I had thirteen hours of natural labor when they came in and said, "This baby's not coming. You're going to have a section." I had never dilated past two centimeters, and the cord was wrapped around Robert's shoulder and neck. At one point, his heart rate dropped and my blood pressure shot up. That's when they decided to do the section. In six minutes they had him out. Even though we were disappointed that we had not had a "normal birth," we were thrilled that the baby was healthy and everything was okay. My husband got the whole section on video—even his first cry.

With my second pregnancy I had some health problems, and my weight dropped down to about seventy-eight pounds. I had checked into a hospital, and they'd released me because they couldn't find out what was wrong. I was in bed for about six or seven weeks when finally I was referred to a doctor who told me that I had Crohn's disease. All the while I didn't even realize I'd been pregnant—I'd stopped having periods for a long time. When we found out, we were thrilled on the one hand but terrified on the other, because I had lost so much weight and had been so sick.

My OB and my gastroenterologist worked together. They wanted to get my weight back up and protect the baby the best they could. They had to do all these tests on me, and they were all a risk to the baby—but they told me I was going to die unless they did them. I didn't have a choice.

They were able to get my weight back up and my pregnancy started going real well. Then, one day, I was taking my son to swimming lessons— it was during the summer, June, I think. I began to have a lot of pain, feeling like I was going to be sick in the car. I thought I was having a Crohn's attack and stopped at my grandfather's house close by. I called my mother, and she came right over and took me to the emergency room. At the hospital, they wanted to find the baby's heartbeat—I told them not to, and that I was having a Crohn's attack. I was so small that they were always having trouble finding the baby's heartbeat—but they kept insisting. I yelled, "Leave the baby alone!" But they wouldn't, and when they couldn't find a heartbeat, I was sent up for an ultrasound.

The baby was gone—his little heart wasn't beating anymore. We later found that he had tied himself up in the cord, literally a true knot. And that's why he died. It was kind of frustrating for us because we'd gone to such great lengths to protect him and finally lost him over something that was totally unrelated to my illness.

They induced labor. My doctor sat with me, almost in tears, in the emergency room until my sister got there. My husband was in school. They knocked me out and induced labor. I had a vaginal birth that I can't remember well, thank goodness—I was told to push a couple of times, and my sister helped me to actually deliver, which was a real sacrifice to her because she wanted children but could never have any.

When the baby was born, they handed him to me. I was in such a drugged stupor that I can't recall much. I wish I'd been more alert. They took him away before I was really ready—I don't think they realized. It's a Catholic hospital and all three births have been here. When the hospital people came in to take him, my first question was, "What's going to happen to this baby?" I was worried that they'd do research or something on him. They assured me they wouldn't and that he'd be buried in their public cemetery where they place all these preborn children in unmarked graves. But it didn't seem right to me. We have burial policies and own funeral plots, so we had him buried in the space that I'll be buried in. When I die, they'll just pull his little coffin out, put me in, and then put him back on top of me. People think it's strange, but it's a comfort to me to think that we'll share that space for eternity.

After that experience, I very much wanted to get pregnant again. The doctor said I should wait a minimum of three months, but really it would be best to wait a year. We didn't want to wait though, and in the third month I got pregnant. I went in and the doctor asked, "Have you missed a period yet?" And I said, "No, but I'm pregnant."

They watched me the entire pregnancy. I was probably in the doctor's office every two weeks. It was a little scary at first—every little twinge, Richard and I would sort of panic. With Crohn's disease, you never know when it's going to flare up. We were nervous and excited, but after the twentieth week, things started going real well, and after the twenty-fifth week we felt like we were home free.

We decided to plan a C-section. It was a relief. After we lost the second baby, the idea of having a vaginal birth was emotionally upsetting to me. The only vaginal birth I'd experienced was unsuccessful, and I didn't want to be reminded and carry fear into this next birth. So I was actually relieved when the doctor suggested it to me because I wanted one and thought they'd feel I was nuts if I requested it—although, I know, some women do.

We made the decision at seven months. We'd talked about it before, but I'd had a fainting spell at seven months, and that clinched it. We made jokes with my doctor, asking when would be a good time for him. Finally, we nailed him down at eight months; we picked a date that was around his vacation so that he'd be there. For a lot of reasons, it was actually quite nice.

We picked a time when my son and my husband would be out of school and planned it so that my family could all be there. It was very relaxed, and I knew what to expect.

The day of the C-section was very nice. We had to be at the hospital at 5:30 in the morning, so we got up very early and fixed my son breakfast. He wore a T-shirt from his sibling class that read, "We had our baby." We took pictures right before we left and then went all together to the hospital. It was a Friday. My sister, brother-in-law, and mother were there. They watched my son and waited out in the hall, just outside—I saw all of them just before she was born.

In the delivery room, everybody was joking and cutting up, until at the thirteenth hour, they needed to find the baby's heartbeat. They started looking and couldn't find it. I kept saying, "It's okay, I felt her move this morning." My doctor called for the ultrasound to be brought quickly into the room. But the baby wouldn't move, and they never found the heartbeat. They decided to go ahead with the section. I was really scared and thought, *Here we go again!* They put in the epidural, and it didn't take. They kept saying, "Do you feel this?" and I'd say, "Yes!" Then, they'd say, "You can't. You're just having ghost pains." But I insisted, "Don't cut me open now, I can feel everything!"

Finally, my doctor came in, and he believed me. He's a really nice man. "Lisa," he said, "We can put in another epidural, or we can knock you out." I really wanted to be awake, so I told him to try again.

The epidural was the worst part of the whole C-section. There's something really creepy about knowing that they're putting a needle into your spine. You can sort of feel what's going on, like when the dentist numbs your mouth, but you can feel things . . . a kind of pressure.

This epidural took. They did the C-section without ever finding a heartbeat, but Anna began to cry even before they lifted her out. As soon as they cut my uterus open, we heard her holler. My husband and I both started crying—her scream was the most wonderful sound we'd ever heard. She was born at 8:36 in the morning and weighed almost seven pounds.

Almost as soon as the baby was born, they let my husband take her out into the hall to see everybody. It was great. It's a very family-oriented hospital. Anna stayed with us in a room practically the whole time. I kept her in bed and she'd nurse on and off constantly. The last night at the hospital, my son came with a sleeping bag and had a slumber party with his new sister. It was real sweet.

I came home from the hospital and things went fine. Anna was a fiery little thing—she's got quite the temper. I had no problems afterwards, and I've continued to work and raise my kids. I haven't had a Crohn's attack since I lost the baby and feel like I have the disease under control. I've even been teased because I'm up to a whopping 140 pounds now!

People think that having a C-section is the end of the world. When I had the emergency C with Robert, it was like, "Oh, I'm so sorry for you." All these women came out of the woodwork to tell me how sorry they were. And I really didn't get it—I was thinking, *What's the deal here? I have this beautiful, healthy baby!* I didn't have this huge sense of loss and deprivation that people seemed to think that I should have. And then when I planned Anna's birth by section, people thought I was nuts. There are all these books that advocate natural birth, so you feel like a failure if you don't have one. We didn't buy into that. We found a book on C-sections that was upbeat and positive. And we truly feel like we had good experiences. I think women need to know that if they have a vaginal birth, well, that's wonderful; but if they have a C-section, that's wonderful, too. After all, it's the end result that counts.

$$\wp$$

Elly lives outside New York City with her husband, Mitchell, and four children: Jillian, age nine; Chelsea, age seven; Travis, age five; and Dylan, age two. Elly spoke about her first V-BAC experience, the birth of Travis. Elly had just gone back to working full-time as an office manager and was in the process of learning how to juggle work and mothering responsibilities.

Fighting All the Way

After having a C-section with Chelsea, I knew, even before getting pregnant with Travis, that I wanted a V-BAC. My first, Jillian, was a vaginal birth, but with Chelsea I had been plagued with outbreaks of herpes and decided to plan a C-section. I didn't want to risk delivering with open sores. After Chelsea, when we were trying to get pregnant again, I knew I wanted a V-BAC, and did my best to prevent having outbreaks. That was my goal.

I took lysine and didn't wear any underwear. Also, I thought positive, happy thoughts. I did have open sores during most of that pregnancy, but towards the last month, they cleared up.

I remember reading *Silent Knife*, and that book gave me the courage to ask all the right questions. I learned that doctors sometimes want to perform a second C-section after a first for a variety of reasons—the incision might not hold up, labor could be too hard physically, the uterus might explode . . . And when my doctor voiced some of these same concerns, I was able to ask him, "Has any one of things ever happened to a patient of yours?" And he said, "No." So I asked, "What makes you think they'll happen to me? I'm a big strong woman." I countered all his negatives with positives.

I also told him that I didn't want a fetal monitor because I wouldn't be free to move around and that might slow labor up so much that they'd do another C-section. Then he wanted to do an internal exam, but I told him that I had active herpes and that he couldn't. Finally, he looked at me and said, "When did you go to medical school?" We continued to argue all through my pregnancy.

I went into labor on a Friday afternoon in April. I didn't realize it was labor; I thought it was just *that gassy belly of mine*. When evening came, I found myself going through my regular routine—getting the kids fed, bathed, and ready for bed. My husband came home in the middle of all this, and I said, "By the way, hon, I'm going to have this baby really soon." He said, "Okay, let's eat dinner first," and we kept going through our normal routine. But I could feel contractions; I could even feel my perineum flex and relax. It was wonderful. I was in no pain. I thought, *I should be timing these*, but there were too many things that had to be done. I didn't have the luxury of sitting around pampering myself.

It must have been 10:00 at night. We're observant Jews, and because it was Friday we had begun the Sabbath. My mom came over to watch the girls, and Mitchell and I decided to leave for the hospital. We arrived at around 10:40. They offered me a wheelchair at the Emergency Room entrance, but I didn't want it. I was doing deep breathing at this point, and walked down the hallway, took the elevator, and went to the labor room—I just walked in.

But suddenly, everything went topsy-turvy. People came with scrub outfits on, trying to throw a fetal heart monitor on me. They came with an IV cart. And I'm like, *What do these people think they're doing?* "Oh no, no, no!" I said. I turned to the doctor, "Remember I told you to wear comfortable pants when I went into labor? I want you to be able to bend down and check the heartbeat with a stethoscope, not a monitor!" I was extremely adamant and very upset. Mitchell was reading a newspaper, and he looked up and told the doctor, "My wife knows what she's talking about. Leave her alone." I had kept him up so many nights explaining all I was learning from all the many books I read. He knew what I wanted and didn't want. I wasn't a sick person; I was having a baby.

The doctor left in a huff and said to one of maternity nurses, "You talk to her!" He made a big production out of shaking his papers, picking up his pen, and filling out all these forms.

I had only gotten a quick internal when I first arrived. I was at six centimeters, and thought, *Well, I have hours and hours of work ahead of me.* But I was wrong—Travis was born by 11:50!

I didn't have any pain. I consciously disassociated from my physical self and concentrated on uniting with the baby inside me. I could focus all my energies on the baby and think about what the baby needed to do. I kept thinking: *Come on down!* like in the TV game show, *The Price is Right*. The MC calls a player up to the stage by shouting, "Come on, come on down!" And that's what I was chanting to myself. *Come on down! We're opening up now, so come on down!*

There was no sense of panic or rush. Mitchell continued to read the newspaper—which was fine with me. When he spoke, his voice was comforting. He just read the newspaper. That's what my husband does. So there we were: Elly and Mitch. And this is how we give birth.

My water broke on its own, and after that warm rush of water, I felt the baby's head. I told the nurse, "He's coming!" She said something about having to wait a moment to check with the doctor. I told her, "I'm not waiting."

I remember people flooding into the room with panic on their faces because it's against hospital procedures to have a V-BAC outside the surgical unit. But that was just tough toodles on them! I wasn't moving! I was going to give birth, and that was going to be the end of this discussion!

I was on my side when my water broke. I hoisted myself up to my butt in a semi-sitting position. I had to ask the nurse for help. Mitchell stood behind me because I needed to push against him. I gave two or three pushes—the baby's head crowned. Someone ran for the doctor. He came in and quickly said, "Okay, stop pushing." I asked, "Is the umbilical cord over the baby's head?" And he said, "Yes." But it wasn't alarming to me. I trusted the doctor enough to know that he could just unhook the cord.

We thought we were going to have another girl. But when Travis came out, the doctor said, "It's a boy!" My husband cut the umbilical cord, and we just sat there together laughing, just laughing.

I claimed Travis as my own right away. I had them put him on me immediately. I started smelling him and letting him nurse. I never tore and didn't need an episiotomy. And Travis was a big baby—nine pounds, eight ounces.

I birthed the placenta—which is always hard for me. It's this leftover blob that you just have to get out. Then, when they took the baby away for a moment, the doctor actually began to yell at me. But I was on such a high that I didn't allow his negativism to affect me. He said the knot in the umbilical cord had been dangerous. I told him it wasn't. He said that I was bleeding a lot, and that maybe my uterus had torn. I told him, "No. My uterus hasn't torn!" It was like he was trying to fool me into thinking I'd been walking on the edge of a high mountain, and I was just lucky that I hadn't fallen off. But I wasn't buying this stuff, and neither was my husband. The bottom line was: I felt great, and the baby was great.

I had argued with this doctor all though my pregnancy, and here we were still arguing after the birth. I don't know what his problem was and didn't really care—I had been too busy giving birth.

In between having babies, I went back to school. For an English class assignment we had to write about a very emotional time in our lives. I choose to write about Travis's birth. This is part of what I wrote:

"The room was charmless, stark, and utilitarian. It contained no single embellishment that couldn't be hosed down and sterilized. It was an icy, cold room, suitable for a dozen various medical procedures—from abortion to autopsy. And it was amidst the pain and passionless stares of an unknown medical staff that I birthed my baby. The aching opening of my cervix was nothing more than a process to them. They were ready to rip, cut, snip, and suction. I needed to be comfortable and be comforted. I needed to breathe, to move, to bellow, and to moan. They were empty and ungiving. Their surgical masks could not cover their desire to drug me into submission. They wanted me still, unmoving, on my back, and quiet. I fought their attempt to invade my veins. My baby needed my blood, rich and warm, not numbed by their steely acids. I grew loud and rude and determined. Frantically, I groaned deep moans that vibrated with the legacy of mothers who had come before me—with the opening of our bodies to bring forth a slick, wet baby born of our volition. And with one final and ancestral scream, my baby burst out into this world, indignantly crying for my arms. I was there to receive him, awake, alert, and on guard."

Looking back, I realize that I had chosen this doctor because he has access to a hospital that's three minutes from my home. That was almost the most important thing to me—that I would be near my other children. I wanted to stay at home and labor for as long as possible without having to run to some sort of New Age birthing center that would be an hour out of the way. I felt that, regardless of the surroundings, I was going to have the birth I sought simply by telling people, "Don't touch me, leave me alone. I know what I'm doing."

I had clearly communicated these feelings to my husband. Mitchell trusted that I knew what I was doing, but the doctor was very patronizing. I told myself that as long as he could honor my desire not to have another C-section, I didn't care about his attitude. It wasn't until I was in hard labor that I realized the extent of his anger with me. I was a challenge to his authority.

Yet I did return to him. When I became pregnant with my fourth child, Dylan. After all, I had had two healthy children with him, and good, bad, or indifferent, he had delivered them. I wasn't planning on marrying the guy— I was only hiring him to help me give birth. I remember that during the first examination, I was lying on the table buck naked and he asked me to sign a waiver giving him permission to do anything he wanted for this next pregnancy and delivery. I'm like, "What? I need to speak to my husband about this." I couldn't believe what he was asking me to do. Mitchell and I decided not to use him—we had our fourth with someone else.

It's a pity that I had to fight so much to get what I wanted. Yet I feel that with every birth comes emotional growth—growth that I can claim for myself, yet share with other women. It's strange, but birth is like the punchline of a joke that men will never get.

Julia lives with her husband, Bill, and son, Joseph, age fifteen months, in a town of about eight thousand in Iowa. Before becoming pregnant with Joseph, Julia taught piano and voice. Bill works as a carpenter.

Emergency C-Section

I waited a while before deciding to marry. I wanted to do many things first. Bill and I went together for about three and a half years—I'm not a gambling kind of person—and I was sure that this was the man I wanted to marry. We were married for about three years before we decided that it was time to get pregnant. I did all sorts of reading and research on pregnancy and birth beforehand; I wanted to be prepared.

It took about four months to conceive. It was weird because I was at the point of thinking, *Oh no, I better go get us checked out,* and then I got pregnant. I knew right away, about three weeks after conception. I kept real good track of my periods, and because we were anticipating this moment for such a long time, I was watching myself very closely. When I was just one week overdue, I thought, *This is it!*

I was in at the doctor's from day one. I wanted to make sure everything was okay—I was being real anal-retentive about the whole thing. During my first trimester, my hormones were all over the place, and I was a real basket case. I was acting very strange, but I didn't want to tell my family until I was three months along. A lot of people I knew had early miscarriages, and I didn't want everyone to anticipate a baby and then be disappointed. I told my parents at Christmas by giving them coffee cups with *grandparents* printed on them. They kind of looked at us and said, "Well, we wondered why you were acting so psychotic."

I must have been awful—very emotional, moody, demanding, and worried. Even after the three-month mark, I was still paranoid for a couple of months. I don't know if it was hormones or just facing the unknown—like I said, I'm not the kind of person who likes to go into anything unprepared. I remember at one point, my mom made an offhand comment about having a baby shower, and I took it the wrong way and almost didn't speak to her for months.

My whole family knows me well, so they gave me a wide berth—whatever Julie wants, no problem. Everyone just backed off. I'm sure it was like walking on eggshells. Bill was great with me; he's really mellow—very, very mellow. It takes him a while to get angry, and I have to make him talk about what he's mad about. But overall, we have a really good relationship; we're lucky.

I never had to throw up during those first three months, but there were certain foods I couldn't eat. Then, after about four or five months, I hit that plateau where you feel great all the time.

For prenatal care, I went to my general practitioner—the one I'd been seeing since I was ten. That's basically all we have around here. We have a hospital and a clinic with four or five doctors in town—so we're very fortunate. But they rotate, and there was a chance that he wouldn't be the one on call when I delivered. He's very grandfatherly and would talk about how to love your child, and that parenting wasn't easy. He also knew a lot about breech birth, unlike doctors today who'd rather just section you than deliver breech. And just temperamentally, I really liked him.

I wanted to start Lamaze classes early and then take Bradley classes after. But the Lamaze people said that I had to wait, and we didn't have access to Bradley here.

When we finally were able to attend Lamaze, it was really good. Also kind of funny 'cause on the first day they show a film of a birth—I guess to get you over the shock, to get you used to it. At the end of the film, some people are crying, some are sitting there with this look on their faces like they'd been goosed, and some don't come back the next week. Some men, that is—the women usually come.

They recommended perineal stretching, and we'd practice that at home. It was a just a real great way for us both to be closer. I really wanted Bill to feel like he was part of the whole thing, and I didn't want to draw back within myself. That was really important to me. This was half his project.

We visited the hospital. They were kind of in transition, setting up a birthing room, building new operating rooms, and using one of the older operating rooms as a temporary labor/deliver room. The birthing room, at the time, was pretty stark, not put together like you'd find at a major, metropolitan hospital. But it was much better than the other room, which looked like a great big tin can. It gave me the creeps. They had this chair with stirrups, and they sit you here and roll you back and lift you up—like some sort of pig ready to be butchered. The floor was concrete, and I kept thinking, *What if they drop the baby? It'll crack its head!* At least the birthing room was carpeted. It was the better option, and that's where I wanted to deliver.

I really had drummed it into my brain that things were going to be different when the baby got here. So I took advantage of being able to do stuff while Joseph was still inside me. I belong to a community group, and that year was our town's 125th birthday. We were planning to put on a play, which turned into a musical. I composed music for this show, and around eight months pregnant, I sprained my ankle. So at the end of my pregnancy, there I was with a cast on, working on musical scores from 6:00 in the morning till 10:00 at night. That's all I did. I gained an awful lot of weight, but this involvement kept me busy, and I probably would have gained more had I not been doing it. I never got the cleaning instinct, but I did sew—I sewed tons of stuff; it was weird. I still have piles of fabric in my sewing room.

The weekend before the show opened, on Saturday night, June 27, I went into labor. Bill and I had been up at the high school since 6:00 A.M., working all day on a set. I had had false labor the night before. Bill was in bed, and around midnight, I began to have contractions. I was up and knew it was labor because the pains were really, really even. I just stayed awake, and about 1:00 woke Bill up. At 3:00 in the morning, we decided to go to the hospital.

They checked me, and I was only dilated to one centimeter. The doctor on call, whom I had never seen before, decided to let me stay. He knew this was my first baby and wasn't sure how labor would progress. It was great; I was the only one on the floor and got the birthing room.

I stayed up all night, walking and going to the bathroom—just doing everything that you're supposed to do. I stayed up all the next day, Sunday, but by Sunday night, I'd only progressed to four centimetres.

They put me on the external fetal monitor every so often and I'd have to lay there for an hour at a time—which really ticked me off. It was supposed to tell you when a contraction was coming, but it never did. I got sick of that stupid machine.

At around 9:00 Sunday night they said, "You need to get some sleep. Why don't we give you something to help you?" I said, "Okay, fine." I dozed for a while, and Bill took a nap. Every fifteen minutes, I'd wake with a contraction—they were really spread out.

By 1:00 Monday, I still wasn't progressing. They gave me something to help me relax. I'm not sure what it was—a pill, I think. Then, in an hour, I went from like four to seven. At the time, I thought, *Alright, this is going to be great. I'm finally going to make it.*

By 4:00 that morning, I had the radio on in the room and we were listening to light jazz and classical. I was going into really hard labor and the contractions were right on top of each other. I said, "Oh, we're finally doing it! This is going to be great!"

Then they checked me. I thought transition was coming, but they said I wasn't going anywhere again. I'd gotten stuck and couldn't take it anymore. I said, "Take me home. I want to go home!" I was getting delusional and didn't know what was going on. I had thought I could see the end of the tunnel, but I wasn't going anyplace, and I lost it.

I was feeling the urge to push, and they kept telling me not to. I wasn't effaced, and I wasn't dilated completely. I was, like, at seven. It was the hardest thing I'd ever done—I had to cross my legs. I was curled up on the bed in a fetal position, and I was screaming as hard as I could trying to hold back.

Bill was with me the whole time—in my face, he told me later. But I don't remember him. At one point, he went out for five minutes after we made the decision to have the C-section. That was the only time he left me.

The doctor was the one who suggested the C-section. At the time it felt like the baby's head was just banging against the inside of my cervix. If I had been able to walk around on my feet rather than having to stay in bed—who knows? You never know what could have happened.

It was like I was in this little brick box, beating my head against the wall. I felt like, *Let me out, let me out! This has to stop!* I couldn't see any way out. By 4:00 in the morning I thought I was on my way to success . . . that I was going to have my baby and there was a way to finish this whole great big project. But now I was in this box, and I just could not get out. He was inside of me going, *bang, bang*—like this battering. When we decided to have the C-section, everything relaxed.

By about 6:00 the surgical team were all there for the C-section. The nurses and anesthetist came in first. He was really good. He very calmly and concisely explained to me what was going to happen—and I was in there screaming at him: "Okay, okay, just do it. I've made the decision, now I just want to get it over with!"

I wanted to be awake, so I had an epidural. I had heard all these stories about how it hurt, but I didn't feel it when they stuck the needle in. The doctor checked me one more time, but I still hadn't progressed. When they gave me the epidural I could just feel this blanket of relaxation creeping up over my toes, my knees, then my stomach. I was concerned a little because I wasn't holding back anymore and assumed my body was still contracting. But the pain and mania I had before, the panic I was gripped by, just let go.

They took me into the surgery room. I didn't feel the cut or anything. It was the same feeling you have at the dentist when he's drilling your teeth. You know what's happening, you feel what's happening, but it's not painful. I just felt this little pulling feeling, and I kept trying to look over the shield that they had. But they wouldn't let me. They were talking about contaminating the field and were firm about that. As soon as they got him out, they showed him to me. Then they cleaned him up and took his Apgar scores. They were really good.

I remember when they first pulled him out. I could hear him cry—it was a gurgly sound—and my husband was there. He had a Polaroid camera—we didn't do any of that video stuff. Bill followed the doctors and nurses just to take pictures all the time, so I was able to see later what he looked like when he was first born. He was perfect, except for a little nick above his right eye—I think from the scalpel.

For about the first three months after having the baby, I was very, very depressed about the C-section. My mom was very mindful of watching for signs of postpartum depression because I'd been treated for a bad depression about ten years before. It was just outpatient care and counseling I needed. And my mother had had postpartum depression when she had us. It got progressively worse with each baby, and when she had her last and third child, my sister, my mom was hospitalized for a while.

My mother's situation was different than mine—she was very isolated. But, nonetheless, I was very concerned and told everyone around me all the signs to watch for. Also, about a month after the delivery, I got a uterine infection. I was having back pain which kept getting worse and worse. Then I started running a high temperature of about 103. I went in to the doctor, and he gave me antibiotics. The infection cleared up within twelve hours.

For a while after Joey's birth, I couldn't watch or listen to the sounds of childbirth. My mom rented this movie and a baby was being born in it. I had to walk into another room—I just couldn't watch. Everybody says, "The most important thing is that the baby is okay." And that's what I kept telling myself, but it sounded so hollow.

I kept feeling that I was being selfish because I didn't feel right about the whole birth experience. I mean, it wasn't what we expected or planned for.

It took me a full year to get over my feelings, to finally come to terms with my C-section. Now, it doesn't bother me much anymore.

What helped me to get over it was the realization that I was not the only person who felt that way. I read and looked for material that dealt with C-sections and V-BACs. I definitely was not the only woman who felt inadequate or that I'd been cheated because I'd had a section. Also, I came to understand that wanting a vaginal birth wasn't a matter of being selfish and that it was okay to feel sad about the whole thing. Also, it helped to take care of Joey; I'd look at him and think, *It was all worth it, no matter what I went through.* And that's the bottom line. I didn't have to feel guilty about feeling guilty. It just happened, and I didn't have any control over it.

ॐ

Jennifer is a third-generation Californian who lives in San Dimas with her African-born husband, Stephan, and their two sons: Cameron, age four; and Caleb, age seventeen months. Her first son was born by emergency C-section, and her second son was born vaginally. Here, Jennifer describes her V-BAC experience, which came after two miscarriages. Jennifer is a stay-at-home mother who used to work as a courier in Hollywood, and Stephan currently works for an oil-drilling company.

V-BAC, I Did It!

Caleb began as a "subsequent pregnancy," which means that I had two miscarriages directly before. The first miscarriage I had in my thirteenth week, and the second I had in my ninth. It made the pregnancy with Caleb high-tension almost the whole time, and it made bonding with the pregnancy very difficult. I was so afraid I would lose him that I'd tell people I wasn't going to announce this pregnancy until the kid's in kindergarten.

It was real hard. I had a serious bleed at eight weeks and had to be on bed rest for about a month. My family was very supportive though, so I was lucky. My mom only lives about ten minutes away, and she was coming and helping.

I'm into herbs and homeopathy. I don't know if the bleeding stopped because of this stuff or if it stopped because . . . well, I don't know. I'll never know what made it stop. Everything I read said that you're either going to lose the baby or you're not. So it's hard to say. I was very leery about getting up and walking around at first, but at thirteen weeks I could feel him kicking, and at that point, emotionally, I started feeling like, okay, this is it—the pregnancy is viable.

Caleb was very active. At sixteen weeks, he could knock the ultrasound machine off my belly. He's a pistol. There were times, as my belly would be growing, that he'd kick me so hard that I'd gasp. And my older son would go, "Oh, the baby must be kicking Mommy." It was a regular experience for me to have painful kicks.

The doctor I went to for this pregnancy was different from the one who delivered Cameron. We moved, but knowing what I know now, I would have wanted to change anyway. There should have been a lot more communication between me and that doctor. And, in the end, he wasn't even the one who delivered me—it was one of the other doctors in his practice. This other guy told me, "I'm giving you a chance." But he really didn't—now I know that I shouldn't have been hooked up to the IV; I shouldn't have been lying on my back; I should have been allowed to eat; and I should have been told about perineal massage. They thought my muscles were too small, too tight—whatever. Although I was in labor for fifty-three hours, there were things that he could have done, or could have told me, but didn't.

When we moved to where I now live, I got pregnant the second time and changed OBs. But I wasn't happy with the way he handled my miscarriage, and then when I got pregnant again, I really wasn't happy with him. I was bleeding four days before Christmas, and he told me to go ahead home and don't worry about it—a lot of women bleed. And this was just three months after my first miscarriage! So that day, I called around and found a doctor who would do hormone testing and give progesterone shots if you needed them. And that was the doctor I had Caleb with.

The communication between me and this new doctor was there from the very beginning. I wanted to know if he felt this pregnancy was going to make it. He was very honest with me, and when we determined that the baby was not living any more, I was able to look him in the eye and say, "I'm not going through another miscarriage. I want a D and C right now." When I got pregnant with Caleb, we continued to have a good relationship all through that pregnancy.

Now, Stephan and I had considered using midwives, but because of all the trauma that we'd gone through with the miscarriages, we were real hesitant to do anything that wasn't mainstream. Because my husband was born in Africa, he knows all about midwives and home birth. But this is his wife and his child we're talking about—and if we can use Western medicine, we'd better do it. If someone in his family in Africa needs medical care, they go to Germany.

Stephan has been here eleven years; he spent his first seventeen years in Liberia. He's seen women walking down the street, nursing their babies with their boobs hanging out. He's very relaxed in that regard. There was never any question for him about nursing our toddler, and I believe in toddler nursing. There are some things that he's uncomfortable about because of our cultural differences, but mostly we're in agreement. Anyway, we decided to stay with this OB, and we both liked him.

The rest of my pregnancy was great. Up until thirty-four weeks, I wasn't certain that I would have a V-BAC. The baby was lying sideways and I told everybody that if he didn't turn, I was going to have a cesarean. That was my emotional out. Because I'm a LaLeche League leader, I felt a little pressure from other leaders to go natural and have a vaginal birth. As part of my League duties, I counsel women to be as aware as possible. And the ethic at LaLeche is very pro-natural.

When it was sixteen days before my due date, they decided to induce. If I was going to try a V-BAC, they wanted the baby to be small so I'd be able to push it out. The size was important. On April 25, I went to the hospital and had a full day of prostaglandin gel. I got lots of contractions, but they really weren't doing anything, so I was told to go home and come back the next day. For two days, I walked around the halls with my husband and Cameron, who was three. In fact, he followed me around more than anybody—which was nice. On the second day, I began to have very hard contractions, but they weren't regular so they sent me home that night—Tuesday, it was. My cervix is really posterior and was behind the baby's head. I was very sensitive, and when they'd hook their finger in there, it would just send me to the roof. So they really couldn't gel me up a lot.

Tuesday night, they sent me home. I was still having excruciatingly strong contractions. I took some herbs to calm the contractions, because as long as I was home, I needed the break. Then, I came up with this master plan. When I saw the doctor at his office on Wednesday night—twenty-four hours after my release from the hospital—I was going to tell him to give me an epidural and then break my water. This way we'd be able to get things going.

Stephan and I were really depressed at this point—we had thought we were going to be coming home with our baby two days ago. So, all day Wednesday, we did family things, and that night we went to the doctor's office. I was the last patient of the day. He managed to check my cervix and said, "If I'd have been in there for two seconds more, I'd have broken your water." I was dilated to three. So, I said, "Well, why don't you just give me an epidural and then go ahead and break my water?" I figured that was the only way he was going to feel able to do it without me hurting a lot. He said, "If that's what you want to do. . . ."

So my plan was set into action. Thursday morning I got to the hospital, and they started me on Pitocin first. Wednesday night, I had taken castor oil to get my contractions moving. I wanted to do everything to get this kid out of me. Between the castor oil and Pitocin, I began to get into a labor pattern. They wanted me to have a good four hours of Pitocin before they broke my water. At noon the doctor came in and gave me the epidural. I told Stephan to have some lunch because I knew that once they broke my water, he wasn't going to be able to leave. He was gone longer than I anticipated, and they broke my water before he came back.

The epidural did not take. The only thing that happened was that my left leg was numb. There was no anesthesiologist; the doctor administered it himself. I remember as soon as they broke the water—a minute or two later—I had this contraction that ripped through my being. It went from these calm, nice contractions where I could breathe through them to this excruciating pain. I screamed, "No way!" Everyone came running. A nurse put something into my IV—probably to calm me. By this time, Stephan was back, and I looked at him and said, "No way, no way!" That's what I said the whole time I was in labor.

I went from three to ten centimeters in three hours—contraction after contraction, without a break. Every hour the nurse would tell me how far along I was. It took me like thirty hours just to get to one centimeter with Cameron, so every time she told me how far I was, I'd say, "No way!" I was like, *This is incredible!* But I wasn't fighting the labor. While I was saying, "No way," I was doing everything I knew to move my labor along.

The epidural still didn't do anything; I don't know why they didn't just take it out. I could have been up walking. And I was screaming so much that nurses would come in and say, "Jennifer, you're scaring the other patients on the ward—calm down!" But I didn't care. It hurt too much. It was like I went straight into transition. I had this horrible kind of pain that only goes away when you push. I kept telling Stephan, "I can't do this." And Stephan's like, "You're already at six—you're going to do this!" It was such a difference from my first labor, because then he just sat there, biting his nails a lot. With this one, I was demanding for him to stand right here and breathe with me. And he got me through it. I mean, really, if it wasn't for him, I would have said, "Give me drugs."

So three hours pass, and the nurse says, "You're almost at ten—go ahead, start pushing." I was like nine and three-quarters. Again, I said, "No way!" At first, I couldn't believe it! I was still in the labor room.

I started pushing, and right away it made things so much easier. I envisioned my stomach squishing the baby out. I was only having about twenty seconds between contractions. I couldn't believe how long they let me keep pushing before they decided to let me go into the delivery room. I wanted to sit up, but they wouldn't let me because of the epidural.

Finally, they wheeled me into the delivery room. I don't know exactly how long we were in there. I think they made me change beds, but at this point, I wasn't really cognizant of what else was going on. I remember I could see the baby's head in a mirror they had there. It was right there. I remember trying to reach down and feel his head. He was having some mild to moderate deceleration because he was crowning for so long—it must have been an hour and a half. The doctor told me he was going to use the vacuum. I still had the fetal heartbeat monitor on, and I was totally focusing in on the baby's heartbeat. No one told me that they'd have to detach the monitor in order to use the vacuum, so all of a sudden, there's no heartbeat at all. I was like, "What happened to the baby?" Then they told me and put on an external monitor and found his heartbeat again. I was able to focus back in. It was a very scary moment for me, and I yelled at the doctor, "Don't ever do anything like that to me again!"

I was pushing, and they were using the vacuum. I lost track of time. I remember how annoying the cloth that they'd draped over me was, 'cause I was sweating and working so hard. They put oxygen on me because of the deceleration—and that felt gross.

The nurse who was helping me was awesome. She kept saying, "You're doing so good; he's almost out!" Finally, I felt his head come out and thought, "Oh, that was his head!"

The cord was wrapped twice around his neck, and that's probably why he didn't come out as readily—he was getting strangled every time he was trying to come down. Caleb was born sunny-side up—the wrong side of his head had been pushing on my cervix the whole time. I had an episiotomy, and once his head was out, I pushed one more time, and he was born.

I wanted to nurse him as soon as he was born—this was a pretty big issue for me, 'cause with my first I had eight hours of separation. I had read about how wonderful it is to nurse right away, but Caleb didn't want to; he just lay there and kept looking around, all over the room like he was trying to find somebody. His eyes went from side to side, but he didn't want to nurse. I put him on my nipple, and he was like, *Forget this!*

The first thing that came to my mind after he was born was, *I did it!* I was crying—I was so happy. Caleb was six pounds, fifteen ounces. All these stupid doctors had told me that I wouldn't be able to deliver anything over five and a half.

I was really proud of myself, and Stephan was so excited that he wanted to run out and call his mom. But I said, "You can't call your mom now," 'cause I wanted him to hold our brand-new baby. He didn't get a chance to cut the cord because it had been wrapped around Caleb's neck.

I watched the mirror as the doctor sewed me up. Stephan held the baby for a moment but was so excited that he had to call somebody and left. To get me out of the room, they had to put me back on my bed. I don't remember when they took the epidural out. They laid Caleb right by me—I was on my belly and up on my elbows. He was all wrapped up in his blanket and his eyes were still rolling back and forth trying to see everything. Then, right in the hallway by the doors to Labor and Delivery, up comes my stepfather with Cameron.

I didn't know this at the time, but they had told Cameron that he had a baby brother, and he was crying and having a fit because he wanted a sister. When I said, "Cameron, this is your baby brother," he looked at me and said, "I wanted a baby sister. It's a girl, Mom, it's a girl!" And I said, "It's a boy, babe, it's a boy."

At that moment, it was like, here are these two kids that I love more than anything on earth and want them to be happy. But Cameron was so sad. I was proud of this baby, and yet I felt torn. It was very weird.

I never had any headaches from the epidural, but my left leg stayed numb until about 3:00 in the morning. At 1:30, I finally let them take Caleb to the nursery. He'd been born at 5:00 in the evening, and it wasn't until 1:00 that morning I felt a little bit tired.

But I woke up after about two hours and realized that there were babies crying in the nursery. I didn't want anyone to give Caleb a bottle, so I go up, stumbled in there—my left leg still felt dead to the world—and tried to find him. I was looking around and really starting to get upset. You hear of all these "switched at birth" stories. But finally, I found him; they had tucked him in this little room all by himself 'cause he was sleeping the whole time and the other babies kept waking him up. I took him back to my room, figuring that he'd want to nurse soon, anyway.

The only real problem I've had with recovery is that I felt a lot of pelvic pressure. I don't know if it's because I had an episiotomy or because Caleb's head was down there for so long and my muscles got stretched. My doctor tells me that my muscles are very, very tight down there, but I have a tendency to carry tension in my lower body—so I don't know. Some days, the pressure is so bad that I really can't stand for very long. You just don't expect this kind of thing to last sixteen months after birth.

Also, there's a period after delivery in which you're not interested in sex. I'd tell my husband, "It's not you at all. It's my hormones and nature telling me not to get pregnant because I have a nursing baby." Stephan felt bad, like I wasn't really interested in him. Not too long ago, I brought this subject up at a League meeting. I was the youngest leader there, and one leader was almost twenty years my senior. When I expressed my lack of sexual feeling and how much a problem this can become, she said, "Romance and intimacy don't always have to end in sex." And I told her, "Yeah, but you know when you're in your twenties, usually, it does."

Two

THE BIRTHING CENTER

ॐ

Some women live in areas of the country where a local birthing center offers an alternative to a hospital or home birthing experience. The popularity of these facilities is growing nationwide as more and more women seek an environment which supports a less institutional approach to birth. Women who choose to deliver in a birthing center environment tend, as a group, to be proactive in terms of their pregnancies and their prechildbirth planning. They often view the birthing experience as a unique personal challenge offering a potential for emotional and spiritual self-growth.

ॐ

Cindy is a civil engineer who lives with her husband, Steve, and their son, Eric, age eleven months, in a rural upstate New York solar-powered cabin. Steve works part of the year as a fisherman in Alaska and spends the rest of the year as a stay-at-home dad. Here, Cindy discusses Eric's birth in a rural birthing center.

A Little Bit Further from Everything

Steve is a fisherman in Alaska and is gone for part of the year. When he's home, his job is taking care of our son. We tried to plan the pregnancy so that Steve would be home for the birth—not in Alaska. We started trying in December and then got pregnant probably mid-February—which was great.

I took an in-home pregnancy test and told Steve by coming home from work and giving him a little stuffed toy. He was very happy. We immediately started thinking about where to go for prenatal care and where to have the baby. I had miscarried right around the time of my wedding—which was not too long before—and I had gone to the Planned Parenthood in Ithaca. They had just opened an OB/GYN practice, the first in the country. And so when I got pregnant—I guess it was last July—I went to Planned Parenthood because I totally supported them; they were an all-female practice and offered affordable care. I had no hesitation. They were wonderful—I mean, when I was miscarrying, I spoke to the doctor at 2:00 in the morning, and she was very thorough and pleasant. So I didn't have any doubt that that's where I wanted to go, although my husband's family is from Philadelphia and most of his sisters and cousins had gone to birthing centers there that seemed really great. I couldn't help but think, *It's too bad we don't have one here!*

And strangely enough, in between the time that I miscarried and got pregnant again, a birthing center did open up. So, I was a little torn—I wanted to support Planned Parenthood, but the birthing center seemed like an appealing alternative. It was only about forty-five minutes away, and they're basically right next door to the local hospital.

I had my first few appointments with Planned Parenthood. Then I began attending something called the Ithaca Birth Group, which was started by a group of lay midwives and ran for eight weeks. Each session is about a different issue: choice of practitioner, breast-feeding, labor, delivery, C-sections, et cetera. I heard some great stories there about the new birthing center, and then heard some stuff about what they'd require at the hospital—the Planned Parenthood group delivered at Thompkins Hospital in Ithaca. My friend had her baby there and she had a C-section. They have the highest C-section rate in the area.

The Ithaca Birth Group really wants to empower women so they can make informed decisions. Steve was in Alaska, fishing, and I was beginning to feel that I didn't want to deliver with Planned Parenthood in the hospital where my labor would be definitely controlled from the minute I walked in the door. I would have to be on their schedule, and if I didn't meet it, then tough—I'd be forced to comply.

I took the hospital tour just to give it a fair shot. The labor rooms were these little eight-by-eight cubicles, and they only had one birthing room. If you didn't get it, you labored in the labor room and delivered in the operating room, which was just kind of this *Star Wars* sterile thing. I was really put off!

Then I went to the birthing center. It's made in this beautiful old home and looks like a bed and breakfast. The director spent two or three hours with me. I never once felt like she was trying to sell me a package—she just told me, "This is what we have. This is what we offer. This is what we expect of you."

I was four months pregnant when I made the decision to go to the birthing center. I remember writing to Steve, "Look, I think we're making the right decision. You'll come back and see. I think this is better for our baby." So, from four months on, my practitioners were at the birthing center.

There were two midwives who did all the deliveries. I didn't have any chance of delivering with a doctor unless something went wrong. They were associated with Skyler County Hospital in Montour Falls—right across the street.

My pregnancy was almost trouble-free. From four to seven months I had a pain in my rib. Everyone kept saying it was the baby, but I knew that he was too small—I was looking in these books to see how big the fetus is, and there's no way something that small could have been hurting me! It turned out to be stress. My boss had found out that he had cancer in his esophagus and needed surgery, and so when he left I was four months along and put in charge of the department. I wanted to do a good job and not let him down. A couple of weeks after he came back, my pain was gone.

Other than that, I loved being pregnant. I really didn't have any complaints; I didn't have morning sickness, just a small bit of evening nausea, but I never actually got sick.

My due date was November 1. Steve got back at the end of July, and I left work when I was thirty-nine weeks. I was exhausted. I don't work in a big office, but I would feel like it took me an hour to get from one side of it to the other! I called myself a "slow-moving vehicle."

During the last three months of my pregnancy, I was getting a massage every week at a recently opened massage school. I even volunteered to get a massage in front of the whole class when they did their pregnancy massage. There was one woman who was very interested in focusing on massaging pregnant women, and I volunteered to help her—it was wonderfully beneficial for both of us. Also, Steve and I took a Bradley class from a private teacher who advertised over at the birthing center. They had a library there, and I'd be checking out books all the time. I had heard that Lamaze wasn't really good, but when I started reading about Bradley, it just made total sense to me. We finished classes the Monday before the baby was born.

During the last week before the baby was born, I had major Braxton-Hicks. Every night I'd get these incredible contractions and say to myself, *Okay, this is the night! I'm going to wake up in the middle of the night and be in labor!* Every morning I'd wake up and think, *Oh, well!* Then, after about four nights of this, I decided I wasn't going to pay attention anymore.

I had been keeping an eye on myself for going wacked-out on nesting, but somehow the Sunday before my labor started, I lost track. I began to want to cook a really big meal. I went to the farmer's market to buy some pumpkins and potatoes. I wanted to cook a ham, scalloped potatoes, and a pumpkin pie! I later realized that this must have been the early stages of labor.

We had a great meal that Sunday and went to bed thinking about how nice it was to have all these leftovers. I was very full when I fell asleep and don't even remember having Braxton-Hicks. At 2:30 in the morning, I woke up having contractions. I was like, *Alright! So exciting!* I just lay in bed and timed them. I kept turning the flashlight on to look at the clock, and they were, to the minute, twenty minutes apart. I couldn't sleep. I went downstairs. According to the Bradley Method, I was supposed to walk, so I got the dog, my husband's watch, and went for a walk. Wanda and I went down to the pond. It was a beautiful evening—the air was just a little crisp, and the breeze felt so good. I was wearing just a flannel shirt over my dress and felt very comfortable. I remember thinking, *Yes, this is what I was totally expecting labor to be like.* It was blissful. Wanda and I played frisbee at around 3:00 in the morning. I think I came back in at about 4:30, and got this book out so I could write down everything about my pregnancy. I didn't want my thoughts to be biased by labor and delivery, so I sat there writing away.

At about 6:00 in the morning, I realized I was holding my breath, and my contractions were really happening. I wasn't supposed to be doing that! I went upstairs and told Steve that I needed him to make me relax. I got into bed and actually slept about an hour and a half.

We got up at around 7:30, and I went to the outhouse. I wanted to have a major bowel movement because, from what I had read, that's what should happen—but I was disappointed. I did have a bloody show and vomit a little bit. I remember coming back into the house and thinking, *Yes, these are all the signs.* A couple of hours must have passed. The contractions went from twenty minutes to ten minutes apart, then down to five minutes apart. We began to keep really close track, waiting for them to be one minute long and five minutes apart. When they were steady like that, we called the birthing center, and Monica, one of the midwives, called us right back. She was so excited, just thrilled! She's a very "up" person, and although I liked both the midwives very much, I really wanted Monica because I felt that she was more liberal and would be able to give me more flexibility.

Monica told us to come on over. But I wasn't ready. I really felt that we were handling things fine. I wasn't uncomfortable at home. I think we stayed home for another hour before I told Steve, "It's time to start packing up the car." We needed to take food and load our bags, which were already packed. I told Steve, "We're not in any rush, so let's just do this leisurely." I didn't want him to be in a panic. I'd heard stories of men driving sixty miles an hour with a woman on her hands and knees in the back seat. I didn't want that.

When it was time to go, I just lay down in the back seat and would say, "Starting," to Steve because I didn't want him to make a sharp turn or do anything weird during contractions. I just wanted to keep relaxing.

Monica met us at the door. She was beaming! The birthing center didn't have any appointments on this day—they were only scheduling them on Tuesdays and Thursdays—so it was just Steve and me, Monica, and the secretary. There are two birthing rooms, and I picked the one that's a little bit further from everything. Then I started to cry, and said, "Monica, I'm so sorry, I don't know why I'm crying." And she said, "Well, you've come to have your baby—you're going to have your baby here! This is probably one of the most important days of your life!" I immediately felt better. She checked me. I was at four centimeters—I was very happy. I wasn't checked again until much later.

We had arrived at 10:30 in the morning, and I labored very subtly through the day—with contractions coming five minutes apart, like clockwork, all day long. They weren't horribly intense, but they were working contractions. I remember thinking at various times, *Is this the point where I'm supposed to feel totally out of control?* Because in every birth story we ever heard about or watched in a video, there was a point when the woman said, "I'm out of control." So, I kept waiting for that feeling. And I never got it.

The Bradley Method tells you to breathe deeply and work with the contractions—they're what moves the baby out. I kept that thought in my mind all day. I took naps in between, had a little to eat—just a piece of pumpkin pie—and some cherry juice. Steve went out to walk the dog a couple of times—she was staying in the car.

Near 8:00 that night, we tried some nipple stimulation, and soon afterwards my contractions started kind of making me thrust forward. Monica asked if I felt like pushing. But I didn't. I felt that I wasn't in transition yet. I kept feeling the need to thrust forward, and Monica suggested she check me again—that was still about 8:00. I was nine and a half centimeters.

Soon, my water started to trickle, and Monica suggested she could push my cervix open that last half centimeter during my next contraction—which she did. The nurse came in to assist around 8:30. The contractions were still only five minutes apart. Monica made me a little mixture of blue and black cohosh roots—they're herbs, and I think I had about ten or fifteen drops in juice. We were trying to get the contractions going strong so I could push.

I was really confused. Here I was at ten centimeters, yet I never felt transition. I wasn't having an urge to push, just that thrusting feeling. I was sitting on the bed with my butt down and my back at about a forty-five-degree angle. My knees were up and I felt totally ineffective at pushing. I tried pushing on the toilet for a little bit, but my husband was incredibly fearful of me having the baby there—we'd seen some movies of that. I tried squatting on the toilet with my feet on a little bench. I tried sitting on a beach ball and leaning over it—that didn't work. I went back to the bed.

In the Bradley Method they tell you to be supportive of your partner. All during the day when Monica and Steve would tell me how great I was doing, I felt totally good. Now when they said it, I was like, "You guys are lying through your teeth!"

At some point in all this pushing, my water bag started to bulge out. I remember Monica saying, "Oh, look at that—very interesting. I wish I could take a picture of this." For some reason I couldn't talk, but I thought to myself, *Well, just take the picture . . . there's a camera!* I was a little confused, but reminded myself, *It's not my job right now to worry.*

This whole idea of pushing in earnest started at about 9:00. The baby was born at 10:30. At some time, we began to be able to see the baby's head through the bag of bulging water. Still, the contractions were five minutes apart. I wanted to push in between contractions, and Monica agreed to let me, knowing that they'd be ineffective. I found that I had to push during contractions and just try to hold the baby from sliding back between them.

With one push I remember feeling his head come out. The bag of water was still intact. My husband and Monica kind of pulled the bag up over his head—Steve described it as like pulling off a T-shirt. With the next push, the baby came out. It was wild! It felt *so good!* All the pressure and tension were gone. They put the baby on my belly and I could feel him squirming around beneath a towel. I had my eyes closed and kept thinking, *I've got to open my eyes 'cause the midwife's going to think I'm a horrible mother not even looking at my baby!* A full minute later I opened my eyes, looked down and touched the baby. That feeling is something I will never forget.

Steve and I were hugging our baby, patting our baby, and then we're like, *Oh, I guess we better look.* We had it in our birth plan that no one would tell us the sex. My husband looked and said, "It's a boy!" And I said, "No, it's not—what you see is all the umbilical cord wrapped up there." I made him look again, and he said, "It's a boy!" I'm like, "Holy cow!" I was expecting a girl because the heart rate was very fast, and everyone predicted it would be a girl.

Twenty minutes later, I asked Monica if I should push the placenta out. She said, "You can try." I just went, "Ugh!" and it kind of fell out. Then we cut the cord. I had torn a little, and Monica sewed me up while Steve held the baby. She was wearing a head-lamp that we'd brought from home. It was really wonderful—she was so at ease with me, working between my legs, squatting on the big bed—it was like having a sister there with me.

The baby was eight pounds, two ounces. I was like, "Wow!" I'm not a big person; I just assumed the baby would be small.

Steve, the baby, and I went into a large tub—not really a hot tub, not really a whirlpool. We didn't stay there long—the water felt too hot for me, and I was hungry and exhausted.

I had a banana and juice. Then Steve, the baby, and I got into bed. He wasn't ready to nurse, and that didn't bother me—I knew that there are cultures that won't even try nursing until the mother's milk comes in.

Monica went home, and the assistant spent the night with us at the birthing center. She checked us only when we were awake—completely following our rhythms. I was really impressed by her. We just really were left alone.

The next morning, after they took a blood sample and we were ready to leave, the first appointment of the morning came in. It was my sister-in-law, and she met us at the door. We were leaving, and she was coming in for her first visit—she'd just found out that she was pregnant!

୫ଠ

Valerie is a social worker who lives near San Francisco with her husband, John, and eighteen-month-old son, Miles. She currently works part-time in a children's shelter for the Department of Social Services. At the time of our interview, Valerie was expecting her second child.

A Good Doula Can Make All the Difference

I began prenatal care with a practice composed of women doctors, a nurse practitioner, and a couple of midwives. They really listened to what women said and respected women's needs. But they were a small group and weren't quite making it financially. There's just so much competition in this field. They split up, and I followed one of the doctors to another group. But there were a few doctors there I didn't care for. I was a bit nervous because you never know who's going to be on call when you go into labor. And if the shift changes, you get someone else.

A couple of these doctors were very conservative. I'm very liberal and have a bad attitude toward most doctors. I certainly didn't want to have anybody telling me what to do.

They have all this technology, and the mindset is, *Well it's here for a reason*. My husband, John, also bought into this, and I had to convince him otherwise. For instance, I didn't want to use an external fetal monitor. I had read a few articles which found that birth monitors don't improve your chances of having a healthy baby but do improve your chance of having a cesarean. Knowing this, why use a monitor?

Even while pregnant, I knew that birth was going to be something really intense, really personal to me, and I wanted to have control over it. I wanted to know who was going to be there and how I was going to be treated.

I stayed with this group because they really had the best reputation in the Berkeley area, and I was already connected with the one woman doctor I had started out with. As it turned out, I was lucky—she was on duty when I delivered.

The birthing center is part of the hospital. The actual birthing room wasn't as homey as I expected. It still looked like a hospital room, but it did have a couch and a private bathroom.

John and I took childbirth classes with a couple of women who call themselves Whole Circle Childbirth. They offer doula services, and one of the women is a midwife. Doulas are popular out here—they're women trained to act as childbirth coaches, and they really know their stuff. I didn't hire one then, but ended up having a doula at the hospital. Now this group doesn't teach Lamaze or Bradley, but they take techniques from different schools of thought and use what they believe is the best. We also went to a three-hour childbirth class with a prenatal yoga instructor. She imitated the sounds of laboring women, and that was really helpful to me. When I was in transition, I made loud, continuous groaning sounds—the same sounds she had told us to expect. She showed us how to use our voices to take focus off the pain—by crying, screaming, groaning. We did exercises in class where we practiced different vocalizations to help with pain. And they worked.

My due date was March 13. I went into labor on the evening of the 16th, and Miles was born March 17. Labor began at 10:30 at night, and John was already in bed. I knew it was labor because the contractions hurt. When I went into the bathroom, I saw blood, and thought, *Oh, this is it!* I stayed calm and ate a celery stick with some peanut butter. I'm one of those people who has to eat when I get hungry. And that was one of my concerns about going into the hospital—that they wouldn't let me eat. I had my bag packed already with Snickers bars.

The contractions were strong and regular—every five minutes, and I started to think, *Well, this is going to happen soon.* But I let John sleep, and I didn't want to go to the hospital yet.

I woke John at around 1:00 and said, "I think I'm in labor." We knew it was going to be a boy and had picked out a name already. John just kind of grunted, looked at me and said, "Oh, Miles, it's 1:00 in the morning!"

It took him a few minutes to wake up. We timed the contractions, and they were still five minutes apart. I've never been one to deal with pain very well. If I get a headache, I go back into bed and curl up in a ball. So, here I am in labor, curled up in a ball on the couch. I'm trying not to move because any movement sets off a contraction.

Meanwhile, John is deciding what he wants to wear. Finally, he picks his sweats because he wants to be comfortable, but they're dirty. So he decides to do a wash! The pains are still five minutes apart and lasting sixty seconds. I'm thinking maybe we should get to the hospital, and he's doing laundry.

This was just the opposite of what I expected. I thought John would panic the minute I went into labor. Instead, I was the one panicking! I'd read all these books and knew that birth was a natural process and one that I could handle, but I became scared, really scared. It had no real focus—just fear of the unknown. It was the pain, and also the feeling out of control. Labor happens to your body, and you have no control. When I get a headache, I feel that I can control it with aspirin, and it will go away. Also, thoughts about cesareans and all the stuff that can happen are in the back of your mind. Everything's such a big unknown.

We called the doctor. By then the contractions were still five minutes apart and lasting about ninety seconds. In class, I'd heard that that's a good time to go to the hospital. And the doctor agreed and told us to come along.

Looking back, I realize now that the pain wasn't that intense. I was breathing normally and could still talk. But I was scared and had nothing to compare it with.

I left the house in my bathrobe—which is like a security blanket to me. I had my clothes on underneath. It was pretty cold outside.

We arrived at the hospital at around 3:00. We had a half-gallon jug of water and my bag with us. John escorted me into the lobby, then left to park the car. A nurse met me and walked me to the elevator. I was very dramatic! I had to stop at a chair and stoop over with each contraction, and I know my face must have been pretty grim.

Then, in the room, the nurse checks my dilation and I'm one centimeter! For weeks I had been one centimeter! I had learned to check myself and could actually feel the baby's head. Now, here I was, still one centimeter— after all that! They talked about sending me back home, but I didn't like that idea. We're only twenty, twenty-five minutes from the hospital, but Interstate 80 gets real backed up during rush hours. I didn't want to get caught in traffic. Finally, I asked her, "Do we have a choice? Are you kicking us out, or can we stay if we want to?" She told us we could stay. So we did.

At 7:00, the nurses changed shifts. That's when my nurse, or doula, Maggie Holiday, arrived. She was great. She really changed my labor. When she checked me, I was between three and four centimeters, and was actually contemplating taking drugs—which was completely against my mindset when I was pregnant. But I was hurting very bad.

Maggie Holiday turned me around and showed me just how helpful a doula could be. And she didn't do anything real complicated—just kept telling me that I was doing great. She also gave me tips about laboring positions and was very cheerful. She'd say, "If you squat during a contraction, that'll help open you up." When it came to the fetal monitor, she said, "The hospital needs this printout for your chart. I'll just hold it up against your belly every now and then." And that's what she did. The hospital was happy, and I was happy. I never had wires or straps or IVs. I was free to walk around.

Soon after Maggie came on duty, Dr. Chince—one of the doctors that I particularly didn't like—talked to her about the possibility of "actively managing" my labor. He wanted to break my water, speed up labor, intervene. My primary doctor, the woman who I really liked, was in surgery at the time, so Dr. Chince just started poking around. But Maggie sent him on his way. She told him that I was doing fine . . . she really stuck up for me!

I didn't want to be touched or bothered. In the birth classes, John had practiced massaging and holding me in different positions. But now, I just wanted to be left alone. I didn't want to talk, be touched, or eat. I did drink lots, but I didn't want to eat—which was strange, because I had gone without eating all day, and I never do that. John helped me by just being there. I don't think he ever realized how helpful he was. He kept my water glass full and offered moral support.

I'm a Buddhist, and I chant in the mornings and evenings. Before I had the baby, I was real diligent, and I never missed morning ghong. I asked John to chant for me in the hospital because I couldn't focus. He did that—and it really meant a lot.

It was morning when Maggie suggested nipple stimulation to help move my labor along. I'd heard about it in childbirth class, and thought, *What the hell! I'll do it.* They had these low benches in the room—I guess for the doctors. I put a plastic sheet over one, sat on it, kind of squatting with my feet out, and began tweaking my nipples. I did that for a while and the contractions got stronger, and I went to six centimeters.

Then, I began standing, holding the edge of the bed—alternating with the squatting position. Meanwhile, the doctor would pop back in every so often and say, "Well, if you're not such and such centimeters by such and such a time, then we'll talk about breaking your water." All of my convictions had gone out the window with all this intense pain. I was like, *Okay, okay, I'll do whatever you say.* That's when Maggie would come up with a new suggestion to get the labor progressing.

When I was still at six centimeters, Maggie suggested that I get into the shower. I did, and that's when things really took off. In a sense, I had been avoiding any movement that would encourage dilation because of the pain. In the shower, I was forced to just stand up and kind of rock and move. Maggie would check my dilation in the shower. She'd say, "Just put your foot up on the side of the tub here." She used a fetoscope to check the baby's heartbeat. And all the while, she kept telling me that I was doing great. She took my fear away and gave me confidence.

The doctor that I really liked was now attending me. You have to deliver between 8:00 A.M. and 5:00 P.M. Monday through Friday to get her. Miles was born at 2:30 in the afternoon.

Everyone was being very accommodating now. I was becoming more and more confident, and I was chanting in my head, *I can do it, I can do it.* Now, when I got contractions I wasn't turning away from them. I was trying to make them hurt even more because I wanted to get on with it. Sometimes I would squat with a contraction to make it hurt. I could feel the momentum of opening.

I remember the doctor coming in and saying that I was nine centimeters. She left, and John told me later that that was around 2:00. I remember squatting. It was awkward. I was in the shower squatting and poop was leaking out. John was all embarrassed. He brought me soap and a washcloth so I could wash my hands. The nurse asked me if I was bulging. I wasn't really able to talk, but I stuck my hand down there and could feel a soft bulge the size of a half dollar. I don't think I answered her.

Somehow she knew what was going on. She began to say, "We've got to get you over to the bed now. . . ." I stood up, and the baby's head started coming out real fast. I never planned on pushing—it just started happening. I was moaning, and the moan would turn into a push. My body was just doing it. I put my hands on his head and said, "He's here." The thought that went through my head is, *He must really be a small baby.* Maggie again said, "We've got to get you over to the bed." And then another contraction came and I was like, *No way!*

Maggie had her hands underneath me, holding his head. When the next contraction came, I just pushed him out and she caught him!

There's an emergency cord in the shower to ring for assistance. I remember Maggie pulling it and yelling, "I need help! I've got a baby here!" All these people came rushing into the room, and she passed the baby between my legs because the cord was still attached. She handed him to John and said,

"Here, hold him." It all happened so fast. Later, John said that he didn't actually see the baby come out, and he was disappointed.

I was still standing. I put my hand against the shower wall, and saw all this blood coming out and going down the drain, but I had no idea that I had torn. The contractions hurt, but as I was stretching, I never felt anything more than a vague burning sensation. They say that all the nerves down there are kind of dead because the circulation is cut off. I ended up with a second-degree tear.

I remember hearing the baby cry and turning around to look at him. They tell you that newborns don't look like Gerber babies—and they don't. But Miles was beautiful, and he looked exactly like I thought he would—absolutely perfect! I stared at him for about ten seconds, and then turned around and sighed and thought, *Thank you, Jesus! Thank you, God!* Even though I'm a Buddhist! Then I turned my focus away from him completely and just gave thanks that it was all over.

I was still standing and wasn't tired. It had been sixteen hours. I hadn't had anything to eat except a celery stick. I walked over to the bed and lay down. There was blood running down my legs. Someone gave a tug on the cord to get the placenta out quickly. Then, I was told that I had torn. I asked them, "How bad?" The doctor told me, "It's not any worse than an episiotomy would have been. You'll be fine."

Maggie was just beaming. She said, "That was so much fun!" And kept saying, "Valerie, you did so great!" But, I think that she was responsible in part. A good doula can make all the difference in the world.

Miles was eight pounds, twelve ounces. He had a big appetite and was a fine nurser. They asked me if I wanted to go home that night. But I was in no condition to leave. I felt like my organs were all out of place, and I had trouble breathing. Then there was the tear—that was pretty bad, too.

We left the next day around 1:00 in the afternoon—almost twenty-four hours after the baby was born. I felt shaky and kind of like an invalid for a couple of days. I couldn't sit and did most of my nursing lying down. John was great, though—he waited on me hand and foot.

ℬℴ

Pam works as an editor and writer and lives with her husband, Jay, and their eleven-month-old son, Zackery. When Zack was born, she and Jay lived in Boynton Beach, Florida, and they had planned to have him at a nearby birthing center. However, complications arose, and she delivered in a hospital instead.

Not a Granola Birth

Before I conceived Zackery, I had two miscarriages, each around eleven weeks. I was thirty-three by the time Zack was born, so I was up there in age and concerned about whether I'd ever be able to have kids. They say one miscarriage is very common, two not so common. After three, they start doing tests—which I didn't want to do and luckily didn't have to.

After the third month of pregnancy with Zackery, I started relaxing and began to feel that the baby was viable, but I was pretty extreme in my concerns—I don't think the average person thinks the things I did.

For instance, at about four months along, I went to my husband's work party at a big park and decided to play volleyball. It was August in Florida, and some older woman kept saying, "You shouldn't be doing that!" I wasn't playing hard or anything, but I got overheated and had to have my husband dump ice over my head. I thought, *Well, that's it—I fried him!* I thought my body temperature had gotten so high that his brain would be fried. I was all neurotic and paranoid about it.

All along, the twitches and things that are normal with pregnancy would concern me. I'd have fears about the baby's well-being. I took extra precautions. I signed up for Bradley classes pretty early on—at around four months. I was real cautious about eating. I had been a vegetarian and started eating meat in order to get enough protein. I became involved with ICAN, which is the International Cesarean Awareness Network. Most women get involved *after* they've had a C-section; I got involved because I wanted to prevent one.

After a while, I settled down, but all my fears came back full force when actual labor began. I remember reading *Spiritual Midwifery* early on—which was one of my first mistakes. I'm a person who does yoga and who'd been a vegetarian, and the book presents this image of a granola birth. They talk about "the rushes"—that's what they call contractions! And I'm like, *No problem!* But the book misled me—it put an image into my mind, and I held that image too tightly. I envisioned myself as being a good "baby-haver"—as one woman in the book says. I had this vision of having my rushes, breathing them out, and doing my yoga. The contradiction is that there's one part of me that wants to be this relaxed person, and another part of me that worries about a lot of things—that doesn't trust the process, so to speak.

I remember that soon after Zackery was born, I read something in a letter from the editor in *Mothering* magazine. It was real simple, like, "Yes, labor is painful, incredibly painful, but it's safe pain—having a baby is safe." And that was what threw me off—when the pain started, my mind said, *Something is wrong. This is not supposed to be!* But, the weird thing is that something did end up being wrong, and now I'm having a hard time trusting myself. Did I know that something was going wrong, and that's why I had this feeling? Or did my anxiety create the problem? In labor, I just went into fear and said, *Something's wrong.* And that, I think, ties into the miscarriages too—I was so afraid I wasn't going to have a healthy or an alive baby that perhaps I caused myself to lose them.

I had a doctor, a woman OB/GYN at the beginning, then switched to a midwife at five months. I'd had some spotting early on and needed to take progesterone suppositories. There were about five physicians with the practice, and I couldn't be assured which one I'd deliver with. I started to see the writing on the wall. Also, I didn't want IVs and other medical stuff that came with hospital birth. Part of me trusted the medical establishment, and part of me didn't. After I was off the suppositories—past the scary part—I decided to change practitioners.

I found a certified nurse midwife who was working with a an OB. She had been a home birth midwife, had gotten her nursing license, her CNM, and wanted to find a practice where she could get a salary and have time off. My husband was fine with the idea of a home birth, but I knew that if something went wrong I wouldn't be able to live with the fact that I'd delivered at home. So, the next best thing was this birth center.

The birth center was right near the hospital and had a big jacuzzi and shower in the room where I'd be. I could have all my food, snacks, videos, and music there—just what I'd envisioned.

Somewhere along, I hired a labor assistant, but she wasn't the personality I needed. I felt this in my gut, but for some reason, I wasn't trusting or listening to myself. In fact, all through my labor, I kept having feelings that I ignored or just didn't do anything about.

Zack was due December 30, and I went into labor on that day. I lost my mucus plug and had a little bleeding. It was nighttime—we were over at some friends' having dinner, and I went to the bathroom and saw blood. I didn't realize that this was normal, and, in my mind, blood is a bad sign. I called my labor assistant, and she said that it was *fine*—but somehow I missed hearing about the blood being normal. I kept thinking, *Why am I bleeding?* A little alarm went off in my head.

Soon, I started having little, crampy contractions. My girlfriend and I began walking, and Jay and I stayed over at their house pretty late. We were all very excited. Although my labor assistant reminded me that this kind of very early labor could go on for a while and that it wasn't necessarily significant, I didn't heed her. We were too excited!

Well, I had four days of this kind of labor—full-out nighttime labor that stopped by day. At night they'd become very strong, five minutes apart, then as sunlight approached, they'd stop. The labor assistant came over a couple of times but left because nothing was developing. On the third night, a kind of dread came over me and never left. It was approaching like 4:00 or 5:00 in the morning. The sun was coming up, and I knew labor was going to stop. I was in a tremendous amount of pain—back labor which I didn't anticipate. I was really getting depressed.

On the fourth day, I needed to know something, so I went in to see the midwife—I was only one centimeter dilated and really bummed. She decided to rough up my cervix with her hand, in an attempt to move things along. That night my contractions were more intense, and I couldn't rest or sleep. Then, during the day, they still kept coming. By the following night, I was exhausted—I felt like I'd been tortured in Vietnam. I couldn't function and decided to call the midwife, who was delivering at the hospital. I told her, "I can't take it anymore; I've got to have something for the pain. I feel like I'm a failure. . . ." She's like, "Calm down, calm down, come in tomorrow at around 7:00 and I can give you something to help you rest and get your energy back. It's not going to ruin your whole birth plan."

I needed her to tell me that. I said, "Okay." She'd given me something to hold on to. I got back into bed, sneezed, and water came pouring out of me. Almost immediately, I went into transition!

Jay called the labor assistant, who came over. It was about 2:00 in the morning. My water didn't look clear to me, and I was concerned. It had a mucky, lake water appearance. I was freaking out, thinking I saw a tinge of green. *Okay, I have meconium,* I thought. *Somebody tell me what to do!* I showed the labor assistant the water on my pad and on the floor. "Look, this is what came out of me!" I told her. She didn't seem alarmed but didn't give me the feedback I needed either. This is where I was neurotic about things.

She told Jay to go to bed to get some rest. She and I were out in the living room, and I was on my hands and knees, just wailing. I couldn't stop wailing. At one point, she told me to try not to let all my energy out with this wailing, but I couldn't stop. People later asked me, "Did you get really pissed and cuss at your husband?" No, I was never in that state of mind—it was fear, total fear, never anger. I was afraid that I was losing the baby.

The labor assistant called the midwife during this. I really could not get control. The assistant said, "Pam is having transitional contractions, and we'll be over at the birthing center in an hour." I started crying, "No! I'm going to die in an hour! I can't make it an hour! Please, let's go now!" When she got off the phone, I said, "I can't do this!" And she's like, "Pam, you're okay."

At some point, I got off the floor and decided to get into the shower. I felt something come out of me. When I took off my underwear, there was a blood clot the size of a fist. I yelled, "What the hell is this?" I got into the shower, and blood started pouring down my legs. I was screaming, "Why am I bleeding? Why am I bleeding?" Jay finally heard me and got up.

The assistant, when she first saw the blood clot, went to find a homeopathic remedy. And I'm thinking, *Fuck the remedy! I have to be in the hospital now!* I began feeling I couldn't trust her, that she'd been trying so hard to keep me from having a cesarean that she'd overlooked a crisis.

Finally, she said, "Okay, we're going to the hospital." Blood is pouring down my legs. Actually, it was the midwife who suggested the hospital—that's where she was, and she couldn't leave. It was a thirty-minute drive. I was in the back of the car with my head down and my butt up, trying to keep the blood flow to a minimum. I was crying and apologizing to my husband, saying, "I'm sorry, I'm sorry." I thought I was dying and that the baby was dying. Jay was crying too, saying, "I love you. It's okay, we'll make it through this!"

We got to the hospital, and the assistant didn't want me to go to the emergency room—she wanted me to walk in. My hair was half wet from the shower, and I looked like shit. It was about 5:30 in the morning. They took me into a room to check me and the baby—he was fine. They said, "Yes, you're bleeding, let's go ahead and find a room." I think they put an external monitor around my belly. I was on my hands and knees on a bed in the labor/delivery room. I was wailing and beginning to hyperventilate—only letting air out, not taking any in. They told me to breathe for the baby, take air in.

I couldn't move and remember having to pee. The assistant suggested that she take me to the bathroom, but I couldn't, and peed on the bed. She cleaned it up, and I thought, *God! You lose all your dignity.*

But I was grateful. People were sort of just letting me labor there. Then, I felt this release, and something came out of me. According to my husband, it looked like a balloon filled with blood was hanging out of me. An OB had been standing in the back of the room, watching, letting people do their thing. The nurses and midwife all gasped, and he walked over, put his thumb in it, and popped it. Blood, water, everything came gushing out.

This was my bag—filled with blood and fluid. I think the water before was just my forewaters. They say that I had placenta abruptio. Blood came pouring out everywhere—so much so that I couldn't sit up without fainting, and my lips were gray. I didn't need a transfusion, but I did lose a lot of blood.

The doctor said, "It's time to get this baby out." I was ten centimeters dilated. He turned me over, and I started bawling 'cause I thought I was having a cesarean. I saw all these tools, the surgical equipment, lying sterile on the little tray.

Then the midwife said, "Pam, I'm sorry, I know this isn't the birth you wanted . . .," and I'm thinking, *I'm having a cesarean!* What he did was give me an episiotomy. He took forceps and pulled Zackery down past my pubic bone and had me push him out the rest of the way. It took me about three pushes, and he was out!

That was it. He was fine—not a thing wrong with him! I, on the other hand, was a mess. Even when he first came out, I was still crying, and they had to tell me, "Pam, hold your baby. You've got a healthy baby, hold him!"

Jay had gotten the camera just before he was born. I was horrified at the thought of him leaving, but luckily he came back quickly and got a picture right at the moment when they gave him to me and I'm still crying—I cherish this picture.

Soon after that, I began to feel like I was to blame, that I had some responsibility in what happened. Did I bring this experience on myself? I was so prepared for this natural birth—why didn't I get it? Why did I have this bleeding?

I haven't resolved my feelings yet, and I'm afraid of getting pregnant again, afraid of labor again. When I speak of my experience, some people say, "Why did they let you go on for so long . . . if they had broken your water earlier . . . ." But I don't know. I think that the placenta abruptio happened during transition, but I don't know. And I don't trust doctors enough to say.

I believe that I didn't create a safe space for myself and that my labor assistant wasn't the person I needed. She wanted me to stay home for as long as possible, and I think I needed to be in a facility in order to feel safe. I also think I needed someone in my face to help me get my breathing under control, give me some comfort in my pain, and give me more nurturing attention. I'm not blaming her; I just realize that I didn't trust myself to know what I needed.

And then there's the pain. I don't believe I'm a wimp, but the pain I had was unbelievable. My sister had two natural births, and she never made a sound. Beforehand, I thought, *Great, if my sister can do it, I can do it.* All these images, all these expectations, all these people who'd given birth . . . and now I begin to feel that they *lied* to me, that there's some secret society, and they all agree to lie.

I feel cheated. I never had the pushing urge—and I wanted to feel that. Also, I didn't want an episiotomy, and after the birth I was left in pain for about three months. My tailbone felt like it had been hit with a hammer, and I couldn't sit normally. People never told me about that. I felt deceived about a lot of things. But then again, maybe you can't really communicate the truth about childbirth or ever really be prepared.

Even though I'm afraid, there's a part of me that wants to go through it again, to get it right—but that's not a good reason to have a baby. All I know is that I will never judge another woman's decision concerning childbirth. Any decision a woman makes deserves respect.

ॐ

Shirlee lives in Woodbridge, Virginia, with her husband, Scott, and their two daughters: Caitlin, age five, and Laurel, age two and a half. Scott works as a cabinetmaker. Before becoming a mother, Shirlee managed a health food store and then did office work for a chiropractor. Her first daughter was born at home, but because of a change in their insurance, Shirlee decided to have her second daughter at a birthing center, where coverage was guaranteed. Here, Shirlee speaks about Laurel's birth and the complications that resulted in a hospital transfer.

Decision out of Fear

We used midwives with my first daughter, and I delivered her at home. It was a good experience. When I became pregnant with my second, we stayed with the midwives and wanted to deliver at home again. Unfortunately, we had changed insurance plans and this one wouldn't cover a home birth. Because of the expense, I yielded to them and made my decision based on financial considerations—we decided to have the baby at a nearby birthing center where the insurance company promised to pay for it.

Both pregnancies were planned. We tried to conceive a month before I actually became pregnant because I was trying for a boy. I'd been using an ovulation predictor, but it didn't work right. I really felt like, since we were just having two children, I wanted one of each sex—everybody says there's such a difference, but I have a hard time believing that. It would have been interesting to see. Also, it would have made my dad and Scott's parents real happy to have a boy.

I was very tired with this pregnancy—more tired than I remember ever being with the first. With Caitlin, I was working long hours. I had more nausea but less vomiting. With both, my blood pressure started going up, and I started swelling and had to lie down a lot—but that didn't happen until around my seventh or eighth month. This second time, it was harder to deal with because of trying to keep Caitlin happy. She was almost three. I relied on friends to take her for a few hours a day and let her play with their kids— that really helped.

We had taken a Bradley class during my first pregnancy. The midwives required it. Most of the educational stuff we already knew; we had read practically every book we could get our hands on. What we really enjoyed was the relaxation technique part. This time, I felt that the course would be really old-hat, so the midwives said that we could just refresh on our own. So we read *Mind over Labor* and practiced doing visualization, just staying in touch with what relaxed means. I came up with this wonderful visualization where Scott and I were alone on the beach, and I was giving birth. It was really smooth and gentle and intimate. I didn't actually use it during labor, but I think it helped me to prepare.

Because my blood pressure was a little high near the end, the midwives were just a tiny bit concerned about preeclampsia—they kept saying, "Well, everything's fine, you just need to get that baby out soon." We didn't choose to have any prenatal tests done. With Caitlin, we had the MSAFP, which is a blood test done to check for spina bifida. And I remember that on the day we had it done I suddenly felt like there was this big cloud over my head, this tremendous weight: *what if it comes out showing that there's something wrong?* I just felt like I didn't want to deal with it. If the baby had spina bifida, I wouldn't know what to decide. I'm pro-choice, but I felt that this kind of decision would be playing God. Finally, I felt that whatever baby we got is what we deserved and what we would deal with. With my second pregnancy, we didn't have any tests done.

It had taken us a full year to get the insurance company to enroll our midwives on our plan—we had to fight them all the way. But they wouldn't cover home birth, because what if a woman lived too far from a hospital and needed to go at the last minute. They gave lame excuses—they didn't care that the CNMs' protocol wouldn't allow them to attend a home birth that possibly presented problems. I asked them, "What if I delivered at home because my labor went so fast?" They said, "Well, if there was a hospital transfer involved, we might not cover it." So, what they were saying was that if I chose a home birth and said it was an "accident" and complications arose that made it necessary for either me or the baby to go to the hospital, they might not cover it. That scared me; I allowed it to scare me—and that's what I based my birthing decision on. I decided to go to Birth Care, which is a birthing center. I really regret it now.

With Caitlin, we had a different insurance plan—it was one of those 80 percent–20 percent deals. All I had to do was to show that the treatments I received were usual and customary, and they paid their 80 percent. I'm on a PPO now, and they insist that I use only listed providers and facilities.

My first labor was eight hours, and I expected this one to be 20 percent shorter, or six hours. As it turned out, my second labor progressed in a similar way. As soon as my water broke, I almost immediately went into labor and the contractions were very strong. I had no real plans about how long I'd labor at home, but the thought of being in a car while in labor really bothered me. We just decided to play it by ear.

My water broke at 2:20 A.M. on a Wednesday morning. I was lying in bed and woke up suddenly as it started gushing. I tried to wake Scott up, but he was out of it. I was trying to tell him to get a towel. It took a couple of tries to get him awake. He got a towel, and I went to the bathroom. After a while, I felt heavy in my bowel, constipated, so I did enemas and even more amniotic fluid came out. I had already called a midwife as soon as my water had broken.

Scott loaded up the car. He made a sandwich for me and packed our box of stuff. We had ingredients for making a cake—we were going to bake the cake at the birthing center. A friend of mine had done that during her labor, and it was really neat. Her in-laws were in the house, and they had to finish the baking when her contractions got too strong. I thought it would be a neat idea to have a birthday cake.

So we took along cake supplies, some food, grape juice, and some snacks for Caitlin. Scott woke Caitlin up, got her into the car, and we all left. Now, we're in Virginia, and so is the birthing center. But the midwife was across the Potomac in Maryland. The only way to the birthing center is over a drawbridge, and it ended up that she came late because she got stuck when it was open. Luckily, the birth assistant came, and it wasn't too much longer before the midwife was able to get there.

We arrived at 4:30. We were the only ones there. I was glad; I would have felt funny if other people were around. We arrived first, then the assistant, and we all had to wait around in the dark until the midwife arrived because she had the key. We only had to wait about ten minutes, but I felt very vulnerable. Just a few blocks away there's a lot of drug dealing that goes on, and it's not a place where I'd walk at night by myself.

The midwife arrived, and Caitlin and I went upstairs while Scott got our stuff out of the car. The birthing center is located in a row house, the last one on a block. It's long and narrow. I got to pick out which room I wanted—I took the front one 'cause it was more homey. They have handmade quilts, and they paint the baby's name and birthdate on the wall with gold paint. It's nice to feel those other births. The hallway is kind of personality-less, and I didn't enjoy walking up and down the hall during labor.

The midwife didn't examine me until about 5:30. I spent that hour holding on to Scott, just kind of hugging him and leaning up on him and breathing. I was focusing on my breathing and I did great. I was so good—only once did I start to feel out of control, and then Scott reminded me to lower the pitch of my voice as I was making sounds. That really helped; it was amazing. When the midwife checked me, I was only at four centimeters. But I quickly got very crabby, and I think I went into transition. I kept saying, "I can't be in transition already—it's too early!" But I really felt like hitting and biting. I started to clamp my teeth down on Scott and almost bit him once. I had to think, *Wait a minute, this is your husband, don't bite him!*

Caitlin was awake the whole time. Normally, she's very hard to wake, but that night all we had said to her was, "You're going to be a big sister today," and she was up. She was happy in the car, drank juice, and wiped my face with a washcloth—wiped and patted me. She went downstairs to the front room and played with toys. Every so often, she'd come up and show them to me. She was so cute. I was really glad she was there—it just felt like the right thing.

When we arrived at the birthing center, we called two close friends. One is a photographer who was to take pictures for us again, and the other friend was going to help with Caitlin. They both live close to the birthing center and got there right away. When I started making noises, Caitlin got concerned, but our friend was there to help.

I was really pleased with myself. I was breathing and staying focused, and as long as I kept the pitch of my voice down, I stayed in control. I felt very powerful and capable. It's kind of funny—with Caitlin, I was at home where I wanted to be but wasn't as comfortable about my labor. I was having a hard time handling it. I was really crabby, and I was whining, "Oh, it hurts too much!" I think back and go, "What a baby I was!" But I hadn't had any sleep and the contractions were more intense. They came one on top of another without any time to recover in between. This time, it was similar but not as intense. That seemed to make a big difference. Also, I knew better what to expect and how to deal with it.

At 6:45 the midwife checked me, and I was fully dilated. In less than an hour, I had gone from four centimeters to ten. I was feeling very positive—I had no fear about the actual birthing process; I knew that I could do it. It didn't seem like that much of a big deal.

She checked me lying down. She had to push the anterior lip of the cervix back—it was hanging on a little bit. Then, by 6:50, I was sitting on the edge of the bed and beginning to push. I had on a special kind of nightshirt.

It was coral pink, very pretty. They all complimented me on it and said, "Oh, this is going to make the best picture!" But later, I think I took it off—I was hot and wanted to be completely naked. I had to push really hard to get this baby out. It was a lot of work.

At 7:00, her head crowned. It seemed harder than with my first. I remember the midwife saying, "Keep going, we're almost up to the eyes." And I was surprised 'cause I thought her head should have been out by then.

After her head was out, all of a sudden, they suctioned her. I could tell something was wrong. I felt that her head could have been a rubber ball pressed up against me, for all the life I felt in it. There was nothing alive there! I lost the urge to push, and kind of started shutting down right then—the contractions were gone. All I remember is the strong physical sensation. I felt like I was in an altered state—like I was watching a movie about people I didn't know. I pushed the rest of her out without any urge.

The midwife lifted Laurel up. Her hands were under her shoulders, and her head, arms, and legs were completely limp. She was yellow, and I thought, *What a weird color.* I don't remember much about what people said. I was just so absorbed in what I was seeing. And I was trying to keep my emotions from coming 'cause I thought she looked dead.

When I looked at the midwife, her eyes were about the size of silver dollars. I can still picture it perfectly. I've never seen anybody so scared in my life. And I thought, *Hmm, she looks scared.* I was completely detached. I heard her talking, but I didn't really understand what she was saying. Finally, I heard, "Talk to your baby and stimulate her!" So, I touched her and said, "Hi, little baby, come on." But I just really didn't get it. I felt fear for a second, then I just blocked it out.

The midwife began to suction the baby. They put something up her nose—one nostril, then the other. It had a bag on it. The midwife was working frantically, and all I kept thinking was that it must hurt the baby jabbing that down her body like that. Finally, Laurel started turning purple, and again, I thought, *That's weird.* Her bottom was towards me, and I noticed that she was a girl. She turned blue and then a little pink, and finally cried.

They gave her oxygen and handed her to me. Then, the birth assistant was told to call the ambulance, and she froze. She was just petrified; she was in training, and it was one of her first births.

Caitlin cut the cord. She was present for the whole birth. She knew that something was wrong—we have pictures of her as the baby's head is crowning, and she's kind of standing in the corner with our friend. At first, she's really amazed, but then she starts to look worried. She still tells me she was afraid the baby was dead. I think she could feel everybody's emotions in the room, and she knew something was wrong.

The ambulance did get called, and the plan was that Scott would ride in front of the ambulance, and they'd take the baby to the hospital. I'd stay with the midwife and deliver the placenta and then go and meet everyone at the hospital after. They wouldn't let Scott carry his own baby down the stairs or hold her in the ambulance. I was still pretty detached. I had cried for a few seconds, and Scott cried for a few seconds, but we still weren't able to just let go because we didn't know if the baby was okay or if there was some serious problem with her.

For an hour, the midwife and birth assistant stayed with me, Caitlin, and our friend while I tried to get the placenta out. And it just felt like nothing— I might as well have not even had a baby. I felt nothing from the waist down.

After a while, Marsha took the clamp off the cord to see if maybe draining some of the blood out could help loosen the placenta. But it was still pumping like an hour after the baby was born. She was walking around, going, "Oh, I think you can go with placenta in for a long time."

I was walking all over the place. I went to the bathroom a few times. I remember looking out the window and saying, "I'm surprised that I'm not more upset about being apart from my baby." That's when Marsha knew what was wrong. She called the hospital and talked to the OB on call to have me transferred.

With Caitlin, the placenta slid out less than ten minutes after the birth. Now, here I was, walking out into the now-busy streets of Alexandria in my jammies with this rope coming out of me. I pulled a little pad up between my legs and got into the car with Marsha. On the way, I asked her what would happen in the hospital. She described manual extraction by saying they would use a gloved hand to peel the placenta away from the uterus. And I'm thinking, *Oh, no, I can't handle that!* The thought of it horrified me. As sore as I was, I didn't want somebody sticking a hand up there.

I tried to will the placenta out in the car—but it didn't work. I was still detached—I was afraid, but I was *thinking it,* not *feeling it.* It was very strange; I'd not experienced that sensation before.

In ten minutes, we were at the hospital. They admitted me through the emergency room because it was easiest. I was taken up to see Laurel in the nursery. She was in a plastic box under a warmer, and there was a probe on her skin. Scott was with her, and he was talking to her, touching her, and stroking her. I got to go in, but they made me sit in a wheelchair, which was ridiculous.

They tried to get Scott to leave several times, but he wouldn't—which I just thought was the most wonderful thing. It made me extra glad that I married him. I knew that Laurel needed Scott. When they had first arrived, the warmer wasn't ready yet, and Scott wanted to warm her on his chest. They let him hold her until it was ready, then said that they had to put her in this box in order to monitor her.

By the time I got there, Scott already knew her a little bit. He said, "Oh, she seems to really like it when you stroke her like this." And she was just fine. Scott said they'd just looked at her in the emergency room and said, "She's fine. Take her upstairs and put her in the nursery."

They put me in a room and brought Laurel to me, thinking that if she nursed, the placenta would come out. By then, we'd been separated for about two and a half hours, and she had completely lost her urge to suck.

Luckily, the hospital has a lot of midwives working there, and the one who was on duty was wonderful. At first, I thought, *What is she doing in a hospital? She should be doing home births.* But after being there, I realized she was doing far more good—she was really needed there. I needed her. And the nurse was really good. They both helped to soften the hospital rules. Also, the doctor had been trained in England with midwives, so he was great, too.

The midwife tried to pull the placenta out by tugging at the cord. The doctor came in and said, "Nope, just let her empty her bladder and it will probably come out." But, I couldn't let go of anything, so they used a catheter and the placenta began to come out. Marsha was pushing on my uterus, and I felt like she was beating me up while the hospital midwife was pulling. It was hard getting it out. For a couple seconds, maybe a minute, I cried and said, "This isn't fair; it's not supposed to hurt."

And once I got out some of those feelings, the placenta came out. It was huge and painful. I felt like I was birthing a baby again. I had a third-degree tear and they sewed me up. In the meantime, my friend was down in the little gift shop with Caitlin, and they both came up with some roses for me.

Then the lab wanted to take some blood from Laurel, even though Marsha had told them to get some cord blood. She had to go down to the lab and speak to them about it. They finally accepted it. I didn't want them to poke my baby unnecessarily. After that, they wanted to do a PKU and hep-atitis B. But we told them that we had arranged with our pediatrician to have the PKU after the baby had ingested some milk. They agreed.

We left after two hours and forty minutes. By the time we got on the road, it was lunch rush hour and the traffic was terrible—Laurel cried most of the way home. It wasn't until three days later, while on the phone with my close friend in Texas, that I broke through the wall I had built—felt the terror and sadness, and really cried.

But even that wasn't the end of it. Laurel had lost her urge to suck and trying to establish nursing was incredibly difficult. We used a syringe and fin-ger feeding, but all that seemed to confuse her more. Finally, we called a friend of mine who's a LaLeche League leader, and she suggested that we try nursing Laurel on a breast that had already let down. She has a nursing tod-dler, so she came over, the toddler nursed, and then Laurel took the breast. She sucked right away—there was nothing wrong with her. It took a good two weeks to get her nursing really well though.

Laurel's birth was an incredible ordeal for me. Ultimately, I feel that because I made my birthplace decision out of fear and allowed the medical establishment to tell me what to do, things went wrong. I feel that my fear of having an emergency transfer brought on the emergency transfer.

In the two and a half years since Laurel's birth, I have thought about it and cried about it a lot. I wish I had squatted, had gone in the ambulance, stayed with my baby. I wish we had left the hospital as soon as possible. But most of all, I wish I had listened to my heart.

And even though I had jumped through all their hoops, it still took the insurance company a year to pay. They gave me all kinds of excuses. At one point, the OB—who had never touched me and only told me verbally to empty my bladder—charged us $700. We almost had to pay for that our-selves! But again, finally they paid $350, and that was the end of it.

There's still plenty of emotional stuff for me to resolve about it all, but I feel that I am healing, that I am stronger, and that I've learned a very impor-tant lesson about living true to one's self. And it's a lesson I hope I can pass on to my daughters.

Three

BIRTH AT HOME

Much of mainstream america considers home birthing to be a rather extreme alternative to giving birth at either a hospital or a birthing center; nevertheless, a growing number of women who wish little or no medical intervention during their pregnancies and deliveries choose to birth their babies in the least technologically progressive place available—home. Yet, for the most part, these women consider themselves very socially progressive, proactive, and on the cutting edge of birthing culture. Some view birth at home as an alternative that offers greater intimacy than does either birth in a hospital or in a birthing center. Many see themselves as trusting their deliveries to fate or God, and tend to feel very relaxed about and comfortable with the experience that awaits them.

Stacey and her husband, Pat, live in the comfortable renovated basement of her father-in-law's house in Connecticut. Because of a state-wide economic downturn, they had moved from California, where Pat worked as a carpenter. Stacey worked with her husband in his carpentry business until she became pregnant with their first son, Teiyko, and had to quit because of preterm bleeding. Pat now works as a postal carrier. At the time of our interview, Teiyko was three and a half, and baby Marion, whose birth Stacey discusses here, was four months.

Rite of Passage

We wanted to have a second child. But just when my husband and I had decided to wait a bit, I found out I was pregnant. I took an in-home pregnancy test. My husband was absolutely thrilled, and I was happy but also ambivalent. I had just gotten to the point where I had some freedom with my older son, and I was considering getting a part-time job to better our situation. I think these very mixed feelings contributed to giving me a terrible first trimester; I was sick with nausea. And I felt guilty—as though my sickness was a direct result of having these evil, ambivalent thoughts.

With Teikyo, I knew immediately that he was a boy. With Marion, I didn't know. People kept saying that we were having a girl, and I became resistant—somehow I didn't want a girl. I think it has a lot to do with my relationship with my mother—which is not good. And also, I feel that a woman's position in the world is kind of depressing. In most cultures, women are beasts of burden, and many girls in this country experience some form of molestation in their lives. It made me very frightened to think of raising a daughter.

That first trimester was very difficult. I remember that Teiyko had this special video that he liked to watch—it's about construction. He watched it at least twice every day, and even now I can't hear it without feeling sick to my stomach.

My father-in-law has been living alone for about thirty-five years. His part of the house is kind of neglected, and in some ways, he's a very difficult man. There are many people he won't speak to, and if you cross him, you're off his list—forever. But it's a great situation for us, and he certainly loves his grandchildren. So, instead of complaining, we try to see the positives.

Anyway, our apartment was about 85 percent complete when I got pregnant with Marion. The first renovation was done in a flurry right before Teikyo was born. And Marion's room wasn't finished until the day before I went into labor with her. My husband is a great carpenter but a bit of a procrastinator. We'll probably need another child in order to complete any more work on the house.

Teikyo was born at home—and his birth was a great success, so we planned on doing the same thing this second time around. After my first trimester, I began to enjoy my pregnancy and look forward to the baby's birth. My husband's oldest friend, Pete, lives close by. He gets along great with Teikyo because they're both train fanatics. As we made our plans for this home birth, we enlisted Pete to take care of Teikyo.

The birth actually began at about 4:30 in the morning of April 24 when I woke up and felt like I needed to go to the bathroom. It was seven days after my due date, and I had made love with my husband the night before in a desperate attempt to stimulate labor. I had spent the previous day at my sister's house and visited with my mom who was up from Florida. I'd had an unusual amount of pelvic pressure all that day, and my pelvis was constantly burning. The baby's head had been engaged, and I had been walking around dilated to four centimeters for about two months. It was like having a bowling ball there, and, in fact, when Marion was born, she had a round glazed area on the very top of her head that was exactly four centimeters!

Sitting on the toilet, I felt a bit constipated, and I thought that if I could just wiggle around I'd be able to move the baby's head so I could poop. I felt a mild kind of menstrual cramping, and I decided to go back to bed, figuring that if this was labor, I needed to get some sleep. But I was too excited. I continued to have mild cramps and began to time them—they were irregular and about twenty minutes apart, but I decided that this must be labor.

It was about 4:30. My husband was still asleep. Every time I'd get a contraction, I'd mouth the word "open" with each exhalation and try to visualize my cervix opening. Around 6:30, Pat's alarm went off, and I told him, "It's a good day to start your vacation." He just asked, "What's happening?" I said, "Nothing spectacular, but I've been having contractions since about 4:30." He didn't say anything and went back to sleep—which was typical of him. I just continued to watch the clock. At some point, I must have dozed off and Pat got up.

At 7:45 I called Barbara, the midwife. There was no answer, so I left a message on her machine. Then I called Pete and caught him just as he was leaving for work. He said that he'd take the day off and be over after doing a few chores. Pat was upstairs with Teiyko, making breakfast. I did some cleaning and decided to call Bev, who was Barbara's assistant, but she wasn't home either. I figured that they must be attending someone's birth. I called Barbara's beeper number, and a little later, Barbara called to say that yes, they had been at a birth since 5:00 A.M. This woman was at about six centimeters and relaxing in the tub. She told me to call her if things changed dramatically or if the contractions were about five minutes apart; otherwise, she would call me after this birth. She then asked if there was someone else I could call. The hair kind of stood up on the back of my neck when she said that! Why would she want me to call someone else when she just said that she'd be coming over? I think she meant to suggest that I call another midwife—possibly a woman named Lynn, whom I knew from a home birth support group meeting. But I wasn't clear about any of it, and I had to put the phone down because I was having a contraction.

Somewhere along in here, time stopped for me, and things became fast and furious. Pat timed my contractions and they were about four minutes apart. He called Barbara around 9:30 to tell her how fast labor was going, and then set up a train video for Teikyo to watch upstairs. My father-in-law, when he heard that I was in labor, said he had plans for the day and left. He had done the same thing with Teiyko. Then Pete arrived and took over upstairs, and Pat and I could be together. Up to this point, I was really alone, suffering through whatever I was feeling. I was very happy to have Pat finally there with me.

I remember clearly that Pete poked his head down to our apartment to say that Teiyko had a dirty diaper. I got up and went over to the changing room to get a clean diaper—and that's where I stayed. I was really in labor now. Pat was with me, except for when he had to answer the phone, which seemed to be ringing all the time. He was very calm—he's my tower of strength. The midwives were constantly in touch, wanting to know what was going on. When they heard that I seemed to be progressing so fast, they said that they'd be right over.

My contractions were very intense by now. They seemed to be constant, and I couldn't get comfortable. I was still standing at the changing table—it was a good height to lean on. Pat was standing with me. I wanted to ask him for a pillow for my head, but I couldn't get the words out. Then the phone rang again, and Barbara said that she had called another midwife to get over here quickly. She was forty-five minutes away and knew that she couldn't make it. Pat came back to me and tried to explain what was going on, but I couldn't focus; I would have agreed to anything at that point. I wanted to yell, *I don't care who you get! Just get out of here and leave me alone!* But all I could actually say was, "Open, open. . . ."

I was trying to focus on something other than the pain. I was standing up, and with each contraction, I'd lift my myself up to my tippy-toes—my toenails. Every muscle in my body contracted and was squeezing the pain out of me. Then I just dropped down to all fours, and began to squat on my knees, which was more comfortable. I began to push. All at once, I felt my bowels release and I pooped. My water broke, and literally, shot out of me with a pressure like from a water hose. I felt this warm liquid on my legs, and I felt something else come out of me with a big plop—it was my mucus plug.

Pat came in—he'd been on the phone, giving directions to the other midwife. I said, "I'm sorry. I think I pooped and the baby's coming." He was very calm and just said, "Alright, alright."

This is the man that I've chosen to spend the rest of my life with. And here he is, right there reassuring and calming me. He suggested that we move into the bedroom with the next contraction, which was coming almost immediately. With a lot of effort, Pat got me up and we made it into the bedroom. I squatted in front of the bed and I felt the baby's head push down with an enormous contraction, and then slide back up. Then, all at once, unbearable pain became the most exquisite feeling, and I began to push out the baby. I pushed for all I was worth, and with the next contraction I felt a burning. It shook me to my senses and I regretted not doing more perineal massage—it felt like the baby was about to rip me wide open! But I couldn't slow down. I just had to get him out. I heard Pat saying, "Do you want to feel the baby's head?" I reached down and felt Marion's head, but it was squishy and soft, and I remember being surprised. After another push, I heard Pat suctioning the baby's nose. We had a birthing kit that the midwife had prepared. I remember being really impressed! With another push, she came completely out, and I heard Pat say, "It's a girl!" And there she was.

Just a couple of minutes before, the pain had been so unbearable that it seemed I couldn't live through this experience. Then the pushing happened so fast, and time just stopped like it would stop forever. She came out with her hand and arm completely over her head. And I didn't tear at all! It's strange, after a few minutes of feeling utterly exhausted, I felt completely alright again—like I hadn't even given birth. My bottom didn't hurt and I felt great.

I remember Teiyko coming down. My father-in-law had arrived home, and Teiyko told him, "Poppy, I'm going downstairs to see my new sister." The cord was still hanging from me with the placenta inside, and Teiyko squatted by me and asked, "What is this thing doing?" It was pretty funny.

Fifteen minutes later, the new midwife arrived. She kept trying to make herself useful, and she was able to help me deliver the placenta.

Marion was born, we think, at 10:45 a.m. Pat had begun timing my contractions at 9:30—an hour and fifteen minutes from start to finish! I was really pleased. Everyone makes jokes about Pat's special delivery—giving him the credit for delivering the baby. They make such a big deal over him, but sometimes I think, *Wait a minute, I was the one who did the work!*

It was a very empowering experience for both of us. I know that whatever happens, Marion's birth will bond Pat and me forever. You know, when people view religion, they talk about women being cursed to suffer childbirth. But I don't believe it's a curse at all. I remember thinking, *This is my experience, completely mine, and no one can ever take it from me.* My midwife told me that no woman is given a birth she can't handle. I think that it's true. Society tries to undermine women's self-esteem by telling them that they're not capable of this or that, by telling them that they'll need medication to handle the experience. But *birthing* is a rite of passage, and women shouldn't be denied that rite.

ℰℂ

Deidre lives on a rural North Dakota farm with her husband, Keith, and their children, Tori, age five, and Karlin, age fourteen months. Here, Deidre bravely tells the story of Karlin's father-delivered home birth and discusses a rape that this birth forced her to reexperience.

I Don't Know Why

I was in school studying education until I had Tori. Then I had a semester break, went back briefly, and quit. I have no desire to study education again, and I have no desire to teach in the public school system. At one point, I was accepted at a school down in Denver to study veterinary science. Keith and I stayed there for two weeks, and he said, "I'm leaving, going back home— you can come, or you can stay." So, I went back with him. If I'd want to study anything, it would be something in animal science.

When I got pregnant the first time with Tori, it was a surprise. We found out a month after we were married. Keith was not helpful, but on my own, I read books, talked with a midwife, hired a labor attendant, and planned a hospital birth with no intervention whatsoever. It was just perfect— no problems. Everything went the way I wanted it to. Tori was never taken away from me, and we went home just three hours later.

Keith was never really supportive during my pregnancy or during the birth. He wasn't into the "daddy thing." But once Tori was born, he felt he should have done more at the hospital. He didn't do anything—just stood beside me and helped hold me when I was squatting. He felt like everybody kind of took over once we got to the hospital—and when we arrived I was ready to push. I hadn't wanted to leave home until it was absolutely necessary. So the moment I arrived, I ripped off my clothes, jumped up on the bed, squatted, pushed, and there she was! That fast! Keith felt like we lost control at the hospital, which was one of the reasons for choosing to have Karlin at home.

Women I knew would often say things like, "I'd have more kids, but it's so hard . . . ." And here's this smug little me going, *Oh yeah, right.* I didn't understand it. I actually thought about becoming a childbirth educator and attended a few births. I couldn't believe what I saw—I mean birth was painful, not beautiful!

Soon, Keith and I were trying to get pregnant again. I had two miscarriages. Keith was away from home a lot, working as a foreman for a gravel-crushing company. When he was home and I was ovulating, we wouldn't use birth control. The miscarriages were difficult. I'd go in to get checked and be pregnant one time and not pregnant the next. Keith has never been real supportive. Female things are female things.

The night Karlin was conceived, I had been crying and really let Keith have it about how he hadn't been there for me emotionally with the miscarriages and all. We talked it out and decided to go ahead and do it anyway. And, of course, there was a baby—Karlin.

For some reason, my health wasn't real good during this pregnancy. I had low iron and all these little complaints that ended up to be a real pain when added together.

I was seeing a midwife, and she wanted to do an ultrasound because she thought there was a possibility of placenta previa. While I was there, I found out that my baby was a boy.

I was twenty weeks along, but I had a feeling that the baby was a boy from the time of conception. And I didn't like that feeling and wouldn't even admit it to myself. It never even stayed inside my head that this was a boy.

Before I had gotten pregnant with this baby, I knew it would be born at home. I even toyed with the idea of having a totally alone birth—just me. Then, about a week after the ultrasound, the baby's heart began to have premature atrial contractions. We didn't know what it was. We'd listen to his heart and it would slow down and skip—arrhythmia, they call it.

I went to the medical library and got all the information I could get. For about two weeks, I just read. Then I went and talked to a neonatologist, and everybody kept saying, "Do not have this baby at home. You don't know how his heart is going to act once it has to pump oxygenated blood."

I wanted to have my baby at home. I felt that if my baby was born and he couldn't live without all this stuff, I wanted him to die. That's when I decided that Keith and I would have the baby home alone—just Keith and me, no one else attending.

Keith was great with this, wonderful—he was getting his boy. His attitude was actually better from the beginning with this pregnancy because it was planned. We talked it out. He was already used to being a dad and had thoughts of filling his house with children. During my pregnancy with Tori, Keith hated my pregnant body—it disgusted him. When I was pregnant with Karlin, it was just the opposite—we had lots of fun.

My folks, at least my mother, knew that we planned on a home birth. She was behind me and felt the same way I did. I had friends who'd given birth to babies with severe problems, and I saw what these kids went through. Being that this was a heart problem, I decided that it wasn't worth it—I didn't want transplants and things like that. I felt we needed to put our trust in God. If the baby lived, it was supposed to live; if the baby died, it was supposed to die. My dad didn't realize what was going on, and Keith's folks knew nothing of anything.

I consider myself a Christian, a born-again Christian. Keith was okay with our decision although he doesn't have a whole lot of religious convictions—he trusts in "the man upstairs," as he calls him, but doesn't get into Bible verses and churchy stuff.

So we left the situation in God's hands. When I'd have a check-up, it was really tough to hear that heart. I'd have this vision of a sick little boy. You know, you expect a boy to be a boy, to play with other boys. You don't want some little, scrawny kid sitting on the sidelines of all the activities because he's got a defective heart. That was a bad picture for both of us. Here in North Dakota there's an attitude—men are supposed to be men, and women are supposed to be women. It's a cross between a kind of conventional Southern Baptist thing, German strictness, and a redneck-cowboy mentality. It's hard to describe, but we pictured this scrawny, skinny boy sitting on the sidelines, and it was a very difficult image for us.

Midway through my pregnancy I had a turnaround. I decided to love this

baby and pray that it would be well. Tori and I called the baby Oliver—
though we actually named him Karlin—and we started talking to Oliver
every night. Well, two weeks before "Oliver" was born, my iron shot up and
the irregular heartbeat completely stopped. I visited my doctor, and he listened to the heart and was like "Wow!" My midwife listened and she said,
"Okay, you've got the green light now. This baby can easily go through birth
the way he's doing now. Just let it happen!"

I believe that God healed my baby. I don't know what was wrong with
his heart—I won't ever know—but I believe that God healed him.

On the tenth of August I began to have a lot of early labor, but I decided
it was nothing and went to Bismark, shopping with my mom. By noon I was
feeling kind of queasy. I ignored it. We were looking for drapes for my living
room, and I had it in my mind that I wasn't going to have the baby without
new drapes.

Mom kept saying, "We gotta get you home! You're in labor, can't you
see?" Tori was with us. I insisted that we go to Wal-Mart as our last stop, and
I found some drapes that were acceptable. Then we went to McDonalds, and
I ate two quarter-pounders with cheese. Two! And a malt, and fries! Why I
ever did that, I don't know. It was some kind of rebellion, I think.

On the way home, I accepted the fact I was in labor. My husband was
working about seventy miles away and living in a trailer close to the job.
Often he'd stay at a job until it was completed rather than commuting every
day from home. He'd left me a name, but not a number, and I knew that it
was going to be hard finding him.

Anyway, when I got home I found my in-laws there. I didn't want them
to know I was in labor because they already told me that they'd zoom me off
to the hospital—they had no idea of our plans. So I'm walking around, trying to pretend I'm not in labor—which is really hard. They're piddling
around—I think she was washing my dishes or something. Also, they were
unloading corn for my calves, and all this other stuff.

Finally, as they were leaving, my mother-in-law turns to me and says,
"You don't look good. You look like you've dropped and you're really, really
white. I think it's going to be tonight." And I'm like, "Oh, no! Not in a million years. Go home!"

After they left, I called the sheriff's department in Stanton because it was
the only one that they were dispatching from. I said, "I need this guy's phone
number because my husband's there . . ." and I explained the situation. They

said, "Just go to the hospital, and we'll get a hold of your husband." And I said, "No, you don't understand; I'm not going to the hospital. My husband is *attending* this birth."

The whole process took about two hours, and Keith finally got home about 10:30. The whole time, I'd been walking around with Tori and not letting myself labor. I was so keyed up. Actually, no one ever called me back to say that they'd found him—he just arrived.

When Keith arrived, he must have had second thoughts about this home birth. He came in, grabbed a couple of beers and went to visit this guy we had staying on our farm in a camper down south of the house. This was a friend of Keith's who was working on a road crew out here and had parked his camper on our property. I was like, "You're leaving!" And Keith said, "Maybe a little bit." But I think he had to compose himself. He got home and there's this woman in labor. He just realized that he was going to have to catch this baby, and that this birth was for real. So he had to get out of here, which I took very personally.

About that time, I started to lose it. Tori began to whine, and I couldn't take it anymore, so I called my mom to come get her. Mom picked up Tori, and then Keith came back. He wanted to turn on the TV. I got mad at that, and he sat there with a pouty scowl on his face like, *I can't do anything!* I went into the bathroom, locked the door, sat in the tub, and made some phone calls from there.

When I came out, I walked around the house a while—from about 12:00 to 12:30. Then, I lay down on the bed and tried to get heart tones with a stethoscope. I was really upset at myself that I wasn't handling this labor well. After I'd come out of the bathroom, Keith was better. By the time I was lying in bed, I was in transition, making all these transition noises, throwing up, and he got more supportive.

The pain was very intense—I hadn't felt anything like this with Tori's birth. It was intense, intense pain, and I told Keith that I was going to die. Keith was like, "You're not going to die! We're going into the living room and have this baby!" I kept screaming at him, "I'm going to die! I'm going to die!" I really thought I was.

He half-carried me into the living room and that helped me to regain composure. Keith had prepared the floor with a shower curtain, a couple of drop cloths, and stuff like that. I squatted on top of these and told him to scrub up his hands 'cause the baby was coming—and it was; I could feel the head crowning.

Keith got back, and I pushed, and Karlin was born. He came out pink and screaming. Later, when we were filling out his birth certificate, I gave him ten on his Apgar. I delivered him squatting on the floor—I held him right away, but then laid him down. I don't know why. I was concentrating on myself, and Keith was cleaning up because it was a very, very messy birth. I didn't have an episiotomy, but there was blood and meconium all over the place. I hadn't delivered the placenta yet. Karlin was just like lying there, obviously okay, but he wouldn't open his eyes. For some reason that scared me, so I told Keith to call the midwife.

So we called—it was probably like a minute or two after he was born. We stayed on the phone for almost an hour. She kept telling me, "Everything is okay, everything is fine." While we were on the phone, I delivered the placenta, which I caught. Keith tied off the umbilical cord and cut it. I was bleeding a little bit heavier than I should have been, and the midwife was telling me to lie back and relax. But I was pretty keyed up and too concerned about being my own midwife to relax.

Karlin wouldn't open his eyes and wouldn't nurse. He didn't want to open them. He could—'cause he'd open and blink them sometimes, but he'd always close them again. With Tori it had been so different—as soon as she was born, I grabbed her and nursed her before my placenta was even out. The cord was still pumping. That's a cool thing. I mean, it's just like a life cycle—she was attached to the cord, which is attached to the placenta, which is attached to me, and then she's attached to the breast.

Karlin didn't do that—he didn't want anything to do with us. He felt better if he was alone, and when we'd pick him up, he'd cry. He never opened his eyes, so I couldn't bond with him.

Keith cleaned everything up, and I finally hung up with the midwife. Then Keith went to bed. It was probably like 3:00 in the morning, and I was still on this high. But there was nobody around—nobody to talk to. At 6:00 I tried to make a few phone calls, but no one would really get up to talk. I decided to take a bath with the baby—an herbal bath. But Karlin hated it; he just wanted to sleep.

I eventually went to bed, but I was still bleeding a bit heavier than I should, and I was afraid that I'd hemorrhage in my sleep. It was tough for me to rest. Keith got up and went to work in the morning, which I guess I had resentment about. It was Friday, and he could have taken the day and had the whole weekend home.

I was left alone and felt totally lost and unhappy after the birth. During the next few weeks, I realized that during my transition I'd begun to feel violated. I continued to have this crushing feeling, really horrid. I don't know how to explain it—I felt like a total failure. I was pretty much a wreck. When Tori was born, there was this joyful, "show her off" feeling. With Karlin, I felt like I wanted to disappear—it was like I had been raped.

The next couple of weeks were really tough on me. Keith was full of how he had delivered his own baby, and nobody gave me any credit. I had planned it all, gone through the pregnancy, and had a baby, but nobody patted me on the back or said, "You did a really good job."

Right after the birth, Keith invited some people over, and I was expected to wash dishes and cook—Karlin was only a day old! I was still having after-birth pains and stuff. They brought over a couple of cases of beer, and everyone sat around and drank. The whole thing was disgusting. Here I was with this new baby, and there's a whole bunch of people in the house drinking beer—I didn't even know them.

Keith basically ignored me, except when I was holding Karlin. It all goes back to that attitude: I was just a baby-box who'd nurse and care for his son until I could hand him over—like he was some kind of king or something who'd hired me to have a baby for him.

I was okay with Karlin as long as I thought of him as a baby. As soon as I thought of him as a little boy, then I'd have these horrid, crushing feelings again. Last May, I started going to counseling—since Karlin's birth, my marriage hasn't been good. Four or five sessions into it, the counselor asked me if I'd ever been raped. I told her no. Then we began to go through some of my past sexual experiences when I was young and came across this one where it seemed like my whole life changed after it. I did some reading and realized that what I had considered a sexual experience was really a date rape.

I was fifteen. This guy was like a father figure; he had lots of money and always treated me very good. But after this sexual thing happened with him, my whole idea about being a woman and being sexual and loving men totally changed. My girlfriends would be sneaking peeks at *Playgirl*, and I'd be dis-

gusted to the point of wanting to throw up. It was the same feeling that I got
when Karlin was born and I saw he was male. I don't know why these feelings didn't come out with my husband, why it took so long to hit me, and
why it would all come out after *this* birth, but it had something to do with
the pain that was involved. Not just the physical, but the emotional pain—
feeling totally out of control and feeling the physical pain on top of it. In a
way, Karlin was like this guy coming back.

I still don't understand why my mind twisted it so. And my husband
doesn't know anything about any of this. When I told him I was doing this
interview, he got all excited because he thinks the spotlight's going to be on
him again. He has no idea. I haven't found a way to open this up to Keith.
Our sex life is affected. Our marriage is affected. I think that at this point in
time it's too much for Keith to even begin to understand. But maybe I'm not
giving him enough credit. I'd like to be free from this horrible cloud hanging
over my life.

*Angie lives in Ocala, Florida, with her Yugoslavian-born husband, Marius, and their four
children: Blake, age ten; Brooke, age nine; Spencer, age five; and Emily, age fourteen months.
Angie is a stay-at-home mom who home-schools and helps run the family's lawn mainte-
nance business. Here she tells the story of Emily's home birth.*

According to My Heart's Desire

Even though my husband and I come from small families, we both wanted
a lot of kids. We have the number seven just fixed in our minds. I guess I take
it literally when the Bible says, "Be fruitful and multiply." Also, my husband
and I truly love children. I know kids are extremely costly, and that my husband is the only one who works, but we've been blessed—God always meets
our needs.

At first, Marius was working for somebody else in a factory job. We were
below the poverty level, and he thought, *Man, I'm working like a dog for some-*

body else and not getting anywhere. He'd been doing lawns on the side and decided to increase those jobs. Finally, he just stepped out in faith and quit his job right in the middle of the winter. God sustained us through it all and tripled his income. Everything we do revolves around our faith.

Now, my first three children were born in the hospital, but with Emily, we had a home birth. When my third child, Spencer, was about a year old, we discovered he was allergic to dairy products, and we all decided to become vegetarians. Later, when I became pregnant with Emily, I went to the library to do some research because I'd never gone through a pregnancy without eating meat. There, on the library shelf, right next to a great book on vegetarianism, was this book on home birth. And I thought, *home birth, that never even crossed my mind as a possibility for me . . . I'm going to pick up this book and read it.*

I read the book, and immediately my heart just said, *Yes, this makes perfect sense.* I felt like the book was telling me that I could have my baby at home no matter what this worldly system says about it. I told my husband, "You're not going to believe this, but I really feel like we need to have this baby at home." And he said, "Well, my mom had me and my brother at home." He was all for it.

I was seven weeks pregnant. I looked in the phone book under "midwives" and "birthing centers," but didn't find much. I called a friend who told me to call someone in Gainesville. I called every doctor, hospital, backwoods clinic, midwife, birthing center, you name it—nobody would deliver my baby at home. I was like, "Oh Lord, what am I going to do? I've got to find somebody 'cause I know that I'm going to have this baby at home."

Finally, I called a health care agency and got in touch with a woman who said that she had done home births before. She was a registered nurse, and we didn't realize at the time it was illegal for her to do what she was going to do. It wasn't until April, a month before my due date, that we discovered we were working underground and going against the laws here. But by that time, we were too far into it to go back; we decided to move ahead, thinking that next time around we'd know.

We met the nurse, Pam, and her sister, Marty, who was going to assist. After meeting us, they went home to discuss our situation. Later, Pam called and told us that they liked both me and my husband and decided to take us on.

Pam did all my prenatal check-ups. I hate needles and IVs—the things they do to you in the hospital. I wanted someone to come into my home and check me every month. Pam agreed to do that; she came once a month to examine me in my home.

For about the first thirteen weeks, oh Lord was I sick! I was home-schooling the children, and I had to end up putting them back in public school. I was so, so sick, throwing up twenty times a day—I couldn't even keep water down. My family was like, *You're going to lose that baby! You need to go to the hospital.* They were just crazy 'cause I had never done a home birth before, and I was sick and a vegetarian. They think I'm a screw-ball, anyway.

Although everything looked pretty scary, I continued to eat fruit, drink water—I didn't want to go to the doctor. I just believed that everything was alright and I'd come through it.

Sometimes I did become afraid, however; I'd feel fear in my heart. But my husband always tried to reaffirm me. During this time, we came upon a book, *Fasting Can Save Your Life*, which showed me that I was toxic and that my body was cleaning itself out of all these impurities, and that's why I was I was vomiting. So, I began to welcome it as a cleansing process, and once I began to look at it like that, I seemed to get better.

The rest of my pregnancy was just beautiful, wonderful, great—up until my due date, which was May 15. On that Sunday morning, everybody in the world was calling me: *Had that baby yet? Having any contractions?* I'm like, *No, just leave me alone.* I hated that! Then one week went by—nothing. Two weeks went by . . . I had only gained eighteen pounds. Pam was saying, "Well, it's okay, you're still small." She wasn't too concerned.

But then, comes the third week and no baby, I started getting people call-ing me: *Something's wrong. You haven't gained enough weight. You were so sick at the beginning of your pregnancy. You're a vegetarian—something's wrong! Isn't your midwife saying anything? Why isn't she concerned?*

They were really starting to put fear in me, and I was beginning to get scared myself. It was well into the first week of June when I asked my hus-band, "Well, what should I do?" He said, "You're not having contractions, and I believe that God knows what He's doing. It's a natural process and who says due dates have to be right?"

On June 16, Pam came over to check me. I'd been having a lot of Braxton-Hicks, and was hopeful that they'd turn into the real thing. Pam said, "I'm going to strip your membranes." I told her, "Fine," thinking that something might happen. She got a little blood on her glove, but I stopped bleeding later in the day.

The next morning I got up and lost my mucus plug. I thought, *Oh, thank the Lord, I'm going to have my baby.* With my other three, as soon as I'd lost my plug, I had them within two days. But not this time—nothing progressed.

I remember the night of June 26. I said to Marius, "I'm really in fear now, and I don't believe I can take this much longer. My due date was May 15th, and here we are more than a month later." He just told me, "We are Christians, and we believe the Word of God. He's going to help us, and He's going to get us through."

The next day I got up and read my Bible. It was June 27, and I read Psalm 27 where it says something about children being a gift from God. They're His reward. I thought, *God, these children are a gift from you, and why would you give me something that's not perfect, not good?*

That night I went to bed. I felt really good. My husband and I had sex. The next morning, the 28th, I woke up in labor! I said, "Yes, Lord, you got me through this!"

It was about 6:00 in the morning. My husband was already at work, and I called Pam's beeper. The contractions were coming three minutes apart. I thought I was going to die! She didn't answer. My heart was beating fast. I called her again—I was sweating under my arms. I called her again. Nothing. Then I called Marius to ask him what to do. He suggested I call her sister, Marty. So I did. She asked, "Are you in labor?" I said, "Yes!" And she said, "Oh my God, Pam's gone to Daytona Beach. Her son's in court there."

Marty said that she'd be right over and told me to get Marius home. I called him, and he was furious about Pam.

Marty got here and checked me—I was six centimeters. She told me to lie in bed, which seemed to slow labor down. When I'd get up, the contractions would start again, really fast. I stayed in bed until 1:00 when we finally were able to reach Pam.

Once we got a hold of her, she was on her way. She said that I should begin walking around, and that she'd be here in about an hour.

At about 2:30, Marius and I went for a mile walk together around the neighborhood. Marty stayed home with the kids. The contractions were coming so fast I thought the baby would fly out of me any minute. When we got home, Pam was still not here, and I got back into bed. At 4:30, she finally arrived. I was almost seven and a half centimeters.

I wasn't in excruciating pain at that point, but it was getting where I couldn't take it much longer. I ran the bathtub full of hot water—I'm talking mega-hot water—and I got in there, put a pillow between my legs, a pillow behind my head, and went through the rest of my labor there.

I had no idea of time. Finally, at some point, Pam said that she needed to check me again. When I stood up, I was like, "Boy are they ever strong! I can't take it!" And Pam said, "My Lord, Angie, there's the head!"

As they tried to help me to the bed, my water broke and I could feel the baby coming down. This was something like 7:45. I was on the bed, on my back, and hurting. I was like, God, I know I'm not supposed to be lying on my back to have this baby, but I couldn't get up the strength to turn over. They had to force me. My husband just said, "You get up. That baby's head is right there and you need to have this baby!" I got on my hands and knees. The children were in the bedroom with us.

I remember Pam saying, "Don't push! Don't push! You're going to rip if you push!" So I didn't. Pam began working with her fingers and the baby's head slid out. She turned to Marty and said, "Don't let her push! The cord's wrapped around the baby's neck!" I could see my husband's face, and I could feel fear in the room.

They tried to unwrap the cord, but couldn't. Finally, someone said, "We're going to have to cut it." I was still being told not to push, but the baby just flew out of me before they could even get the scissors to cut the cord. I hadn't been pushing—the baby just flew out, and it was all Pam could do to catch her!

Later, I was told that while Emily's head was out, she had her little eyes open and she was looking around. When she was out they were able to slip the cord around and didn't need to cut it. Immediately, we were all rejoicing and crying! I put her right to my breast and just nursed her. The cord was still attached. She latched right on!

You know, when Pam came so late, the first thing I said to her was, "You know what? I'm going to kiss you now because I'm glad to see you, but after the baby is born I'm going to kick you in the butt for doing this to me." She laughed at the time, but right after I had the baby I said, "Well, get this baby off me so I can kick Pam in the butt now."

I quickly delivered the placenta—it came out in one whole, beautiful, perfect piece. We put it in a bowl. My kids ran out into the neighborhood. They were crying and telling everybody. Before I knew it, I had the whole neighborhood in my bedroom.

Everything had gone according to my heart's desire. I had no anesthesia, no needles, no IVs, no episiotomies, no stitches, no nothing. I had torn just a little, but didn't want any stitches. Pam told me it would heal by itself. God had pulled us through.

We buried the placenta and planted a tree on top of it for Emily and in remembrance of my grandmother who died in our house exactly one year before Emily was born. It was a holly because my grandmother loved holly trees.

Sue is an artist and runs a successful embellished-clothing business from her home in Key West, Florida. She sells her work to area retail shops. Her husband, Tony, is a real estate broker. At the time of our interview they had two daughters: Amanda, age two, and Emily, age four months, whose birth is described here.

Birth Standing Up

My second pregnancy was difficult. Before Amanda reached her first birthday, we found out that I was pregnant again. It wasn't planned—we hadn't made the decision to have another baby. My husband was shocked. I had gotten pregnant with my first child just four months into our marriage—and now I was pregnant again.

I know that some men think their wives are beautiful when they're pregnant, but my husband doesn't feel that way. And personally, I don't feel very beautiful myself. I was tired a lot of the time and couldn't pamper myself like I had with the previous pregnancy. Also, I had to keep up with a toddler who couldn't understand. It's a miracle to watch a young child grow and change, but after a while, I stopped being able to appreciate her; I was too tired!

Tony believes that he is a good father, and I think he is, too—the girls love him. But he'll only take the kids if I plead with him. And lately, he's working more and more . . . because it's easier . . . and he's got the excuse that he's doing it for the family. It's definitely an ego booster to be successful in the outside world—you get acknowledgment. At home raising kids, you don't.

With this second pregnancy, I decided to have a home birth. My first child was born in a hospital with a midwife attending, and I had to be induced with Pitocin. Overall, I hated the whole thing—being in the hospital, being induced, and being treated like a patient. My second child's birth was very different.

Labor began on the day before Easter. I was taking Amanda, who was one and a half at the time, out for an Easter egg hunt. Before I left, I began to have what felt like menstrual cramps, and I was kind of nervous. But the pains weren't strong or regular, so I decided to go on with the day's plans. At about six o'clock, dinner time, I was still having the same irregular contractions. Then at about 9:00 that night, I lay down to rest and felt that we needed to call one of the midwives. The pains were getting stronger.

I was tired, and my husband and I had a little argument. We had a hand-painted cradle that we'd made for our first daughter, and my husband was cleaning it up and putting fresh sheets on the little mattress. I was belly-up in bed and kind of telling him what to do and how to do it. We had a few words about this, but really we were both a bit on edge. Amanda was asleep in her bedroom. At 10:00, we decided to take her over to our friends' house. They had agreed to watch her for us. I remember Tony holding her, and Amanda barely awake, waving good-bye to me over his shoulder as he carried her out. She was sucking her thumb. I blew her a kiss.

The midwife came at about the same time. I remember feeling so relieved. She was instantly in control, and I relaxed. The timing was great. My husband came back in a few minutes—our friends live just around the corner—and we were now assembled for the birth. I decided it was time to go upstairs to the bedroom; I wanted to make sure we were in the right place and I was comfortable.

I had read somewhere that a woman in labor should greet each pain, kind of welcome, rather than resist it—that's what I was trying to do. I had heard that if you can keep your lips soft, that meant that your insides were soft too. I was trying to help my body, but it was hard. The pains were quickly becoming intense, but at least I could catch my breath and rest in between them.

I must have gone into transition downstairs. I went to the bathroom and pow! I needed help to get upstairs, but the pains were so bad that I didn't want

anyone to touch me. I remember being at the bottom of the stairs and holding on to the banister. It was a long way up. I finally did let my husband help
me. I made it to the bed, and he positioned himself behind me, holding me.
One or two contractions later, my water broke in a big gush! Thankfully, we
had remembered to put the rubber sheet over the mattress!

At about one in the morning, the other midwife came by. These two
midwives often work together. I remember Beth checking my blood pressure
and telling me that everything was going well—which was very good. Before
the birth, I had been worried that if something went wrong and we weren't
in the hospital, it could be dangerous. But these women were totally wonderfully and capable. During the birth I had no worries at all; I had given my
trust completely to them.

I labored with my eyes closed. I didn't want to see anything. I used all my
consciousness to feel what my body was doing, and I concentrated so as to
be able to experience all sensation. It was a very natural thing to close my
eyes.

One of the midwives suggested that I might help labor by squatting on
the floor. Across the room near my worktable we had a futon down, and I
thought that I'd like to squat on it so that if I needed to, I could lie down
quickly. The midwives went to get it for me, and my husband helped me to
stand up. A really big contraction came, and I felt like I was going to bite his
neck! Then, holding onto him, standing up, wham! The baby came sliding
out of me!

I never had the urge to push. I just felt like another contraction was coming, and then—there was the baby. I remember that the contraction was
incredibly hard, and I screamed with it. Beth had to dive to catch the baby. It
was wild giving birth this way! First, there was silence. Then someone yelled,
"It's a girl!" I was totally surprised. During my entire pregnancy, I thought I
had been carrying a boy. I was still standing up when they cut the cord, and
I was face to face there, holding my husband.

They laid me down on the futon, and handed her to me. She was crying
and wanted to nurse right away. This new baby felt immediately comfortable
to me. I delivered the placenta, and the midwives realized that I had torn. I
remember that getting the stitches to repair me was more painful than the
actual birth. I don't think that the numbing medicine they used was strong
enough. I screamed out with every stitch.

Beth cleaned the baby up. The midwives were very clinical and organized. The baby was born at exactly 3:33 on Easter morning. It was all very relaxed and natural. Even though she cried, Emily seemed very calm from the beginning, and I'm sure that having her at home contributed to this sense of calmness and ease. The midwives stayed with us until 7:00 in the morning. They wanted to make sure that everything was just right before they left.

৪০

Sarah is a full-time mother and lives in a small town in Florida. She has three children, two of whom she delivered at a hospital in her hometown of Boulder, Colorado. Sarah chose to have her last baby at home with midwives attending. At the time of our interview, her first child, Charlotte, was twelve years old, and her middle child, Justin, was nine years old. Chloe, her home-birth baby, was about to celebrate her first birthday.

Here I Go Again!

My third labor began just like my first two—my water began trickling out. This time, it happened about 5:30 in the morning. I remember it was just becoming light outside.

The contractions hadn't started yet, and I just lay in bed, getting nervous. I kept thinking: well, here I go again! After nine years, I don't know if I can do it!

I was doing my slow-breathing exercises, trying to relax myself. Then at about 7:00, I woke my husband, David, and told him that we should probably get things ready. David had breakfast, and I ate only a little. I got the bed ready—we put a shower curtain down under a fresh sheet. We also have another bed, a waterbed, and I got that ready, too, but I didn't feel I really wanted to give birth on that. Also, we borrowed a hot tub, fixed it up outside, thinking that I might want to have a water birth. I called the midwives, just to let them know. My contractions were very weak and irregular. They didn't feel that they needed to visit me yet. After the preparations, David and I decided to go for a short walk. The day outside was warm and beautiful.

Later that morning, things really began to pick up. By this time, I wasn't nervous because I had told myself, *Well, I just gotta go through with this—labor is here! There's no use in fighting it!* I remember thinking back on my previous labors—the first one was forty-four hours long and the second was seven and a half. I told myself foolishly that I'd make it a short one again—as though I had some control!

Seven hours went by, though, and I hadn't progressed very much. It was afternoon, and the midwives were coming by to check me every now and then. David was with me, helping. We continued to walk and try to keep the contractions going. The interesting thing was that whenever the midwives would come over, we'd have such a good time talking that my contractions practically went away. We actually had to tell them to leave so that David and I could get the contractions started again. I'd bring out my pictures—the midwives had never seen photos of my kids who live in Colorado. We were having a grand old time! But finally, I decided that we couldn't just sit around and have parties. The midwives would leave and sure enough, the contractions would pick up again. I would walk for a while, then rest. I knew that I had to have some strength left. Also, I drank lots of good juices and teas, thinking that I needed the energy.

The midwives, I remember, came back in the evening to check me again. Nothing. But right after they left, I suddenly felt like, this is it! And sure enough, as soon as they left, this time the contractions started to pick up. The midwives came back at about 7:00. When they checked me, I was somewhere between five and seven centimeters.

Then, whammo! All of a sudden, the contractions really got going! I tell you, I didn't remember how incredible labor could be. Good ol' amnesia, you know. Even after two births, I had completely forgotten how intense Mother Nature can get.

I stayed pretty much in the bedroom—the one with the regular bed. My good friend was there to help, so there were four of us. And it's a good thing—we actually needed everyone. My friend and my husband moved the hot tub inside as it was getting cool out. They began to fill it up, but I didn't want to move.

I was just lying in bed. The midwives were giving me ice and Popsicles. I couldn't believe how strong these pains were. And then something funny happened. I had never experienced this, and I don't know how many women ever have: I felt the baby wiggling in the birth canal! Literally, it felt like she was trying to move her head. I couldn't figure out how she was doing it, but

I found that I was getting mad at her. In between contractions, I felt her kicking and moving that little head. It hurt, and I was angry! I remember trying to talk to her, "Hey! You can't do that, it hurts!" But boy, I tell you, she was just determined! Up until the moment she came out, I swear, she was wiggling. Literally, even with her legs and head in the birth canal!

It was really tough. And this wiggling certainly added to it. I had to have a lot of eye contact with somebody—which I had never experienced before either. Also, I needed to vocalize. David would begin to make a sound that I could follow. These noises were kind of gross and high-pitched, which wasn't good because that meant that my breathing was too shallow. So David would try and make a lower sound so that I could get my breathing back down. Really, I had to make these sounds, and it was comforting to have them.

It was getting toward 9:00, and I was beginning to get into transition. I was dizzy, almost delirious. The contractions were real strong, and I didn't know what was going on around me. I remember shouting, "Oh God, I want to get out of this!" It's pretty intense. I don't care what anybody says, it's pain!

Then I distinctly remember having a tingling or funny sensation down in the bottom there, and I knew it was time to push. I've had this sensation in all of my births. I could even tell the midwives exactly when I'm at ten centimeters—and at each birth, when I was checked, I'd be right.

For me, there's always this feeling that takes over, a feeling I can't help but respond to by pushing. It took everything to push this baby out. I had David hold one of my arms, my friend held the other, and the midwives were down at the end. I was on my bed. Everyone helped me up so I could lean over and push. My knees were up, and I was grabbing my friend and David so hard that later we could see finger marks on them in our birthing pictures.

In my previous labors, the need to push would come in spurts; this time, even when I had to stop pushing to catch my breath, the actual urge to push never stopped. At one point, the midwives told me to stop pushing because I was about to tear. They were very good at guiding me, and it was comforting to be able to muster up enough strength to hold back for a few seconds. I never tore, and I'm really grateful for that.

The actual pushing and delivery only lasted about half an hour, but I couldn't believe how hard it was to push her out. Once I was at it, I got a kind of motion going. It was very difficult, but very exciting too. And when the baby came out, she had her eyes open! I remember saying, "It's a real baby!"

Somehow, I had lost perspective and stopped believing that there was a real baby inside me. Women just get so involved in their own bodies during labor, and then, all of a sudden, there's this baby—a new person.

Right after she was born, the midwives placed her, stomach down, on my belly. Somehow, I had forgotten to ask about the baby's gender. One of the midwives said, "Don't you want to know if it's a boy or a girl?" The lights were low and everyone was very quiet. Gently we rolled her over. I thought it was going to be a boy. But no, it was a girl, and we all start screaming, "It's a girl, it's a girl!" We startled the baby, and she began to cry. I gave her my breast, and she immediately latched on and stopped crying. It was amazing. I remember thinking, *Oh God, I did it again!*

There were no problems. She was nine pounds, very alert and ready to rock and roll! She was beautiful. Her Apgar was great, and she didn't need to be suctioned much. Now, the neat thing was, once they got me cleaned up and the baby cleaned up, we went over to the hot tub, which was filled with warm water. David got in with her, and they spent half an hour together in that water. Chloe was just—I hate using this hippy language—blissed out. Arms, legs so free, and eyes open! It was wonderful to watch. I think that dads need a little something like this in order to make a real connection. Someone put a rose in the water and lit candles. It was like being in love all over again.

Andrea currently lives in Ohio with her husband, Doug, and two children: Chelsea, age four, and Amanda, age two. The birthing story she describes occurred in Staten Island, New York. Chelsea was born at a local medical center; Amanda's birth, described here, offered Andrea a very different kind of birthing experience.

Standing Where Nobody Has Stood

Before my daughters were born, I worked full-time at an environmental department store called Terra Verde. I was also a graduate student at NYU, studying environmental conservation education. I graduated and became pregnant in the same month. My mom always taught me to finish what I've been working on before moving to the next project.

I stopped working soon after I became pregnant with Chelsea because of the nausea, and I haven't worked outside the home since. Currently, I do volunteer work as a LaLeche League Leader. We've lived in Ohio now for about a year. My husband decided to move to the Columbus office because we wanted to be near our family. My parents and all my grandparents are here; so are my husband's parents. This is where I grew up.

My first birth experience, with Chelsea, had been rather traumatic for me. When my water broke, it was thick with meconium, so the hospital staff insisted on using internal monitors. Nobody would really tell me what was going on. I felt alone, and it was kind of scary. After my water broke, the contractions intensified, and they wouldn't let me off my left side. I thrashed around and asked for a C-section. Thank goodness, they wouldn't do that. Instead, they decided an epidural was in order. I told them, "Whatever. Take the pain away." First, they had to lower my blood pressure with magnesium sulphate, and then they administered the epidural. I had an internal monitor, a catheter for my urine, a catheter for the epidural, and a continuous blood pressure monitor. I laid on my left side the whole time—nobody told me to change positions. When the epidural started to wear off, I began to have the urge to push. But I was told that only half my cervix was dilated. I had to roll over onto my other side and let the doctor ease the lip around Chelsea's head. I pushed for a couple of hours. The doctor stretched my perineum out—that was good. When I finally delivered Chelsea, I didn't need an episiotomy.

But I was exhausted. I thought I had come close to dying, and that the hospital staff had saved me. That's the state of mind you get into when you're in the hospital. They took Chelsea to the nursery for observation. She was born at 4:00 in the afternoon, and I didn't get to nurse her until the next morning. And that's what traumatizes me still—realizing that didn't have to happen.

At first, Doug and I said, "No more!" But then I realized that the experience of Chelsea's birth wasn't my body's fault, it was a problem with the care I received. Shortly after Chelsea's birth I began to think about how things could be different.

I explored herbs and homeopathy and decided that for my next pregnancy I'd go to a midwife. There was only one midwife who'd attend births in Staten Island, and she lived on Long Island. My friend had just used her and liked her a lot, so I tried her out for my regular yearly pap smear and liked her very much, too. When I got pregnant, I called her right away.

Staten Island is very medieval as far as childbirth goes. The hospital where I had Chelsea referred to my Bradley instructor as "that witch."

But at some point, I decided that I myself wanted to become a Bradley instructor. My goal was to achieve this before Amanda arrived. As part of my final training, I had to teach an actual class. I did, and my students were two pregnant friends. As part of the class, we went to visit a local birthing center. It was alright, but I still didn't like the idea that I'd have to leave my home to have the baby. I feel like that's the first intervention.

Doug was scared to have the baby at home initially. But I explained to him just how I had felt with Chelsea. He understood. I told him that if we were going to have any more children, they'd have to be born at home. He understood how important it was to me and didn't argue. It helps when your husband trusts your judgments.

I had problems with colds all that winter. I was trying to become a Bradley instructor, trying to keep up with a toddler, and trying to keep up with LaLeche League stuff. And I was pregnant! I'm not always a particularly happy pregnant woman. There's something about the hormones that turn me into a bit of a bear sometimes. Some women glow, and some women don't. I didn't—and that's how I'd characterize my pregnancy.

Amanda was due June 25—my mother-in-law's birthday. I went into labor on June 13. I don't remember much of that day, but after supper, around 7:30, the Braxton-Hicks I'd been having started feeling different. I remember giving Amanda her bath and reading while she played in the tub. I could just feel a pull in my tailbone—it's hard to describe.

Doug and I just went about our normal business. I asked him if we should stay up. He said, "No, that was our mistake last time. Just go to bed and sleep." So we went to bed. All night I could feel contractions coming— not very close together and not lasting very long. We just rested as much as we could.

At 6:00, I got up to call Janette, the midwife, and let her know what was happening. Doug decided to stay home from work. After breakfast the contractions stopped for a couple of hours, and I got some good sleep. They began again around 8:00 or 9:00. We did normal stuff. We went for a walk in the park. When I'd have a contraction, I'd just stop and wait for it to pass, then keep on going.

We had made arrangements for Jane, a good friend, to watch Amanda. She has a daughter who's in her play group. They came over for lunch that day—now it was Tuesday, June 14. I was feeling alright. The contractions kept coming, not very close together, and again, they wouldn't last long. I made lunch for us all, and we just talked. It took me longer to eat. Every now and then, I'd stop and look away. My friend would say, "Are you having a contraction now?" And I'd say, "Yes." She'd had a bad experience too, and was kind of in awe of the whole thing. I seemed to be handling it all so well.

We talked the entire afternoon. My water still hadn't broken, so I felt cautious about even calling it labor. That evening we all decided to nap. My friend went home with her daughter, Doug took Chelsea back to bed, and I flopped on my beanbag chair to rest. I decided to have a little talk with the baby. I said, "Okay, if this is for real, you're going to have to let me know. I'm getting to feel a bit unsure here." But nothing changed; the contractions just kept on coming.

We made it through dinner, and I ate very lightly. The contractions began to feel a little more intense, so I suggested that this would be a good time for Chelsea to go to Jane's house. We packed up her stuff, and Jane came over to pick her up. After that, everything just took off.

It was 8:30 in the evening. I remember feeling really sad because it was the first night that Chelsea was away from me. I paced around the house, crying with contractions. I laid down on my bed, and when I started to get up, I felt a pop. A little bit of water trickled out. I went to the bathroom and noticed that it was lightly green.

I called Janette right away. I was worried that it was meconium, and that had been what happened with Chelsea. It was 9:30 now. Janette said she was on her way. I stayed on the toilet and in the bedroom for a while. I would kneel on the floor, kind of rock during the contractions. It felt good to be on my hands and knees rocking—I felt like I was soothing Amanda inside me. I was worried that she might be a little stressed out with the meconium. But it was very light, and I told myself that if it were something that needed worrying about, Janette would worry when she arrived. It takes an hour for Janette to get from her home to our apartment—we'd have a full hour to wait. I knew that fear could make labor worse, make it more painful and stressful, so I told myself not to worry.

Doug began filling our birthing tub immediately. We had rented it from Janette. It was a huge, oval, hard-sided one, with soft liners on the bottom. You could put down pads underneath the liner and custom-fit it that way. The hard sides allow support while laboring. My friends had had their baby in it at home, and had come over the previous weekend to help set it up.

Janette arrived at 10:30. She and Doug ran around preparing the baby's clothes. I had washed them six weeks earlier, put them in Ziploc bags, and tucked them into the drawers. Janette checked me vaginally only one time. I was eight centimeters dilated and almost completely effaced.

I was really happy, because with Chelsea the contractions got awful at five centimeters, and here I was at eight and didn't feel that bad. In fact, I had thought to myself, *I guess these contractions aren't really doing anything.* They didn't hurt much and never got more intense than they were at 8:30—that, I remember, was the peak.

Janette asked if I wanted to get into the tub. I said, "But what about the meconium?" Some midwives feel that if there's meconium, you shouldn't get into water. But Janette just said, "Oh, don't worry about it."

I got into the tub at about ten minutes to 11:00—it was wonderful. The water was warm and completely supported my pregnant body. In between contractions, I sat on the bottom of the tub and just leaned against the hard side and rested. When I felt a contraction coming, I sort of swam to the other side and kneeled. That was my favorite position. Holding onto the side and kneeling, I could push my legs far apart and deal effectively with the contractions.

Very quickly though, the contractions became pushing contractions, and my body started pushing. It scared me because I'd never felt the full intensity of this before. I could feel my rectum moving back and feel the pressure like I was about to have a big bowel movement. I got scared and screamed and tried to clamp my legs together because the sensation was overwhelming. Janette was great. She said, "Just open your legs, relax." I had to let my body do the pushing with each contraction; I couldn't help them along because it would hurt too much.

I was in the kneeling position. I remember reaching my hand down and feeling Amanda's head. Suddenly I realized, *This is the baby! I'm going to have a baby!* I remembered how wonderful it was to nurse a baby and that soon I'd be able to again! Chelsea had weaned when I was six months pregnant. After all this stuff went through my head, the fear just went away. I was able to just relax with each contraction, and I let everything stretch out on its own. I didn't have to do much work.

We had expressed a desire to catch the baby ourselves, so Janette suggested that I might want to lean over and switch into a squatting position. But it didn't work—I had to return to kneeling. I asked Janette if it were possible to be in transition and yet be pushing at the same time. She doesn't really believe in the stages of labor, so she said, "Yes."

Then suddenly I was able to gently help the pushing. Amanda's head came out, and Janette asked me to wait a minute because Amanda's hand was up by her head. She said, "Wait, and just ease the baby out slowly." So I pushed very slowly, and Janette caught Amanda, slid her up between my legs and said, "Here's your baby!"

I was on my hands and knees, lifting Amanda out of the water. When I opened her little legs to check if it was a boy or girl, she peed and I couldn't really tell. Water babies are very calm. They don't cry right away. It's such a gentle way to be born.

Janette wanted me to rub her back to stimulate her. But she didn't cry. As soon as Janette touched her, however, she did cry. She got mad that somebody else was touching her.

I continued to rub her back a while, and then looked down and saw it was a girl. I looked up at Doug and said, "Amanda." He took my picture then. That's the one I have on my desk.

They clamped the cord and cut it. I got out of the tub and sat on one of those birthing stools. Janette began the newborn exam. I watched from the stool and my placenta came in ten minutes. I was hardly aware. It just came—plop, there it was. Amanda cried during the exam. Right after my placenta came, they wrapped her up in towels, wrapped me up in towels, and I got into bed with her. She nursed, and we started making phone calls.

A few days later, I realized that Amanda was tongue-tied. The membrane that attaches her tongue to the bottom of her mouth was too short. I had to try to find a doctor who would snip it so that she could nurse properly. A few days postpartum, I had to drive an hour out to Long Island. There was no one nearby who would do it for me. One doctor said that I could have an appointment in three weeks. Another said he didn't believe I could diagnose the problem. So we went to this doctor, who snipped it right away. Amanda was sore a little bit, but was soon fine. This little escapade shattered my dream of being pampered in bed with my two girls, but you do what you have to do.

Janette came the day after the birth, and again on day five. The regular scheduled check-up is supposed to be on day three, but with all this tongue-tied business, it was later. I was tired but doing great. In fact, my uterus had shrunk amazingly back, and I must say that I had done something that must have significantly helped.

On my last prenatal visit before Amanda was born, Janette asked me, "So do you want to eat some placenta?" I said, "Well . . . ." But the intellectual part of my brain said, *I don't know about this!* And I just told her that I'd see how I felt after the baby was born. Then, since it was a home birth and I wanted to make sure everything went right, I told Janette that I would try a little. So I chewed on the placenta a bit. It was very fibrous and hormonal tasting, and I couldn't swallow. But I did chew it. I believe that's why my uterus went down so quickly. There's an interaction between the placenta and saliva that helps stop hemorrhaging and brings the uterus down. And I think that's why in nature, animals eat the placenta. My bleeding stopped in three days—not six weeks. But this subject is rather taboo. The other day I was surfing the Internet and when we discussed this, they felt it was cannibalistic. This is not something I'm very comfortable talking about because so many people are judgmental.

We live in a very fearful society. Giving birth the way I did and making the decisions I made helped me to lose my fear. During my experience training to be a Bradley instructor, I had to write about what birth was all about for me. I wrote that I felt birth was like walking to the edge of a cliff, standing where nobody has stood, and then coming back. It changes your whole being.

Four

DELIVERING IN UNEXPECTED PLACES

ဆၢ

THREE OF THE WOMEN in this section had planned to give birth in hospitals or birthing centers, but, because of unexpectedly short labors, ended up giving birth in unusual places. The ability of these women to remain flexible and positive in stressful situations helped them to have positive outcomes and unforgettable birthing experiences. The last woman in this section is the wife of a wildlife photographer, who, with her husband, followed the natural migration of the animals throughout the year and had no "real" home. Although the realities of this woman's life might not appeal to everyone, as she accepts her circumstances, she actively decides that her birthing experience should be not only memorable but also should provide all participants with a good time.

ဆၢ

Elizabeth lives in Hillsborough, North Carolina, with her husband, Eric, and their three children: Hanna, age six; Ingred, age three; and Ansel, age two. Elizabeth talks here about the unusually quick labor she had with Ansel and the strange place where she gave birth.

A Really Major Gas Pain

Hanna was the perfect baby—always happy, always laughing. My second made up for it: Ingred started screaming on her fifth-week birthday and didn't stop until she was about eleven months old. Ingred couldn't sleep unless she was lying on someone's chest, and when she was awake, she always seemed to be screaming—it was just a matter of how loud.

After her, I thought that I wanted to have a third child, but my husband, Eric, really only wanted two. I would pray, *I want one more baby, please Lord!* But then, I began to make peace with just having the two, so I sent up another prayer, *Lord, cancel the order! I don't want another baby!* And immediately, I got pregnant. I was devastated. Ansel was the only baby that we didn't try hard to have.

I remember soon after I knew I was pregnant, Eric and I went on a kayaking trip. We were out on a big rock in the middle of the river and I said, "What would you think if I told you that we were going to have another baby?" And he said, "I think it would be kind of nice. I'd like it." I said, "That's good, cause we're going to!" He was thrilled. He said that he wanted to become the perfect daddy—and really, he has. He was deliriously happy through the whole pregnancy.

But I was miserable. When I become pregnant, I get extremely ill. Some pregnant women say, "Oh, I never felt better in my life." I say, "I never want to feel this way again!" When I would tell people that we were having this unexpected baby and explain how I felt both physically and emotionally, they'd ask, "Well, why don't you get an abortion?" I'm morally opposed to abortion, and although it was a trying time, I was committed to having the baby.

My midwife was in nursing school and couldn't help me with this pregnancy. I begged her to do the birth, but she couldn't. My first baby was born at the home of our midwife, Mamie, and the second was born at our own home. This third we wanted to have at home, but after checking around, there was no one available I could trust, so Eric and I decided to bite the bullet and have the baby at the hospital with the midwives there. We weren't real happy. I'm scared of hospitals, and Eric is too.

When we toured the hospital, the nurse kept talking about all the things they did to identify the baby—so that no one would steal it. And that didn't make us feel any better! Eric described the birthing rooms as medieval—something out of *One Flew over the Cuckoo's Nest* with wallpaper! It wasn't nice, and we weren't pleased. Also, we didn't like the way the midwives were handling us. I think they felt a little distrustful because we had had home births and they were afraid that we'd use them for prenatal care, drop them, and have the baby at home.

To complicate things, I'd had a thyroid condition as a teenager. It wasn't a permanent condition, and I was well over it. But the tendency is to panic when you see that on my records. I kept telling them that I would know if my thyroid got low. It's real clear to me. But they ordered tests, and I refused to have them done. They didn't like that. I just felt like they were being invasive—not allowing me to trust myself, and that made me distrustful of them.

We wrote up a clear birth plan and contacted Mamie again. She lives in the mountains, and we didn't want to go to her house again because we had two young children and it's so far away. But Mamie knew us, knew what we wanted, and was happy to come and advocate for us. She's a southern woman—polite, but with steel behind it. She'd certainly be able to stick up for us.

And this whole time I kept praying, *Now Lord, I know it's not safe to give birth at home with just the two of us, but boy would I love to have my water break, go into labor and have this baby so quickly that there'd be no time to get to the hospital!* Then, a couple of weeks before Ansel was born, I had a dream that it had happened.

But really, we made plans to go to the hospital. My parents came down from Indiana to take care of the children. I remember the night I went into labor, we all stayed up late to talk. It was January, before my due date. My last baby was late, and with both children, I had about two weeks of labor pain that would come every night before the actual birth. This time, I didn't have any nighttime labor, so we weren't expecting anything to happen.

A few days before, I had some gas pain, but the midwives decided not to check me—they told me it was normal, and that I'd surely be able to recognize labor. I liked the fact they didn't want to check me, but looking back, I feel that if they had, they might have seen some signs.

Anyway, we were up talking that night. And I made a joke that when women are really exhausted, they go into labor—at the worst possible time. "I'll probably go into labor tonight, ha, ha, ha!" I joked. We all went to bed around midnight.

Then, sometime after 2:00, I started to have that gas again. My husband suggested that I put my bottom up in the air so the gas could rise. I tried that, and it didn't really help. It began to hurt pretty bad, instead. I went to the bathroom, but quickly came back into the bedroom because I hurt so bad. Eric, said, "Well, you're being kind of noisy about this. You probably woke your parents up!" He went into the other room to check on them. They were awake and wanted to know if I was okay. Eric said, "Oh, she's just having gas." But then I made a noise, and my mother said, "She's in labor!"

When I heard my mother say this, I realized that I *was* in labor. Eric came into the room, and I told him to start the car. It was the coldest night of the year—typical with my children. Hanna was born in May after a tornado, and then we had an unseasonable snowstorm right after! Ingred was also born on the coldest night of the year.

My dad went down to start the car to get it warm for me. Eric went to call the midwives. I decided to use the bathroom and empty myself, so I wouldn't have to go in the car. But then I made that noise again and felt myself open up almost instantly. I could feel myself dilating. I had Eric come and check me. Having had home births, he knew how.

We were in the bathroom together, and next we hear this popping noise and then water. Eric asked, "What was that?" We just looked at each other! We knew what it was! He said, "Let me run down and tell your mom." She was on the phone with the midwives. But I said, "Don't leave me! The baby's coming!" Eric said, "I know, don't panic." And he ran down and then back up very quickly.

I could feel that baby heading down. I was kind of stuck on the toilet. I couldn't move. Eric looked down and saw something. I yelled, "It's the head. Catch it!" The baby's head just popped out, and the body quickly corkscrewed around and out in one smooth movement.

It was pretty amazing. It was everything I had prayed for—just perfect! The baby was healthy. He cried right away. Later, my mom said there was only one drop of blood on the floor. It all had gone into the toilet. Cleanest labor I've ever had!

From the moment that I knew I was in labor to the moment Ansel was born, only ten minutes had passed! You don't think much of anything in the middle of a situation like this. You're on autopilot. People are always saying to Eric, "Oh, you were so brave to have caught the baby." But his answer is, "There wasn't much choice. Either me or the toilet."

I remember looking up soon after the birth, and my dad was standing there. He had never been around my mother when she gave birth to either me or my sister. And there he was. He had heard all the commotion and came up—he found me with a baby on my lap. He was so thrilled! The other children got up, too, and came over—they didn't miss out.

I waddled over to the bed with the cord still attached, whacking me. We have a very high bed and I had to let the cord pass through my legs in order to get up. We got me and the baby covered. We turned the temperature up in the house. My mother was still talking to the midwife, who had heard the whole birth on the telephone.

I wanted to birth the placenta and then go to the hospital and get checked. But it wouldn't come. I drank some herbs. My mom had called Mamie, who came right over. I could hear Mamie saying downstairs, "Now, don't you have this baby without me!" She came up, and I began to deliver the placenta at the top of the stairs. Mamie caught it! I guess it was the next best thing to catching the baby!

We took the placenta in case they wanted to inspect it, and we all piled into our Volvo station wagon. I lay with the baby and nursed him on the way. My father had bought a fish scale to weigh the baby, but we had forgotten to use it. They didn't know what to do with us at the hospital.

They said, "Either women have their babies at the doorstep or they make it up to the delivery room." They never come in with the baby in their arms! But I wanted to be checked and have Ansel checked. With my other two, I had had a piece of the placenta stick, and I wanted to make sure that everything was okay and that there were no after-delivery complications.

They agreed to check me, check the baby, and then release us. The doctor in charge was very laid back and supported our wishes. We were extremely grateful. Later, I wrote a letter to the hospital thanking them for their help.

You know, often you hear these stories about women who can't tell labor pains from gas pains. And you think, *Yeah, right!* But for me, it did feel like a gas pain—a really major gas pain! Everyone thought that with a third baby I'd certainly recognize what labor felt like. But I didn't. And even though I wanted to have him alone at home, I never actually thought it would happen.

਍

For most of the year Sandra lives with her husband, Mike, and their son, John, eighteen months, in a tent near Billings, Montana. John is a wildlife photographer, and the family follows him around as he records the life patterns of the animals he photographs. Here, Sandra talks about her all-natural birth in the honeymoon suite of a motel.

Birth in the Honeymoon Suite

My husband, Mike, is a wildlife photographer. In the summer, he works as a river guide and runs river trips down the Yellowstone. In the spring, he does the birthing of baby animals, and in winter, he often follows their migrations. I used to go with him all the time, but since John was born, I don't go so much anymore.

We have some property right outside Yellowstone, and this last summer we lived there in an eight-man tent fully equipped with a queen-sized bed, La-Z-Boy chair, TV, and VCR. It was wonderful—we had electricity and were near a creek.

When John was a year old, we figured he had traveled 25,000 miles. But probably we'll get more settled; we plan to build a log cabin and photograph mostly around Montana.

Mike and I have been married five years. We were planning to wait another two before starting a family. It's funny because we were not careful just one time, and that's all it took.

I found out I was pregnant because one month my breasts were very tender. I went to Planned Parenthood to check it out. I was late with my period, but I didn't worry 'cause I'm always late. My grandmother had died of breast cancer and I got really paranoid. I went to the clinic and said, "I think I have breast cancer. Check me out." They said, "Well, we have to do a pregnancy test on everybody . . . ," and I said, "No, no, no; I don't want to pay for that." They told me it was free and that they had to do it. I was like, "Well, okay, but I'm not pregnant"—I had forgotten about that night. So I took their little test and was sitting there when the worker comes back and says, "You're pregnant!"

I nearly fell off the table—I was really sad and started crying. I began thinking about all I was going to miss out on. I thought, *My life's over!* I didn't realize that children were so portable.

That week, we were living in an apartment. I bought some baby booties, wrapped them up, and gave them to Mike. I think I'd seen that done in a movie sometime. Mike was thirty at the time and more ready than me; he was really happy about the news. I felt like a little girl still. I thought, *I can't have kids, I'm too young!* I was twenty-six but felt like eighteen.

For the first part of my pregnancy, I had the funnest time—I loved being pregnant. I'm really thin, about 112, and when I got pregnant I developed boobs and gained 45 pounds. Everyone said I looked so much better. I always wanted to gain weight and was not uncomfortable at all. I even had stretch marks—but they didn't bother me. And I didn't want my due date to come. I wanted to be pregnant another nine months. When I was in labor, I said, "Oh, good-bye baby"—it's even on my video tape. I felt so connected with the baby that I mourned the loss of him inside my tummy.

When I was ten weeks, I went to a wedding where the maid of honor was nine months pregnant. We began to talk about childbirth. She was going to have her baby at home with a midwife, and my first response was, "You're crazy! What if something goes wrong?" She explained how safe birth is at home, how the midwife comes with all this equipment she rarely has to use. At home, the process happens more naturally so that complications don't arise as frequently as in hospitals. She said, "Believe me, you're strong, you can do it, and it's wonderful." So, I thought, *Hmmm. . . .*

I'd been going to a regular OB/GYN group. When I returned from the wedding, I began to see them in a different light. I asked questions and didn't like the answers. I looked in the Yellow Pages for a midwife and had a two-hour consultation. I felt very good about it. My average OB/GYN appointment lasted ten minutes.

Mike and I went to the library and got every book on midwifery and home birth we could. Then, we went to Canada to photograph there. I read in our little cabin for a full month. Boy, was it an eye-opener! But my family was really concerned about my changing to a midwife, so for a while longer we stayed with the OB.

Sometime before Christmas, we bought a house in Three Forks, Montana—a tiny town of less than a thousand people. I was really stressed out about mortgage payments, and we had to have renters in the rooms above us. I wasn't used to it; I'd been so loose and fancy-free, and the renters had kitchen privileges and were in our space.

I wasn't eating or drinking very well. Then, the day before Christmas Eve, I went snowmobiling, and went into premature labor the next day—Christmas Eve. I had been visiting relatives in Jackson Hole, Wyoming, and it was my brother-in-law's idea to go snowmobiling. I was seven months pregnant and had to be life-flighted out. They sent a small airplane because I'm afraid of helicopters—I saw my father crash in one when I was twelve.

I remember the flight: It was a beautiful night with a full moon, and I looked out at the Tetons, which were all lit up. The plane was very cramped and Mike had to sit in the tail of the plane. They landed at the airport in Salt Lake City and had to take me by ambulance to a hospital. Mike and I prayed the whole time.

I stayed in the hospital for seven days and called a midwife, who suggested I drink five glasses of milk a day—for the magnesium—and lots of this special tea to quiet my uterus down. I concentrated on being relaxed and not stressing out. After a week, I seemed fine and was told I could leave.

I had to have modified bed rest, so over the next three months I stayed in my in-laws' wonderful little cabin in Story, Wyoming. There was a TV, a VCR, washing machine, dryer, garbage disposal, refrigerator, dishwasher—to me it was a palace! For a while, I could only walk from the couch to the bathroom. I'd just kind of shuffle around, paranoid that I'd go into labor again. The time in the cabin gave Mike and me a chance to research more about home birth, and we decided that we wanted to have one.

I found a midwife in Billings, Montana. I thought about giving birth in the cabin, but she didn't want to; Billings is three hours away, and she wasn't comfortable leaving her other pregnant women who were due about the same time as me.

Kathleen was a lay midwife—only thirty-three years old and really beautiful. She looked like a wrangler or a barrel racer—very western, with this cute figure and hair down to her waist. Maybe I'm silly, but I thought, *Don't look prettier than me when I give birth!* She doesn't wear any makeup to your birth and puts on these big glasses and an apron, like she's going to cook a roast—pretty cute! She suggested that I give birth at her house or at a motel. I didn't want to go to her house because she's got four kids—I wanted privacy.

We drove around Billings to find a motel. We didn't want a Motel 8 or anything like that—it just sounds kind of tacky, *Oh, my baby was born in a Motel 8!* We wanted something nice for the birth certificate like The Dude Rancher or The Silver Spur. We finally settled on The Ponderosa Best Western, and joked about calling the baby Little Joe.

It was the honeymoon suite, with a separate living room and bedroom.

It had cherry wood furniture and was on ground level, so we could park the car outside and unload discreetly. Also, it seemed really soundproof and was only about ten minutes to the hospital, just in case.

The week before I was due, I began to make motel reservations—I'd call ahead and book a room for the following night. Then, I'd cancel before 4:00 so I wouldn't be charged on my credit card and make another reservation for the following night. We kept this up for a week. The management never got suspicious.

Then, on March 31, Mike went into town to have breakfast with a friend who said, "Mike, you need to go to Billings, just check into that motel, and stay there. Do it today!" So, Mike came back and said, "Let's go—even if we have to stay a week." We packed up and drove to Billings.

In town, I went to see the midwife 'cause it was time for a prenatal checkup. She has a room in her house and wanted to check my dilation; midwives usually don't like to give pelvic exams, but she felt that if my cervix wasn't soft and I wasn't dilated, I'd probably be better off going home rather than hanging out at the motel for a couple of weeks.

I was three and a half centimeters dilated, and she said, "Good thing you came!" I didn't feel anything. I must have been dilating slowly over the last week.

Mike and I took a walk downtown, and I started to feel contractions. We checked into the room and went out to dinner, but nothing sounded good because I felt nauseous. By 7:00, we went to our room. My contractions were really coming—like five minutes apart and real regular. We hurried and unpacked the truck, which was just loaded with stuff. I had all these cute little gowns for myself and an outfit for my husband to wear during labor. I bought him these off-white sweats and some cool clothes for him in case he got too warm. During the birth I wanted him to change into shorts, but for labor, I had these new sweats—and some new socks—everything had to be new and clean. I even had Mike get a haircut about a week before, so he'd look good for the video.

I had two camcorders with tripods, about three cameras, New Age tapes to listen to—all this stuff I planned when I was on bed rest. We even had printed directions on how to use the equipment taped to the cameras.

Everything was positioned toward the bed, and Mike remarked that if the maid came in it would look like we were shooting a porno movie. That night, I just labored and ate. I had brought my toaster oven and vegetable steamer. I also had little ice juice chips—papaya and orange. I laid out fruit and was up till about midnight getting all this stuff ready.

The midwife had given me red raspberry tea and herbs—they're supposed to take the edge off the contractions. We relaxed; I drank tea while Mike timed my contractions. At some point, I fell asleep.

In the middle of the night I woke up; my contractions were getting stronger and stronger, closer and closer. I'd been keeping a journal, and about 3:00 in the morning I wrote, *This might be it*—it was my last recorded thought while being pregnant.

I just kind of lay in bed. I had too much on my mind to sleep. Mike was snoring logs and didn't wake up until around 8:00 or 9:00 the next morning. I wasn't in a hurry for the baby to be born. We kind of hung out and ate breakfast. I remember thinking, *Gee, these contractions are getting stronger and stronger, I'd better go curl my hair.* But my hair wouldn't curl that day; it's weird—maybe it was the hormones. Meanwhile, the contractions were so strong that I had to stop a couple of times and relax. Then I thought, *I haven't shaved my legs!* So I got into the tub and tried to shave my legs but couldn't reach over my belly to get my bikini line. *Oh, bummer,* I thought; I wanted a nice bikini line for the video. Next, I decided to put on makeup. I had bought this Maybelline waterproof mascara—I thought if I cried or sweated it wouldn't run. And it didn't—that mascara was great!

Kathleen had told me to drink and eat, because labor would be one of the hardest things I'd ever have to deal with. So, after the makeup I began to eat and drink, but quickly realized that I was tired and needed some sleep.

The contractions weren't what I would call painful, but I couldn't sleep. At some point during the morning, Kathleen came over, and my water broke. I was going to the bathroom when I heard a *plop, plop,* which didn't sound like pee. But, I was in denial a bit and still thinking, *No, no, I can't be having a baby.*

Kathleen checked the fluid with litmus paper. She told me if it turned blue, it was amniotic fluid. The strip turned bright blue, and I thought, *Oh my gosh! I can't be in denial now!* She told me to try to sleep and that she'd be back around noon. This time, I was able to doze off.

When Kathleen came back early afternoon, she listened to the baby's heartbeat. It was doing great. Midwives don't like to do pelvics because some women fret over how far along they are. This way you can just go with the flow instead of thinking you've got to perform.

Kathleen just hung out in the living-room part of the
assistant, Karen, with her by then. I was in my own world—the
were pretty strong, and I wasn't focused in on what anybody else w.
It was like tunnel vision; I was only into myself and my body. I remem.
that I wanted to be in a dark corner, like a cat having her kittens. I crawled
between the bed and wall. We had the lights off, and it was pretty dark down
there. My husband stayed back, and I just kind of laid there, curled up in a
fetal position—off like a wounded animal. I asked for the heating pad and
held it next to my stomach, and I remember that I just wanted to feel pure
and warm.

Then, I got this sudden burst of energy, and I got up and started cleaning the room. My husband had made a mess while I was off by myself for a
couple of hours. There were banana peels and stuff everywhere. I was busy
straightening up when Kathleen looked at me and said, "I think you're in
transition."

I was surprised 'cause everyone told me that was the hardest part, dilating from seven to ten centimeters. I told her that it didn't feel like transition,
but she said that the herbs I'd been doing had probably helped. So, I thought,
Wow! and started laughing. It's on the video—the whole scene. Kathleen
said, "You're supposed to be crabby. Women in transition are crabby." And I
was laughing! In fact, my whole labor was filled with me saying, "I love you,"
to my husband; I never got out of sorts.

At around 5:00 in the evening, Kathleen suggested I get into the bathtub.
She said, "Without fail, if I put a woman in a tub of water, she'll come out
dilated to ten." I got in; it felt wonderful. I had a cushion for my back and
probably stayed there for an hour. When I came out, Kathleen checked me;
I was at ten.

Much of this time was like a dream. Somebody got me out of the tub.
Kathleen had stripped the motel room bedding off so we wouldn't get their
stuff dirty. She put a pink shower curtain on the floor by the bed and had a
birthing stool—a plastic step-stool like you get at Wal-Mart—with flowered
pillows nearby.

All of a sudden my back hurt, and I got on all fours and started rocking,
rocking. During my labor, I had on four different gowns for different parts of
labor. Now, I was wearing this cute little lacy one that came down to my
knees, but Mike knew I wanted to wear this antique camisole that I had
bought in an antique store for the actual birth, so somebody helped me

change into it. It was white, and I remember thinking, *I wonder if some woman in the 1800s wore this to give birth.*

I had my hair in a ponytail tied with white ribbon. I had lace and ribbon everywhere. I sat on the birthing stool off to the side. Then I got this sudden energy again, and I was out of my dream world—I came to. The contractions were like eight minutes apart, and in between them, I felt great.

I started giving orders to everybody. I told Karen, who was like a little mouse, "Okay, this camera's for this, and that camera's for that. . . . I want you to take a picture when the head comes out." I told Mike to change to a fresh roll of film so we wouldn't run out.

Somewhere in there my in-laws arrived. We had made reservations for them to stay next door in an adjoining room. My water broke again—this time with a pop and lots of blood. I was lying down, and Kathleen had my leg over her shoulder. And this was when my mother-in-law came in to say hi. I was embarrassed she saw all that gross stuff, but she left because she knew I wanted to be alone with Mike.

I sat up Indian-style. I was at ten, but with no pushing urge. So we all just waited an hour or so, kind of joking around, talking, and I felt really good. When a contraction would come, I'd rock.

At one point I said to Kathleen, "Doop-da-doo, when's that pushing urge going to come?" She suggested that I put my arms around Mike's neck, stand up, and give a little push to see how it felt.

I stood up and tried but felt totally uncoordinated. I couldn't feel the baby; it felt like I was four months pregnant. I told Kathleen, "This baby's not ready to come. I can't feel his head down there, and I can't push!" Then she said simply, "I can do all things through Christ who strengthens me." It gave me courage to hear that. Kathleen had me try to push from the stool. I tried, but part of me felt like I was going to hurt the baby, crush his head. I don't know why. I wanted him to stay in my stomach, safe—and for me to be pregnant forever. I wouldn't push. I was afraid.

An hour and a half passed. Then Kathleen said that she'd put her fingers up me and that I could push toward her fingers. It felt really good. I told her to leave her fingers there, and I pushed like that for two and a half hours. She must have been really sore! My husband said she used up two tubes of K-Y jelly.

I was getting tired. Kathleen asked, "Would you like to try some oxygen?" She had a tank with her. So I tried it, and it gave me a lot of energy. I had it on for an hour. I just kept pushing, and finally Mike said, "Push, Sandy!

The baby wants to see the wide open spaces of Montana." That gave me encouragement.

They all were saying nice things, and nobody hurried me. I lost track of time. I thought I'd only been pushing for thirty minutes or so. Later, they said, "No, Sandy, you pushed for two and a half hours!"

I was standing, and Mike was holding me up under my armpits. He noticed my feet were turning blue, but I felt fine so Kathleen told me to keep going. I pushed and his head crowned. Then his face slid down, and Kathleen said to him, "Oh, you're looking at me—I'm the first person you see, poor thing!" My eyes were closed for this last part. They had a big mirror, but I didn't want to see myself opening up like that. Kathleen had me feel the baby's head, but I didn't like it—it was freaking me out to have a head come out of my body. I just concentrated on pushing.

I remember Kathleen saying, "Are you ready to hold your baby? Get ready. He's going to be born!" I had my eyes closed and was so numb down there that I couldn't feel anything. He slipped out, and when I opened my eyes the baby was on my lap. In the split second after the birth, Mike had helped me to sit back on the stool—and there he was, so slippery that I was afraid I'd drop him!

He was incredibly clean, with little blood or that white cheesy stuff. I held him by his bottom—the only part I could hang on to. Kathleen put a warm blanket over us, and we just hung around for fifteen minutes until the placenta was out. Then they cut the cord.

I asked Kathleen if it was a boy or a girl—it didn't occur to me to look. She said, "Find out yourself!" So I looked and was surprised to find it was a boy. My husband and I wanted a girl, but the minute we looked, it was like, *Oh yeah, this is what we want—a boy!*

His eyes and nose were clear. He was eight pounds, three ounces, and twenty-one inches long with a fifteen-inch head—the size for an eleven-pound baby, Kathleen said. And lying there looking at him, I thought, *He's so pink and perfect; he'll never be this perfect again.* In fact, everything was perfect, and I imagined that I was Queen Victoria—I felt like the queen of the whole world, the most important person on the planet.

⬦

Originally from Florida, Karen met her husband, Tim, while attending a boarding school near her present home in western North Carolina. She is the mother of three children: Brian, age nine; Katie, age five; and Shelley, age two and a half. It was about Shelley's unusual birth, which took place in a car en route to the hospital, that Karen chose to speak.

Car Birth

I got pregnant with Shelley when Katie was about two. We had discussed having my tubes tied, and Tim was considering a vasectomy. I think I got pregnant while using a sponge. I guess we must have been careless. It was a real shock! Tim was dumbfounded—we worried how in the world we were going to manage with three kids.

There was a local group of midwives that had just started practicing. Some of their patients were migrant workers, and they had Spanish-speaking personnel in the office. It was kind of nice. We decided to use these midwives and associate with a hospital that was closer than the one in Asheville that we'd used for my other two kids. With Katie, I went from three centimeters to complete delivery in an hour and a half, so I was advised to find a closer facility in case this next one came quick. It wasn't the most progressive hospital, but they read over my birth plan and signed off with the promise to do their best to honor my wishes. They had a tub I could labor in—I had done that with Brian and liked it very much. So that was very positive, and I thought it would all work out.

Also, we hired a lay midwife, Nancy, who had gone with us when Katie was born. And we decided not to take childbirth classes, figuring we'd done it twice before and didn't need a refresher.

My mother came up from Florida during the first week of October. The baby was due October 5. She had been there when Brian was born but had missed Katie's birth because she was working at the time. She was really excited to be coming for the birth. I'm an only child, and I think that binds us pretty tight.

I went into labor on a Saturday night. My husband works third shift and had the weekend off. I had been having contractions off and on all day—nothing to write home about, but Nancy came over in the evening just to check. It was eightish. The kids were settling into bed. We decided that I wasn't really in labor and prepared to have a normal night. The midwife left, and everyone went to sleep. But later, sometime before midnight, I went downstairs to the kitchen to call her again. I was still having these irregular contractions, and I thought I should tell her before it got real late. She said, "Well, I'd better come over and check you to put your mind at ease."

I took a shower and woke Tim. We let my mom and the kids sleep. I was still having contractions, but they weren't regular and weren't particularly intense. Nancy arrived at about 12:30. I lay down on my bed, and she told me that I was doing something because I was somewhat effaced and about four centimeters. Then, right as she pulled her hand out, I had the most God-awful contraction. I mean WHAM! She told me to lie still and went out into the living room and told Tim, "We're going to the hospital." She knew how quickly I'd had Katie and didn't want to take any chances.

I was wearing my housecoat. She told me to put my shoes on "NOW," and that we had to leave. I wasn't in such a hurry. It's strange. I knew that I was definitely in labor, but I didn't rush. In fact, just as I began to look for my shoes, I said in a kind of offhand way, "We're not going to make it." And she's like, "Get your shoes on now! We're leaving!" I didn't have my hospital bag packed and wasn't dressed, so I said, "But I have to put my clothes on." All Nancy said was, "Karen, get into the car!"

I had been folding laundry before I went to bed. Nancy quickly grabbed a handful of towels off my couch and put them on the front seat of her car. Tim got my mom and the kids up, and I got into the midwife's car. Tim was going to follow in one car, and my mom and the kids in a separate car.

Also, I had a girlfriend who was supposed to videotape the birth. But they wouldn't let me call her. I was really pissed off because when Brian was born, my camera was left in the car. And when Katie was born, the camera malfunctioned and we were left with an almost black photo of a crotch shot.

Anyway, I wasn't very happy at this point. In fact, I was coming up with all kinds of excuses just to avoid getting in the car. Unconsciously, I was resisting.

Later, Nancy told me that she also considered not getting into the car and having the baby at home. But my mom is extremely resistant to the idea of home birth. I was a preemie, and she had heard all kinds of horror stories. Anyway, once my mom was awake, Nancy figured we needed to get to the hospital. She quickly called the other midwives and told them to get prepared—again, because of my history with Katie.

The drive to the hospital is twenty minutes. Nancy was driving like a bat out of hell. The contractions were still not very regular. And with Katie, by the time we were going to the hospital, they were very regular. So I didn't know what to think. Nancy gave me the option of going to a closer hospital, but I didn't want that because I'd end up with whoever was on duty and everything would be out of my control.

We were on Route 25 north. We passed the office where Nancy works. She thought about stopping there, but her office is at the top of a flight of stairs and there was no way she could get me up there. I'm a pretty big woman, and Nancy is tiny. Things were just rushing through her mind, and she decided to keep going. A little farther down the road, we picked up a cop. I mean, we were going very, very fast. Nancy just laid on the horn, flashed her flashers and just kept moving—through red lights and all!

So, now we have this cop chasing us with his blue light. Nancy's like, "I'm not stopping! He can just follow us and find out what's going on. . . ."

I remember thinking, *Okay, I'm cool with this. Let's go!* We kept driving, and my water breaks. Now, I'm having to pant and I feel like pushing. I yell out, "The baby is coming NOW!" Nancy whips to the left side of the road— not the side we're on because there's some really yucky houses and railroad tracks on that side. She ends up in the parking lot of this little, one-horse used-car dealership. And you ain't never felt anything till you have a baby crowning and somebody puts on the brakes!

The cop pulls over right beside us. Nancy jumps out and runs over to my side of the car. The glove box is broken in her little Subaru wagon, and like I said, I'm not small. She tells the cop, "I've got a lady here who's fixing to give birth." And the cop is like, "Yeah, right." Then he takes a look at me and realizes we're serious.

Well, Nancy gets out her birthing kit and dumps it on the dash. We're not talking sterile conditions here! I have to lift myself out of the seat, hold on to the roof of the car. I was wearing a sanitary napkin and panties. I remember Nancy asking, "Is it okay if I cut your panties?" I'm like, "Cut away!" And out comes Shelley's head. The cop meanwhile is trying to hold my hand. I remember shoving his hand away and screaming, "Get off me!" I don't know what his family situation is, but I was trying to concentrate and didn't want some stranger touching me. In retrospect, I feel kind of bad—he was only trying to help.

And so the baby was born. Nancy left the cord attached and handed

Shelley to me all wrapped up in one of the towels she'd grabbed from my couch. We opened my nightgown and laid the baby skin-on-skin with the towel wrapped around us.

Then Tim arrives. He comes up to the driver's side, and I pull the towel back and show him the baby's head. I remember feeling around and saying, "I think it's a girl!" But I didn't look. It was cool out, and I wanted to keep her covered up.

After Tim came, an ambulance pulled up. They cut the cord somewhere along in here because they needed to take the baby from me in order to help me out of the car. I still hadn't delivered the placenta. While they were trying to decide what exactly to do with me, my mother pulled up across the street and just waited there. She didn't want to get the kids out—I guess she was afraid that they'd see too much.

By this time, there's three or four police cars along with the ambulance—everyone wants to see what's going on. They help me from the car, get me into a wheelchair, and onto a stretcher. They want to take me to the hospital right away. They don't even want to check me. But Nancy wants me to deliver the placenta and is really concerned. She keeps insisting, and they finally hand her a bowl—but they aren't happy. Then, my uterus won't go down. Nancy has to keep her hands on me, and the ambulance driver doesn't want to move until we're all strapped in. But Nancy doesn't feel safe taking her hands off me. She told them, "I can't let go of her uterus—she'll bleed!" And once again, they let her have her way.

Nancy stayed with me. Tim drove her car because he wanted to clean it up. Actually, it wasn't really all that messy—between the towels and the sanitary pad.

Everything worked out fine. The story of Shelley's birth made the newspaper the next day. And during Christmas, just a couple of months later, people were still talking about her birth. I remember my husband's Christmas party at work. I came in carrying the baby, and everyone kept saying, "Oh, there's the baby that was born in the car!"

Sherrie was working for the military and living in Virginia with her husband and daughter, Tiffany, at the time that Ricky, her second child, was born en route to the hospital. Since then, Sherrie has divorced, changed occupations (she now works as a kindergarten teacher at a private school), and lives alone with her two children, Tiffany, age eight, and Ricky, age five.

Tunnel Birth

My husband and I lived very busy, hectic lives. Richard was in the navy, and I was an officer in the army. Right before I found out that I was pregnant with Ricky, I had been promoted to a very stressful job that many men want and very few women get. I was in charge of scheduling all the operations for an entire battalion, and my job required a lot of traveling and a lot of responsibility. At that time, I really enjoyed being in the military and considered making it a career. After Tiffany, we didn't plan on having any other children. But then I found out I was pregnant with Ricky.

We had a great baby-sitter for Tiffany, and I was able to juggle both my job and parenthood. But after I got pregnant with Ricky, I no longer wanted to make the military a career. I planned to get out as soon as I finished my current tour in Virginia. It's hard to find people to watch your children when both Mom and Dad are in the military—you never know when you're going to have to deploy or how long you're going to be gone.

Usually, when I had to be gone for long, my mother would come up from Fayetteville and stay with Tiffany. But around this time, my brother became terminally ill and my mother needed to be there for him. I no longer had a person available, a member of the family, to come and assist me. Again, I did have a wonderful baby-sitter, Tiffany's godmother, to help, but it wasn't the same.

My brother, who was dying, also lived in Virginia Beach. In fact, my husband and he used to play raquetball all the time. He developed a rare form of cancer that causes cholesterol to build up in your bloodstream. It blocks the arteries. First his hands went numb, and then the arteries behind his eyes became blocked, and he went blind. Six months later, he died. It was very hard on our family.

During the time I was pregnant and my brother was dying, my husband, Richard, was very supportive. My mother came and stayed with my brother who was being treated at Walter Reed Medical Center. He died a month before Ricky was born. In a way, I felt that Ricky was a blessing.

Towards the end of my brother's illness, I had trouble visiting him—he had been such a vibrant man. The combination of his illness and the medicine made him hallucinate, and I couldn't deal with that very well. My husband would go and visit him while I'd stay at home with Tiffany and other kids from the family. I always say that God knows who to pick because I couldn't have gone through what my brother went through.

When I was about six months pregnant, I changed jobs within the military. I interviewed and was able to get a position that was easier to manage. It was really a higher level job, but my boss there was more understanding and didn't demand me to be away as much. With that other job, I'd always have a suitcase packed, and early in my pregnancy with Ricky I traveled to Honduras, Hawaii, San Francisco, Missouri. I was constantly going. I wasn't happy with this, and neither was my spouse. Luckily, I didn't really start showing until almost six months, so I did all this traveling and held my job without having to tell anyone. They really do frown on pregnant women who have positions of authority, so it was best not to say anything until I made the decision to get out. When I had been pregnant with Tiffany, I was stationed in Korea until I was eight months. Then I came back to the States to have her. Three weeks later, I was back in Korea. It was hard because Richard wanted me to breast-feed, and I didn't have time to bond with my baby—really, it was miserable.

We had taken Lamaze classes to prepare for Tiffany's birth. And I wanted an epidural. But Tiffany came too fast—in four hours. My doctor, who delivered both my children, said, after Ricky was born, that I was a spontaneous birther.

Both my pregnancies were good experiences, but before Tiffany, I used to say I never wanted any children. I liked what I was doing in the military and was older than many women who were having kids. But my husband really wanted to try, and when I found out that I was going to Korea, I felt like I wanted something to tie me to him. I decided that I wanted to have a child.

I used to drive a sports car, and my husband and I were on the go all the time. We were never home—we were very free spirited. When I had kids, all that changed. I've always been good with children, and when Tiffany was born, she quickly became the most important thing in my life.

I'm glad that I didn't have children when I was younger. I wouldn't have been able to give up that kind of life. When I had my children, my life changed, but I didn't feel like I was missing anything. And I do think that I'm a good parent. Better than a lot of parents I see. I enjoy the life that I live. But if you're not ready for parenthood, you can easily become a very miserable person. I don't think that a lot of women know what's ahead. And I certainly didn't. But fortunately, I had a foundation that helped me to understand the joy of birth and becoming a parent. When you speak to some women about birth, you hear all these horror stories, and I can't relate. Both of my pregnancies and births were easy for me, and I don't have anything negative to say.

Richard and I went through a childbirth refresher course. And, then, at the same time, he got a new job in Washington, D.C. Our marriage was already beginning to become troubled. I think it had to do with both of us. Right before he got this job we were living together—really for the first time—though we'd been married for eight years. But we were always separated, going different places. Then, when we lived in the same house, I found out how different we were. And there were some trust problems involved.

If I hadn't had Ricky, I might have divorced even sooner than I did. When I found out that I was pregnant, things were already not great. But I said to myself, "Well, I'll try a little longer." Really though, I knew it was over.

I think that there were other women. Not that I ever really saw; I never had any concrete evidence. But I would get phone calls and people would hang up. There were other tell-tale signs. Money would disappear, for instance. When I'd confront him, he would always deny it, but I couldn't believe him, and if I couldn't trust him, then I couldn't give myself completely to him. You know, everybody, all our friends, thought that we had the perfect relationship, and they'd come to us with their problems. When we split up, they couldn't believe it. We lived together until very near Ricky's birth. Then Richard moved to his job in Washington, and we were physically separated. He was planning to be there for the birth, but it went so quickly that he arrived at the hospital right after I had Ricky.

I went into labor on a Saturday morning—at about 5:00 A.M. The night before, I could feel some contractions, but nothing too strong, and my water hadn't broken. My mom was staying with me. I couldn't really sleep well, and when I got up at 5:00, I woke my mother and told her, "It's time."

I had been to the doctor's the day before for an ultrasound, and I just felt that I'd have the baby over the weekend, though they scheduled another ultrasound for Monday. After that last appointment, we had gotten the stroller that I had on layaway and prepared my bags. That night I called

Richard and told him that I thought I'd deliver over the weekend and to come back home. The drive from D.C. is about three or four hours.

My mom drove her car and Tiffany sat up front; I got into the back seat. The contractions were coming pretty strong. We lived only a few miles from the hospital, and driving through one of the tunnels that connects Virginia Beach to the mainland, I must have screamed. I don't remember screaming— Tiffany told me that later.

I do remember yelling, "Hurry up! I'm going to have the baby." But my water broke, and Ricky came at the same time. I was in the back seat, up on one knee with the other leg stretched out. I had pulled my pants down because I could feel Ricky coming. My mom always keeps these white towels in her car, and she told Tiffany to reach under the front seat and hand one to me. She couldn't stop driving; we were *in the tunnel*.

His head must have come out when I screamed because I remember trying not to push. I could see that his umbilical cord was wrapped around his neck, so I slipped my finger around the cord to free him, and then placed him on the clean towel. I was scared.

When we got out of the tunnel, there was a service station right there. We pulled over and called the ambulance. They came right away. I just stayed there, up on one knee 'cause I was too scared to move! Tiffany helped me a lot 'cause she didn't scream or cry. She remained real calm. Now, when she sees women on TV giving birth, screaming and hollering, she says, "Mommy, you didn't do all that." When the ambulance came, they didn't cut the umbilical cord. They put Ricky on top of my stomach and took us to the hospital that way. The doctor was waiting for us when we got there.

I didn't tear or anything. Ricky was seven pounds, four ounces. My contractions had gone from being eight minutes apart to *here he comes*. When I left the house, the contractions were eight minutes apart and not real severe. I had Ricky in the next fifteen minutes. Only during the last ten minutes did I have any pain. Looking back, I don't think I could have done anything differently. I feel really blessed and glad that nothing happened to him, and he was born healthy. I couldn't have gone to the hospital any earlier because the contractions really weren't coming, and they didn't hurt me. I'm not a great one to tolerate pain. I really didn't have any pain until the last few minutes.

I remember that it hurt to deliver the afterbirth—in fact, it hurt more than delivering the baby. After they cleaned Ricky up, they put me in a recovery room. Richard arrived around thirty minutes later.

It was a sunny, June morning. Because it was Saturday, the traffic hadn't been too bad. Ricky's tunnel birth made the news, and my grandmother in New York saw it on TV. For the longest time, everyone called Ricky "the tunnel baby." He got a lot of extra special gifts 'cause of the unusual place I had him. To me, it wasn't anything extraordinary though because it wasn't difficult; it had happened so fast. My mom thought the whole thing was amazing—she had had a hard time delivering her babies. I'm just really glad she had that white towel there!

I stayed in the hospital for two days. Then I came home, knowing that we'd be moving to D.C. to join Richard in just two weeks. I still had that feeling that my marriage was over, but I said to myself, "Well, I'm going to try."

We remained together for a couple of years. He was a real good dad to the kids and spent a lot of time doing stuff with them. I stayed at home, but just being a wife, I wasn't happy. I didn't nurse. I hadn't had a lot of success nursing Tiffany, and really it's never appealed to me. Having a baby hanging off your breast seems kind of gross, although I know that there's nothing wrong with it. It just isn't right for me.

When Ricky was seven months, I told Richard that I was burned out and wanted to visit my mother. But in my mind, I knew I wasn't going back to him. We stayed at my mother's for three weeks. Then I did go back—the kids missed him, and I guess I wasn't really ready.

I left for good when Ricky was two-and-a-half. I just told Richard, "I'm leaving. I want a divorce." It was a very difficult time for us all. Richard would make things happen that would require us to be back and forth—from D.C. to my mother's. And he wasn't real reliable about money. We argued a lot. Finally, I saw a lawyer who told me that if I didn't accept money from him, Richard would have no rights. So I stopped taking money and put in for unemployment benefits. My self-esteem was real low. I hadn't lived with my mother since I was eighteen. When I got married, I never thought it would end in divorce.

I put Tiffany in a private school and began volunteering there. Soon they offered me a job teaching kindergarten. I had a degree in education and social work but needed to be recertified. So I took the refresher course and began working there; I've been there ever since. I make enough to be able to support us. I'd certainly like to have more money than we do, but I'm not ready. We manage, and I love what I do.

Five

WOMEN
ON THEIR OWN

&

FOR SOME WOMEN, the choice to become a mother is not connected to marriage or even to a long-term relationship with the baby's biological father. In today's society, we are experiencing a shifting away from old paradigms of motherhood. The stories that follow illustrate some of these shifts: a paraplegic woman who chooses to become a mother outside of a long-term relationship or marriage; two lesbian mothers who opt to form a family on their own terms; a woman who, married during conception and through birth, finds herself nonetheless alone; and a young single woman who makes the difficult decision to give up her baby for adoption.

&

I spoke with Frances at a friend's house in Chapel Hill, North Carolina. Frances owns a small silk-screening business and devotes as much time as possible to Emma, her three-year-old daughter, who played quietly and watched public TV during our interview.

With a Little Help from My Friends

When I first got pregnant, it was a big surprise. Emma's father, Wayne, and I weren't married or living together. And then, when I was about five months pregnant, he pulled away and pretty much abandoned me. I knew he would be hesitant about having another child. He has three other children and had been married before. Although he said that he wanted another family, it just was not good timing for him. I often tried to get him to talk about his feelings, but he never would.

He ended the relationship around Christmas time. I had gone to Portland, Oregon, to visit my family. After this trip, Wayne met me at the airport to take me home, and during the trip back he told me that his father was in town and that he'd have to just drop me off. He promised to be in touch with me soon. But right after he left, I found a letter in my purse telling me that he didn't have the love or passion for me that was necessary to make me a happy woman and that it was best for everybody if he was not involved with me anymore. I was stunned. He had never said anything like this to me. In fact, he was always saying just the opposite.

Well, when I got this letter, I jumped into my car and drove to a phone booth. "Be a man about this," I told him. "Don't write me a letter . . . come talk to me right now!" We met. And we talked. I found out that he was seeing another woman. When I heard, I told him, "I'm holding my hands behind my back so I won't slap you across your face!" He said, "I'd deserve it." So I reached over and slapped his face. It was so vivid. I get chills thinking about it—because this kind of behavior so disrupts me.

This was the most devastating thing that had ever happened to me. It was at this point that I decided to move to Oregon. I wasn't going to tell Wayne that I intended to move; instead, I hired a lawyer to draw up a support agreement.

I went to see my doctors because I wasn't sleeping or eating properly, and I felt like I had to take care of my baby. He told me to take Benadryl, but it didn't help. They lined me up with a counselor—a psychologist—and I went to speak with her. She was great. In fact, Wayne met us there one day so that we could all talk together. I needed to try to understand his motivations. I needed some kind of resolution. And frankly, I was surprised that he actually showed. But he never would sign a support agreement. I kind of knew he wouldn't. He doesn't have a whole lot of money. I revised this agreement three times, asking less and less. But he never signed.

And then I had a major bleed. I was living alone in a rural cabin at the time, and I had to drive myself to UNC [University of North Carolina] Hospital. They said that I was in premature labor. I was only six months along. I called Wayne from the hospital, and he told me not to worry and that everything was going to be okay and that he'd see me soon. But he never showed. I had to stay in the hospital about four or five days. Medicaid covered the bill. I didn't have insurance, but the hospital had counselors come up and help me with the forms.

I have many wonderful friends here in Chapel Hill, and they all came to visit me. People kept calling me, bringing me things . . . little teddy bears, flowers . . . it was incredible. I received a lot of support, and that made me feel that everything was going to be okay.

When I was released from the hospital, they told me that I would need to be on bed rest for the remainder of my pregnancy. So I couldn't stay by myself in the cabin. A close friend of mine, Buck, who's separated from his wife and has joint custody of his two kids, had just built a house and had an extra room. He said, "Why don't you come and live with us. We'll take care of you." It was great. I moved into his house. I still had much to take care of though, so I wasn't too strict about my bed rest. I couldn't be.

It was a special time. I spent about three weeks in his house. By this point, the doctors told me that they wouldn't let me travel, so my whole plan to move to Oregon got killed.

Then one night, I remember, it was the night of the Super Bowl, and Buck's kids and I were making pizza. Michael Jackson was the big halftime entertainer. It was a lot of fun. But afterwards, when I went to sleep, I had a dream that I was in Wayne's house, talking to his children about why Wayne is so angry. And when I woke up, the bed was covered in blood. I yelled for Buck, and he called a neighbor, another close friend, Lourice, and she took me to the hospital. Buck's kids were spending the night, so he couldn't leave them alone.

It was three or four in the morning, and I was scared. When I got to the hospital, they said it was premature labor again and that I would have to stay in the hospital until the baby was born. This was late January, and the baby wasn't due until late March. My doctors had to relinquish their care to the staff at UNC because I was a high-risk pregnancy. So I had these doctors who I had never seen before coming to visit me. All the time I'd hear, "You know, you're a high-risk pregnancy and we need to do an amniocentesis" . . . and they'd go on and on . . . wanting to do these invasive measures. And I just said no. I spoke with my doctors, and they respected me and said, "You do what you think is best for you. Call if you need us."

I felt safe in the hospital. The bleeding had stopped; I was in bed, being fed, and I felt strong. I used the time constructively. They have an art therapy program there, and I was brought papers, pens, and markers. It was around Valentine's Day, and I did all these handmade valentines. I also read and did other things in bed. I had a south-facing private room, and it looked like a garden in there—I had so many flowers. And cable TV. I watched the Carolina basketball game playoffs. It was terrific; I felt so loved and taken care of again. I was lucky. My family called me. My sister-in-law, who I respect and admire, called and gave me strength and hope. And I would go down to the chapel and get people to take my wheelchair outside.

My parents were very supportive of me during all this. Of course, they would have preferred me to have been married and all, but they let me do whatever I felt was right.

I grew up Catholic, and my father is very devout. He goes to church every day. My mother, on the other hand, is not Catholic, and she only goes with him on special holidays. I don't consider myself Catholic, but I consider myself spiritual. I gained much hope, faith, and strength with prayer— whether I prayed in bed at night or in chapel. I was looking for some answers, some peace and forgiveness . . . for Wayne. Although I felt surrounded by love and support, this was a very stressful time. I didn't know if there was anything wrong with the baby, and I didn't want to undertake the risks of any tests.

Before I became pregnant, I was involved with a women's cooperative called Womancraft. It's an organization that allows women to sell their arts and crafts retail in a store downtown. Members are required to work a certain number of hours a week, and each member is assigned a work partner. My work partner was Bev, and we became close friends. She had experience teaching the Bradley Method and agreed to be part of the birth. Along with Bev, I have another friend, Odie, an old boyfriend, ex-boss, whom I also wanted to be present at the birth—I wanted to have a male presence there.

Okay, we're in February. I've made all these arrangements to take care of myself for the upcoming birth. Bev and Odie were coming to see me a lot. Bev would bring Bradley Method books, teach me about relaxation, breathing, and talk about birth. I'm still planning on doing it naturally . . . no medications. That was my goal as far as the physical part of it. I wanted to be completely drug-free and free of any invasive measures. They were still saying that I would be able to use the birthing room.

Then, on a Friday night, my friend Bob came to visit. We were sitting there, and I remember not feeling too good. My stomach was bothering me, and I couldn't tell if I was having contractions. I was tired, and Bob held my hand, stroked me, and just let me lie on my side quietly. That night I had another bleed when I went to the bathroom. The next day, Saturday, they decided to take me off antilabor drugs. They gave me a shot of steroids to enhance the baby's lungs because they were afraid that they weren't sufficiently developed. I was hooked up to an external monitor and told, "This might be it."

I called Odie, but he was out of town. I left a message: "Please call me!" I called Bev, and she was sick with some kind of flu. I told her not to worry—nothing was really happening yet and I'd call again later.

Oh, and I had had dreams that it was going to be a girl. The first was a beautiful dream where I was swimming in a luscious blue lake. I swam up to the shore and lay on my back, and there, half in and half out of the water, I gave birth to a baby girl—all by myself. I remember looking down at her, and she looked up at me. She had beautiful dark skin, dark hair, wonderful blue eyes, and perfect little lips. It was a very peaceful dream—with the rhythm of swimming and then the cool water and sunshine on me. In the other dream, I was in a car and there was my baby daughter in a car seat next to me. I remember stroking her and kissing her. I was convinced that I was going to have a girl.

I don't remember much more of Saturday. Sunday morning, Bev showed up and they moved me to the birthing room. I had to put on this little hospital gown. They said that I was in active labor, but I had been having so much tightness in that area that I couldn't tell. I wasn't prepared. When I got into the birthing room, I had to go to the bathroom. I was hooked up to these monitors and had to roll everything along with me. When I came out of the bathroom, I just looked at Bev and started sobbing. And she said, "Jesus, what's wrong?" And I blurted out, "I'm having a baby!"

I had finally realized, *Oh God this is going to happen. It's happening right now!* That was Sunday morning. Emma wasn't born until 10:54 that night. But the day moved quickly. At one point, they lost her heartbeat on the external monitor and said that they needed to use an internal one. Bev agreed and assured me that there was no harm in using the internal monitor. I wasn't clear. I was having contractions, and I was doing the breathing—which helped. In fact, the few times that the contractions caught me off guard and I wasn't doing the breathing, it hurt immensely. When they went to put the monitor in—and I should have known this—my water broke. They quickly got a heartbeat, but all I felt was this rush of water. And I thought it was blood. But when I looked down, it was clear, and I was instantly relieved.

My friends were all there in the birthing room. They were all petting me and stroking me . . . every part of my body was being massaged. I just shut down. I could sense everybody there and hear everybody's voices, but I couldn't communicate verbally. Labor was a totally physical experience.

And Bev was great. She would say, "Frances, you're such a pro, you're doing this so wonderfully." She encouraged me all along the way. And Buck, who's a musician, asked if there was any music that I wanted to hear. I was able to tell him to get this special tape from my hospital room—Sean Colvin. It's kind of spiritual, folk, alternative music. And that really comforted me also. Then, all of a sudden, someone said, "Hey, you're plus ten! It's time!"

But now they told me that they were going to have to take me into the delivery room and that I wasn't going to be able to deliver here. Only one person could come with me. Odie made the decision, "Bev," he said, "you go with her." And I just said, "Okay."

They wheeled me down to delivery in the birthing bed, and the most excruciating pain of the whole ordeal was having to move from the birthing bed to the delivery table. I kept reaching for a nurse who was standing nearby—I was trying to grasp her hand. But I couldn't verbally tell her, "Help me!" It was a horrible, excruciating pain trying to get onto that table.

But then in the delivery room, it all happened so quickly. Within a matter of minutes, I heard them shout, "Push, push!" I pushed once, and I pushed twice, and I pushed a third time, and there she was! In just a matter of minutes she was born. Bev and I were both crying. I had my feet up in stirrups—the whole traditional thing. When she was born, someone yelled, "It's a girl!" Bev and I looked at each other and screamed, "Yes! It's a girl!" The cord was wrapped around her neck, and they were a bit afraid for her. She was tiny—five pounds, one ounce. They held her up for me, then whisked her away. They did all their little things to her and were about to take her to neonatal intensive care, but I told them that I had to hold her first. They put her into my arms, all wrapped up in a blanket and, as I held her, she looked right up at me—into my eyes with her so-blue eyes. I had never been so high in my life.

After they took her away, they put me back into the birthing room and let all my friends come in. We celebrated until they took me back to my hospital room—it was about midnight. I wasn't tired at all. I was as high as ever, even after this incredible day of physical exertion and changes. I called my family back in Oregon. And then I wanted to see my baby. They let me walk down to the nursery and when I went in, they were playing Elvis Presley. It really cracked me up. Odie and I used to work together, and we had this Elvis fixation together—we'd wear these T-shirts about Elvis's resurrection tour. So it was hilarious. They had a rocking chair there. I sat with her and rocked and rocked and looked at her and thought that she was the most beautiful little thing that I had ever seen. I felt that this is what I had lived for my whole life . . . this incredible love and joy. I just couldn't believe that I had lived so long without it.

ॐ

From her home in California, Christina spoke to me about her pregnancy, the birth of her only son, Bruno, now twenty months, and her marriage, which began to fall apart at the onset of her pregnancy.

Good Delivery, Bad Marriage

We wanted the pregnancy, but I don't think my ex-husband, Alan, expected it to happen that fast. It's funny, he kept on asking, "Are you sure you're pregnant?" And I was like, "Yeah, I'm sure." When the reality finally struck, he became very distant. But I just thought, *Oh well, some guys just don't like their wives being pregnant. Things will change after the baby's born.* That didn't happen. The bigger I got, the more distant and scared he became.

He had opened a new restaurant a few months prior to my pregnancy. Things were booming there. It was really taking off. Now, two years later, he's opened up a second restaurant, and he might open up two more in different states. A real success story. Like most successful businessmen, he has incredible drive. But what makes him great in business makes him terrible in personal relationships. It's very hard for Alan to become intimate. And when I became pregnant, that really meant an additional commitment to me—our lives were becoming more connected. But he was still spending sixteen to eighteen hours at work.

Before I got pregnant, I could wait up until very late for him, but then I couldn't; I'd have to go to sleep. He'd be like, "It's 3:00 A.M., and I'm home, so it's time to talk." And I'd be, "I'm sick, I'm tired, I need to sleep." He didn't understand what it was like for me to be pregnant. I tried not to feel pregnant. I hated my body. I used to work out and stay thin. Now, I felt bumpy and fat.

I was working as a waitress at the time—at a couple of different restaurants. By the time I was about eight months, I cut down until I worked no more than about ten or twelve hours a week.

My mother, a banker, had recommended a nice doctor who was a client of hers. I went to him—he was a nice guy—but by the end, we had differences of opinion. I gained a lot of weight, sixty-five pounds. Every time I'd go to his office, the nurse would say, "You're fat. That's not good. The baby doesn't want fat." I felt really terrible. At home, I was very hungry, and I wasn't eating junk food—mostly fruit, potatoes, and vegetables.

My doctor was in private practice, not associated with any group. Usually, he dealt with Hispanic women, and I'm part Hispanic, but I don't speak Spanish. I was like his gringo patient.

Alan came with me to a few appointments. It was nice, but he was always pretty nervous. He was worried because I have a twin sister who is mentally retarded. It's not organic, not hereditary—something happened during birth. Although the doctor tried to reassure him that everything was fine, he was still worried. The minute I got pregnant, Alan didn't want to have any kind of sexual relationship with me. For the first few months, I was feeling so lousy that it wasn't a problem. But then, I began to feel, *What's the matter with me?* The doctor said sex was fine, but Alan wasn't interested.

In the beginning, I was a little worried about birth because of my twin sister, Jill. We're fraternal twins. She was born six minutes earlier than me. But what I was really concerned about was something else—I had contracted herpes years ago, and was afraid of passing it to my child during a vaginal delivery. The doctor said that as long as I didn't have an outbreak, I'd be fine; I could deliver vaginally.

When I stopped working at about eight months, I began to do a lot of reading. Before that, I just kind of didn't want to know. I was too scared. Reading about childbirth was like reading a Stephen King novel. The thought of my cervix opening would make me want to shut the book—*Oh, God, that's not going to happen to me!* But at eight months, I felt, *Okay, let's get down to business.* I read about natural childbirth and began to feel that I wanted an unmedicated birth. My doctor supported that. I remember feeling helped by *A Good Birth, A Safe Birth,* and I found *The Womanly Art of Breastfeeding* at a used-book store.

The most important book I found was about the Bradley Method. When I read that book, a lightbulb went off in my head. I went back to my doctor and started asking him about epidurals, Demerol, episiotomies. He said, "Well, you actually might need these things." I had the feeling that he was soft-selling me on an epidural. He kept saying that childbirth was painful, some women really need the relief. Also, I was very fearful of an episiotomy—like men are afraid of castration. Being cut just terrified me.

I had been going to Lamaze classes, but once I read the book about the Bradley Method, I wanted Bradley. It was too late to start classes, so I called a Bradley instructor and had one class. I worked on relaxation. That was my biggest problem. Neither my mother nor Alan were very patient; it'd be five minutes and, *Okay, we're done.* When I would try to relax myself, I'd just fall asleep.

I told my doctor that I was going to use the Bradley Method. His reaction was, "If I had known that, I wouldn't have taken you on as a patient." Doctors usually don't like Bradley women because they have strong ideas about what they want and don't want for their births. I walked in with a birth plan—*no drugs, no episiotomy.* The doctor read it, but didn't sign. I guess that says a lot.

Alan didn't yet know if he wanted to attend the birth. We'd go back and forth. If it made him uncomfortable, I didn't want him there, but in the end he really didn't have much choice—I kept hanging onto his arm and wouldn't let him go. He'd keep trying to sneak away and have a cigarette because he was so nervous. And I'd yell, "Alan, Alan, where are you?" I just wanted someone's hand to hold. It was the most painful experience of my life, but also the most joyous—being able to feel my son come out of me—nine pounds, fourteen ounces! You know, every time I pick up a ten pound sack of potatoes at the supermarket, I just think, *There's my boy!*

I was four days late. My doctor had been out of town and was due back the day that Bruno was actually born. My mucus plug fell out on Wednesday. I remember his office called to check on me. I told them about losing my mucus plug. I was so excited that when I went out to walk the dog, I locked myself out of the house and had to climb back in through a tiny kitchen window! I thought, *Well, this ought to get labor going.* But my contractions were very mild all the way until Thursday night.

My mom came over Thursday. Alan was working, and my mom and I watched *Seinfeld*. All of a sudden, I had to begin to really concentrate on the contractions. I couldn't watch TV. I was listening to my body, trying to walk around, and eat a little. At around 10:00, I told my mom that I was probably not going to give birth until morning, so she should go home and get some sleep. My husband came in around 1:00. I was timing the contractions. I'd get big ones and little ones. I only timed the big ones and that was probably a mistake. At about 3:30, I had a bowel movement, and I knew from reading that that was a sign that I was being naturally cleared out for delivery. My husband was trying to fall asleep on the couch, but I told him that we had to go to the hospital. He insisted on taking a shower first. I was like, "Hurry up! Hurry up!" I was holding a pillow, and dressed in a nightgown and bathrobe.

We got to the hospital at around 4:00. I gave them my birth plan. They're like, "Uh huh, just don't let the doctor on call know you're a Bradley mom." I was put in a birthing room. It had a bed with stirrups and a raisable backrest, a shower, and a comfortable chair. It was more like a labor-delivery room.

I was really progressing. I came to the hospital at seven centimeters. I felt proud of myself. But the pain was becoming very bad. And I couldn't relax. My mom and husband just kind of left everything up to me. I had two coaches and neither were helping me—I had to deal with it all.

My mom was trying to be helpful and would say, "You're doing great!" But, I just felt like telling her, "Shut up, please be quiet!" I was holding on to my husband, but I couldn't even look at him. I was in so much pain.

Transition was the worst, just hell. I had no breaks in between contractions. I was screaming. The doctor wanted to check me and break my water, but I was having a contraction and yelled, "NOOOOOO!!!" So, he obviously didn't. I think he wanted me to progress even faster. After he left, I asked the nurse, "How far along am I?" and she said, "Eight centimeters." I was like, "Why does he want to break my water then?" And she says, "Well, there are other women needing to have their babies in the hospital now." You know, most of the time, I'm a pretty good sport, but during birth, I felt, *Screw every-*

body, this is my time! I didn't care if he needed to deliver ten other babies at ten other hospitals. My baby was going to be born my way.

Then, it came time to push. There were five people going, "Push! Push! He's a big baby! Push!" I heard the doctor say, "I think we're going to have to do an episiotomy." When I heard that word, I pushed so hard that I pushed him out—and I tore. The doctor seemed kind of angry with me and said, "Well, you tore anyway. What's the difference between an episiotomy and a tear?" He wanted to fight. Then he scared my husband, who still talks about this. The doctor yelled, "She's hemorrhaging, she's hemorrhaging!" I think I was the only person who knew I was really alright; I wasn't worried. I mean, all that pain was gone! They sewed me up and everything was fine.

Bruno had some meconium in his system, and they had taken him away to aspirate it from his trachea. I kept saying that nursing him would help, and they just kind of grumbled, "Yeah, yeah." Twenty minutes later, they handed me Bruno, and he nursed. Man, was he a champion! He tried to get the whole nipple in his mouth, and I'd have to pop him off. But then he just latched on and kept nursing. He just wanted to nurse. But after a while, they took him away.

I was suddenly starved. They gave me things I would never eat, and I loved them! Eggs, yucky toast. I ate the whole tray! Then, I asked for the phone. I called my dad. I called my brother. I called my old boss. I was completely awake and had no pain.

My husband was gone. When the baby was born, he really didn't want to be there. He didn't want to see the baby being born. The doctor asked if he wanted to cut the umbilical cord, and he said, "No," and left the room. I didn't see him again for hours.

I felt like I was carrying too much of a load—all during pregnancy and birth. All through my pregnancy I was really alone. Alan wasn't there for me, and I just blocked him out. I told myself, *I'm alone. I'm just doing this all alone.* Then I felt like I had to tell the nurses and doctors what I wanted up until the time of transition. Then my body just took over. I feel that I willed this baby into the world.

My mom had done the best job she could. But she seemed to always annoy me. I shouldn't really pick on her because she thought she was doing a wonderful job. I guess what was really annoying was that she was trying to comfort me and my husband wasn't.

I wanted Alan to feel as happy as I felt about the experience. But he, I think, just wasn't ready to have a child—wasn't ready for the responsibility. He was scared to the core. He came back to visit me later that day. He looked awful—haggard. Like he'd been drinking, but he doesn't drink.

After that, he spent only two nights at home. Sometimes he'd call me. He'd come home at around 2:00 in the morning, sleep on the couch and leave by 6:00. Finally, the third night he came home, and Bruno was very fussy. I was in tears. Here he was, my new, beautiful baby, and all he does is cry! I'm nursing him, but he doesn't sleep, and I'm tired and all alone. When Alan came in, I asked, "Don't you love me anymore?" And he said, "No."

Alan moved out. I told myself that it was better this way, better now than later. I don't think he wanted to bond with the baby. Maybe he was protecting himself. I see things in retrospect that I didn't see before. Alan had two terrible relationships with fathers—one his biological, one his stepfather. His biological dad disowned him. Alan looked up to him and wanted to emulate him, but this dad didn't want to be a part of Alan's life. His stepdad kicked him out of the house when he was sixteen. How can you be a father if you've never been fathered?

In our marriage, we never fought. But we never communicated either. I should have seen it all along. I feel a loss for Bruno. For Alan, business always comes first. This morning he was supposed to come over, but he never showed. Bruno and I went to the park, and when we arrived home, there was this phone call. Alan had business. Business is always his priority.

But it would be unfair to put down my ex-husband. He gives me almost twice what the state requires him to pay in child support. I can be a single mother and stay at home with Bruno. We live with my mom, and it's a good arrangement. I can parent Bruno the way I want, and I'm very thankful for this.

Diane lives in Memphis, Tennessee, in a married relationship with her same-sex partner, Ginger. Diane works very part-time as an instructor at a medical college and as a social worker. The two women have two children: Maxwell, age two years, and William, age eleven months. Each woman has birthed one son.

Two Moms

Ginger and I met in the fall of 1988 at Texas Women's University. We were friends for about a year and then began dating; there was something very different about the energies in our relationship, and I knew Ginger was someone I would want to be with for a long time. We had very clear communication and were very tuned in to each other. We could fight and resolve our problems—which was important. Also, because of our friendship, we were able to discuss ideas about marriage and children. At that point, both of us were seeing other people, but we would always get back together.

Our relationship got rather intense and after about six months, I proposed to Ginger. She accepted, and we planned a wedding for a year later. Even then we knew that we each wanted to *birth* a child—not just be a parent—so part of our agreement from the beginning was that each of us would conceive, and we would have two children.

It took us a while to find the best route to get pregnant. We tried some very casual donor situations, drew up papers, and made sure that donors would be tested for STDs [sexually transmitted diseases]. We had a known donor for our first choice—an older man with no interest in parenting. He'd give us his sperm in a baby food jar, then we'd go home and use a lab syringe or pipette to insert the sperm right next to the cervix. But it didn't work; Ginger didn't get pregnant.

We had read some books to help us. One book, geared mainly for single women, was called *Having a Baby without a Man,* and there was a chapter in it on special situations for lesbians. Also, there's some gay and lesbian publications that touched on different ways to achieve parenthood—through formal adoption, informal adoption, through known-donor insemination, and through agreements where couples join and do group parenting. Sperm banks were a little too anonymous—although we actually, at one point, did try one—and I wanted to know more about the physical characteristics of the father.

Sperm banks are a real business. They screen donors, but men can easily lie about a family history of alcoholism or mental illness or inheritable disease. Also, Ginger and I wanted to be able to show our child a picture of his or her dad. We wanted to know if he was tall and skinny, or dumpy. Did he have straight feet, good eyesight?

Anyway, Ginger got pregnant with our known donor, but miscarried. Then we had his sperm count checked and found that it had dropped. This donor clearly wasn't working for us. So we moved to a sperm bank next—but it was expensive and emotionally sterile, a medical procedure. Also, it's strange: although we were very open about the uniqueness of our situation, they never asked us anything. And we didn't know if that was out of respect or because they didn't really know how to handle us. We gave up the sperm bank idea pretty quick and decided to try finding a donor on our own again.

How we found our donor is a sweet story. We were at a birthday party for a local bookstore that's in an area of the city that's being regentrified. They have a small following of loyal customers, and we were all outside eating cake. The store is so small that they couldn't set up inside, and we'd have to take turns going in to do our book shopping. Everyone there knew we'd been trying to get pregnant—at this point—for eleven months. When we'd meet someone, we'd be asked, "Oh, are you pregnant yet?" The pressure was intense, and we were really feeling discouraged. Then, we decided to ask the people who would ask us about becoming pregnant, "No, we're not pregnant; do you know where we can find a good donor?" Ideally, we were looking for someone about six foot two, 180 pounds, dark hair, blue eyes, fairly good-looking, and willing to be a known donor with no parental rights or responsibilities.

We were kind of joking around that day with this one guy who said he was going out dancing that night. I told him, "Just look around for someone who fits that description." He was like, "Okay, yeah right." But he seemed puzzled, and I thought that I might have offended him. Later though, he came up to us at the party and said, "What about me?"

We tentatively agreed and decided to speak to our respective attorneys. But it ended up that we had the same attorney, so we all met to talk about it at a little Mexican-food place we all love. The attorney had mixed feelings about representing both parties, but no one wanted to switch. She actively advised one party to find another attorney because she felt that we were all walking into unknown legal territory. But we were all on the same side and our feelings were pretty adamant.

We proceeded to drink very heavily that night because we were so nervous. We went through many margaritas. We threw caution to the wind and decided to trust each other because that's what it's really about—a known donor is someone you trust, someone who knows you well enough to respect your wishes, even when the chips are down. We were very fortunate to feel comfortable with this man and knew that we could build a relationship.

Going into this agreement, we originally thought that our donor would be a gene tool and then step aside and just have some very casual, distant relationship with our children. But it hasn't gone that way; he's built a relationship with the kids and knows them real well.

Anyway, we began trying to get pregnant with him, and after three months we were successful. He'd do his thing, and we'd pick it up and insert it, wait ten days, then do a pregnancy test.

At first, we made trying to get pregnant romantic. But it became very stressful—just like it is for many infertile couples. It became an act in and of itself. Certainly, our love for each other kept us going, but there was no champagne, mood music, or candles. It was more like, "The time is right; he's home from work; let's go get the sperm and try to get pregnant."

This was, of course, for our first pregnancy, Ginger's. Then, after Maxwell turned one, I began to have incredible cravings to get pregnant. It was sooner than Ginger had hoped—we had both planned for two-year spacing. But we hammered it out and agreed to go ahead.

I approached our donor. He was reluctant at first but then agreed and actually became very excited. We all wanted a girl and kind of bartered with the gods and said, "Okay, here's the deal. We want a baby, and we want a girl." I got pregnant right away, then miscarried. It was over Christmas, and I was about five weeks along. We waited a couple of months, and I took a fertility drug, Clomid—I got pregnant.

I was very excited to be pregnant and wanted to wear maternity clothing right away. I knew it was going to be my only pregnancy, and I wanted to savor it like a good bottle of wine. I found that I didn't want anything around my waist; I gained a lot of fat weight early in my pregnancy. I have a very slender waist, and it's always been my selling point. So I enjoyed wearing maternity clothing and shopping for maternity stuff at yard sales. I began talking to our little boy about having a baby sister or brother. He was very young and didn't understand; he thought that everybody has a baby in their uterus. He'd go over and pat other people's bellies and say that they had a baby there.

Then, at about twenty weeks, I was lying in bed on a Saturday morning when Maxwell decided to hurl himself on my belly—he was playing Hulk Hogan. I had really sharp pains right away and began to have contractions. I ended up having an ultrasound and being put on bed rest for a day. But they did subside.

Soon after that, I went to visit my parents who live seven hours away. I didn't feel good while I was there. I was real light-headed, real dizzy, and I couldn't figure out what was wrong. I stayed a week. When I got home, I still wasn't feeling well. Then, one night, coming home from dinner, I began to get bad contractions and had a hard time keeping the car on the road. When I got home I called a friend; I didn't want to tell Ginger because I thought she'd get angry with me.

My friend just screamed and yelled over the phone and told me to call the midwife. She asked if I was bleeding, and I said, "No." Then I finally told Ginger, and she called the midwife. When I went to the bathroom, I began to bleed.

We had a hard time trying to reach the midwives. We made a lot of phone calls that night. In fact, we finally had to call our OB backup, who's a good friend. He said that we should probably go in to the hospital to be evaluated. We had a friend come over to watch Maxwell and we left.

At the hospital, they did an ultrasound, and they said that it was a girl. We hadn't wanted to know, but were very happy. I stayed at the hospital until late, but came home feeling much better.

I continued to bleed a little—it wasn't real bright or real heavy, but just enough to give me the message that I should stay in bed. The midwives wanted me to stay in bed for the remainder of my pregnancy. This was very hard with a toddler. And I felt fine. I had a lot of cognitive dissonance because I felt okay, and felt in my heart that things were going to be okay, and that it was overkill to stay in bed. Basically, I made everyone's life miserable because I wasn't getting the answers that I liked. Ginger suffered the most.

After a month, I was taken off bed rest. I worked at this time as a social worker, counseling women at a medical clinic and teaching a class for medical students. Both jobs were part-time. I was told by both the midwife and the OB that I could continue to work, but I'd have to go back to bed if I had more than four contractions in an hour.

I spent this part of my pregnancy juggling contractions, bed rest, and work. I'd have a rough day and have to take it easy the next. I really wanted to be enjoying the pregnancy and was really struggling against these restrictions. It wasn't how I wanted to spend my pregnancy. I'd have to go back to the hospital to try to stop contractions, and they'd put me on medication. Finally, one night when it was pretty bad and the bleeding had started again, I stayed in the hospital for five days—and I actually ended up having the baby.

When this happened, I was thirty-four weeks along. The midwives will only deliver if you're between thirty-eight and forty-two weeks. It was clear that I wasn't going to make it, so I transferred to my OB. I knew that I probably wasn't going to be in control—that I'd be hooked up to monitors and have IVs—but my OB knew what I absolutely, positively wouldn't go for, and I knew that he wouldn't ask those things of me. I understood that my birth was going to be a medical birth—I was out of the normal range: only thirty-five weeks' gestation with preterm bleeding.

I had pretty realistic ideas. I'd visited the hospital before I'd even gotten pregnant and hung out with my OB friend from 10:00 P.M. to midnight. This is a real high-risk hospital, and it's associated with the university in which I was teaching. In fact, one of my rules was that none of our med students could come in and see me. When I had to come into the ER with some of my preterm complications, some of the students would say, "Oh, she looks familiar. What's she doing here?"

They were giving me steroids to help the baby's lungs, and magnesium sulphate to stop labor. But my body had already begun labor—not gripping, overwhelming, but slow and steady. The drugs can have many side effects, so I had to be monitored. But the bottom line is that the drugs weren't working and finally they said that they'd have to let me deliver.

One of the issues that interests me and that I've thought about exploring for an article concerns the notion that there's really no such thing as prepared childbirth for preterm delivery. There's always this sense of *I don't want to commit myself fully*. It's like having a loaf of bread in the oven and wanting to have that bread, but knowing that the bread isn't ready yet. I wanted to have the baby, but I also wanted to be pregnant longer.

I was diagnosed that week with a partial placental abruption. I finally let them do an amniocentesis and the amniotic fluid was so bloody that it looked like burgundy wine. Although they said that if the contractions would stop for twenty-four hours they'd let me go home, at some point I realized they weren't going to let me.

I remember Ginger came with Max. I don't know if we kind of talked about it or just silently agreed, but it was clear that we both had decided to go ahead and have the baby. I let Max climb up on me and nurse to stimulate labor.

Although I wasn't supposed to get up, I walked Ginger and Max to the elevator. We thought it would be easier for Max to say good-bye this way. Ginger told me that it wasn't until they reached the ground floor that Max figured out that I wasn't going to be there when the doors opened. She said he howled, but I couldn't hear him, of course. I walked back to my room and began to have contractions. I didn't tell anyone. I laid pretty low about it. That was around 8:00. At midnight, my bleeding picked up and my water broke. They transferred me down to Labor and Delivery. I knew that I was going to have the baby because they weren't going to let me go too long with ruptured membranes and a chronic abruption.

In the labor room, they decided to give me Pitocin. They wanted to get the baby out. The contractions got pretty strong, and I was struggling with the labor because I felt very confined. I was tired of being there. It wasn't fun. The Pitocin contractions were overwhelming, and I became increasingly unpleasant to be around.

The room was small. And although the bed was wonderful, I couldn't get it adjusted right. I was spewing amniotic fluid and felt gross. I was tethered to many machines: I had a fetal monitor, and IV with a Pitocin piggy-back. I wanted to walk, move around with the contractions, but I couldn't.

They'd called Ginger for me, and she was there. I was very cranky. I took some Stadol. The nurses, I found, had a very intense desire to completely relieve my pain, probably because pain-free patients are much easier to care for. They gave me too much Stadol, and I had to fight to stay conscious. Later, they gave me some more, and I actually did fall asleep.

When I woke, the contractions were just overwhelming. I hadn't been able to build up to them. I moaned and cried to Ginger, tried rocking and a variety of positions. She kept telling me to *go with the contractions, go with the contractions.* Finally, I grabbed her by the neck, and told her that if she said that to me one more time, I would scream! I never got to the point of being able to do prepared breathing. I did some relaxation, but I felt my body getting more and more tense. In retrospect, I think a lot of it had to do with the physical space I was in.

Labor is overwhelming. Your body takes over and you can't control it. You can only be a witness to the roller coaster; you can't control where it goes. I think I could have felt better if I'd been able to move with the rolls. I felt like a caged animal.

One of the nurses suggested that I have an epidural. We discussed it. The nurse was sure that it would bring relief, but I said, "No." I didn't think I needed that kind of relief because all I could see was: *Oh great, premature labor, chronic abruptions—if I get this epidural, the chances of having a C-section skyrocket!*

It was now Sunday morning. And just to complicate the story, a front-page article on our family had just been released. The new shift had already read it. The nurses had to keep people at bay who wanted to come in to see us because they were curious.

They sent in an anesthesiologist to speak to me about having an epidural. He had read our story and said, "I really like the article but don't know if you will." That helped, and I began to trust him. Also, the fact that he was gay. We really bonded with him. We talked about the epidural, and he felt fairly certain that he could give me one without hurting my back—I have a bad back from a car accident. I decided to have an epidural.

It didn't hurt to get it—I was very surprised. Epidurals can hit or miss— this one certainly hit. Once I had pain relief, I gave in to my exhaustion and slept. My labor progressed. They'd check on me, and when I came to, I asked them to cut back on the epidural, and they did. Every once in a while, my OB came in. He'd walk into the room and say, "I want the Pit up." I began to call them the "Pit Crew."

Sometime in there, they put me in the birthing room and I felt better— there was more space and more light. I was unhooked from the IV and epidural. I was still fairly numb and slightly concerned about my ability to push.

I began to get urges. When my OB came in and asked, "So, I hear you want to push?" I was like, "Yeah!" I think I pushed three, maybe four times, and we had a baby.

I remember the cord was tight, and they had to cut it. The floor nurse who was assisting, quickly yelled out, "Well, ladies, it's a boy!" We all just cracked up. Then, she asked, "Well, do you have a name for him?" And we did: William.

Ginger took some pictures. I delivered the placenta—which felt great. I got to hold the baby right away and keep him in the birthing room. Everyone got to talk and laugh and enjoy the fact that this big ordeal was over.

William had some minor problems—with respiration and his bilirubin. But basically, he was great. I got a second-degree tear, but it was nothing as far as I was concerned. With all my complications, I felt incredibly lucky. William came home with me in a couple of days; my mom was there and we all celebrated.

∞

Michelle is a young woman who, toward the end of her senior year in high school, found herself unexpectedly pregnant. After much deliberation about what to do, Michelle decided to birth her baby and give it up for adoption. Now a student at a small liberal arts college in Georgia, Michelle is making progress toward a BA in communications.

I Think I Did the Right Thing

I'm a twin; my sister and I are very close. I grew up in a family with a mom and dad living at home. My sister is my only sibling. Since I graduated from high school, my parents separated. Now, my dad lives in Texas. My sister and I both attended college here at first, but she quit 'cause I guess she wasn't ready. I live on campus in a dorm.

Back in high school, before I got pregnant, I had just a regular relationship with my boyfriend—we'd go to the movies or to special places together. He was the first person I ever had sex with. It felt natural at the time. I didn't think of it as a meaningful thing. We only had intercourse once, and I ended up pregnant. My boyfriend never pressured me into it or anything—it just felt natural to be with him. He was real sweet.

About a month after we had sex, I started getting sick. I didn't know what was going on. I began to think I was pregnant, and I was scared to tell my mom. I had missed a period and took an in-home pregnancy test—it was positive. It never occurred to my boyfriend or me to use birth control.

I had my friend take me to a clinic to find out for sure if the test was right.

My friend had been pregnant twice—she kept the first one but had an abortion with the other.

The day I went to the clinic, I was very scared. I knew I was pregnant, but I was still hoping it wasn't true. I had a lot of mental anguish. They did a blood test. I remember sitting there on the exam table; my friend was in the room with me—I was really nervous. When the doctor came back and told me I was pregnant, I started crying. I didn't know what I was going to do. My friend tried to comfort me, and the doctor was trying to calm me down and tell me how to take care of myself. He also told me what I could do—different options and stuff—but I wasn't really coherent and heard only some of it.

It was a weekday afternoon, after school—maybe Wednesday or Thursday. When my friend took me home, I couldn't get out of the car; I was crying and nervous. Then, I just said to myself, *Well, maybe this is my fault, and I have to face the consequences and tell my parents the truth.*

So, I went into the house. My dad was sitting on his sofa chair, and my mom was sitting on the couch. They were watching TV. I went up to my mom, and she turned around and saw me, and she was like, *What's wrong?* My dad was looking at me also. And that's when I had to tell them that I was pregnant. My dad didn't say anything—he couldn't. But my mom began hugging me and trying to calm me down.

She didn't blame me for anything. She just asked me if my boyfriend knew. I told her, "Yes." I had told him after the in-home pregnancy test. My mom said that the decision about what to do was up to me. We discussed abortion and adoption. I come from a really God-fearing background—they believe in God. My mom wasn't too keen on me having an abortion—she wanted me to give it up for adoption—so, right there, I decided to have the baby and give it up. I made the choice that day. I kept thinking, *It's not the child's fault. I should give this baby a chance to live and have a family that will take care of it.*

The next day, my dad came around, and we started talking. He was comforting me also and apologizing for the way he acted at first. I just started crying again. He agreed that maybe giving it up for adoption was the best thing for the baby and me. I'm thankful that my parents were so supportive.

It was kind of embarrassing to go back to school—everyone knew. But I just brushed it off. I turned eighteen in April and found out I was pregnant in May, so it was pretty close to graduation. At first, I found myself crying a lot. I felt very sad. But then, I tried to think about the good things—how the baby was doing, what would be best for it. I agonized the first few months, but really, the later months were worse. The closer I got to giving birth and having to give up the baby, the more difficult it seemed.

I never went back to the clinic. I went to a regular doctor at the hospital for prenatal care. He gave me stuff to read about birth, and I attended Lamaze classes where they teach you how to breathe and stuff. I wanted to have a natural childbirth because it was the first time, and, I guess, I wanted to see how it was.

My delivery wasn't until March. I lived at home after graduation. I was thinking about going to college after the birth. My boyfriend was out of the picture, really, as soon as he knew I was pregnant. My parents talked to his parents, and there were some real arguments. They would fuss and fight and argue all the time—both sets of parents. It was hard, and I just said, "Well, he's obviously not going to take care of it, so leave him alone." It wasn't doing any good—them fighting, arguing—he didn't want to have anything to do with me when I became pregnant.

When I had first told him, he was shocked. He was like, "Well, how do I know it's mine?" He changed. When I first met him, he was really sweet and nice, but after, he was like cruel and mean. I had only been with him—how could he question whose baby it was? It hurt. I'd pass him in the hallways, and we wouldn't say anything to each other. He had his friends and I had mine—they would argue. It was bad, a mess.

As I got closer to my due date, it got harder for me. I kept wondering if my baby would hate me because I gave it away. Also, I kept thinking about the new parents—if they would be nice to it, take care of it. Also, would they tell the baby he was adopted, or let him find me if he wanted to later on? The adoption was arranged through the hospital. They were as helpful as they could be. I decided on an open adoption, and I got to meet the parents two weeks after the baby was born. It was weird at first—it didn't seem real. They were a nice couple, but the whole situation was unreal. My parents went with me to their home. We all got along well. The adoptive parents told me that the baby could come see me when he got older if he wanted to. And they would tell him he was adopted when the time was right. I feel very comfortable with where my baby is.

I was into labor on my actual due date. It was around 9:30 or 10:00 at night. I was sitting down at the table, and my water broke. I was in some old clothes that I wear around the house—shorts and a T-shirt. I was scared.

My parents rushed me to the hospital that night. We live in another town, so they had to drive a ways. When we got there, we went up to the front desk and the lady saw that I was in labor. They brought me a wheelchair and took me to a room. I was in pain the whole time and trying to breathe right and stuff, but it wasn't working.

They put me in a labor-and-delivery room, on a table. They gave me some medication through an IV to try to calm me down, reduce the pain some. It helped a little bit. A lot of doctors and nurses came in. It was scary to see all these people around you when you're in pain. My legs were stretched out. It was very hard, and I was hurting. My labor was very fast.

The baby was born at like 12:00 or 12:15 that morning—not much time from when my water broke at like 9:30, 10:00. I don't remember much. I was hurting all the way through. I screamed a lot. I asked for my mom to be there. She came in and helped. I had an episiotomy. When the baby came, they told me it was a boy and asked if I wanted to hold him. I said, "Yes," and held him for only a second and gave him back to the doctor. It was the last time I saw him until the visit to the new parents two weeks later.

I stayed in the hospital about four days. I was very depressed and sad. I kept wondering if I was doing the right thing and if the baby was going to be mad at me and think that I owed him something. Nobody from the hospital came to help me with my feelings. My mom was the one who talked to me. She was real understanding, and she told me that I'd be alright and that the baby was healthy and had parents who would love it.

It took me really a year to deal with all my feelings and move on in my life. After this experience, I decided not to be sexually active anymore. I'm waiting now till I get married to have sex and a family. And I don't hate men; I don't have any harsh feelings against them or anything. I still have male friends, and I still talk to them, but I don't have a boyfriend.

Some of my old friends from high school got pregnant and kept their babies. But I don't think I could have handled that. They have to work minimum-wage jobs and depend on their parents to take care of their kids. And that's bad. These parents have already taken care of their own children, and now they have to take care of their children's children. It's not fair. You have to be responsible.

I think I did the right thing. I know that I'm better off here, getting an education, instead of working some minimum-wage job and not being able to support myself and my child.

ℰℂ

Shannon is a single mother who lives in New York City. She is confined to a wheelchair as a result of a 1987 spinal cord injury that left her paraplegic. Her son, Ethan, is now eight months old.

Coping

I was twenty-two when I fell off a balcony and broke my back. It never got better. You always hear on TV about the person who gets terribly injured and then recovers. You hear words like "courage" or "belief." But most people who get better improve because their injury isn't bad enough, not because they have some special courage or belief. What's a person to do? Commit suicide? I don't think many people would do that. An injured person is the same person he was before his injury: if he was a hard-working person, he'll remain a hard-working person; if he was a lazy person before, he'll be lazy afterwards.

I'd gone to college for medical records administration. But I wasn't sure if I wanted to do that. I was at the point of losing interest. I think, looking back, I was depressed.

I was a senior when the injury occurred, and I had to be in the hospital for a year. After that, I had physical therapy for another year. I knew that I didn't want to live on Social Security for the rest of my life—that's hardly any money at all. So I went back to school for dietetics. But actually now, I do medical transcription. And this works out for me because I can work at home on my computer.

I always thought more about getting married and having children than having a career. But it just didn't happen. I had a boyfriend in high school, but we broke up after my first year in college. And then after the injury, I started going out with somebody for about two and a half years. We were going to get married, but it was all wrong.

Before I got pregnant with Ethan, I had two miscarriages. After these I really was wondering if I would ever be able to have a baby. But I hoped to get pregnant again—and I did.

My boyfriend, the one I was going to marry, was the father in all three pregnancies. He's Korean, and I met him while he was working at a store in

Manhattan. We had a lot of problems. Korean men usually don't get involved with American women, and when they do, they usually don't think permanent relationship. He was divorced and had a son in Korea. He used to drink. When I got pregnant the third time, I didn't tell him. Finally, he noticed when I was six or seven months. He wasn't mad or anything. He came to visit the next week, and then once the week after. That was the last time I saw him. He was beginning a new job somewhere in New Jersey. I didn't get his address or phone number. I can't think of a way to find him now. He might have moved back to Korea.

Before he left that last time, he told me he'd like to see the baby. I never thought that I'd get monetary support, but I did think that he'd like to see the baby—he likes children. I know he'd like Ethan if he saw him.

Now, I live alone in an apartment, and basically, I went through my pregnancy alone there. My aunt came to stay over and spend weekends maybe twice a month. I was working throughout, except when I had problems and had to be hospitalized.

The first time I was about six months along, and the second time I was close to seven months. In between these periods, I had a bacterial infection that caused bad diarrhea. I don't have real good control over my bowels, so this was a problem, and I had some accidents. After my first hospitalization, I would bleed just a drop or two here and there. And I actually stopped taking showers and started washing myself because every time I'd shower, I'd bleed.

About three weeks after my first hospitalization, I had pain in the side of my back, fever, and terrible chills. I'd get really cold and have to pile blankets on. Then, I'd get really hot and sweaty. I had a doctor's appointment coming up, but by the time I arrived and they examined me, my temperature was normal. I was told to go home. As I was waiting to be picked up, I began to feel sick again. They started monitoring the baby and decided to admit me. They thought I might have a kidney infection.

This was at Mt. Sinai hospital. They have very nice facilities there, and I was glad that they decided to keep me, because if anything went wrong, doctors would be right there. They monitored me three times a day, and if I went into labor, they'd know. This hospital has one of the best neonatal intensive care units in the country. If the baby came early, he'd have a good chance. I was always afraid of going into labor alone and not being able to tell. If I called an ambulance, they'd just take me to the nearest hospital.

The first few days in Mt. Sinai, I felt really sick because the fever hadn't gone down yet. Then I started to go into labor, which they were able to stop with medication.

There were some bad things about being in the hospital—I lost two months of work, and I had to borrow some money. Also, they don't have wheelchairs for patients to use for the bathroom, and even the commode chair wasn't accessible because it had sides—I couldn't get into it without two people lifting me. Most of the time I used a catheter. I had to do bowel movements in the bed, and somebody would have to come and clean me off, which was terrible. But I did have a private room, and that was great.

I was there during November and December. I missed spending Thanksgiving and Christmas with the family. Also, there was a big party for a relative who turned eighty. It was up in a big lodge in Massachusetts, and I couldn't attend that either.

I kept missing out on the fun of being pregnant. I always thought that I'd have this big stomach and everybody would notice my pregnancy, instead of my wheelchair. But I didn't start showing until my fifth or sixth month. Most people would just think I was wearing a blousey top. In the hospital, all the people who saw me already knew I was pregnant and there was no need to say anything.

People did visit. My father came in from Long Island every few days. And my aunt, who lives two hours away, would come. I basically watched a lot of TV and read some books. Sometimes I'd just sit and do nothing. But TV pretty much filled the schedule.

They decided to induce labor at thirty-seven weeks. At first they were going to induce at thirty-six weeks, but there were some scheduling problems. It was all okay with me. I wasn't that anxious to end the pregnancy—the longer the baby stayed inside, the healthier he'd be. And, I kind of liked being pregnant and didn't know if I'd have the chance again. I enjoyed feeling the baby kick and watching the little waves roll across my middle.

They planned a vaginal birth for me, knowing that they'd have to use forceps at the end because I couldn't push. I don't think they have many deliveries with paraplegic mothers. There are probably doctors who specialize in it, but they're private doctors I can't afford.

My due date was January 23, but Ethan was born on January 3. He wasn't premature—thirty-seven weeks isn't premature. They woke me up early that morning to go to the labor floor. I wasn't excited; I was afraid that something would go wrong. It felt like any other day—I had been to the labor floor when I had gone into premature labor and for various prenatal tests. And I wasn't an active part of the process the way I would have been if I were able to push and feel pain. I never felt any pain. They gave me an epidural right away. I just sat there during labor with an IV in my arm while they monitored the baby. I watched TV. My cousin came to be my labor coach, but there was nothing she could do. I couldn't feel any contractions unless I put my hands on my belly. I just hoped I wouldn't have to have a C-section.

They induced me at around 10:00 in the morning; Ethan was born at 7:30 that evening. It went slowly at first. The doctor would come in, check me and say, "Soon." And then another hour would go by, and he'd come in again. But when my water broke, it all happened at once.

I was in a labor-delivery room. There were about ten or twelve of them—very little, each with a TV. I could hear women screaming over the intercom from other rooms. I was thinking, *Well, that's not going to be me. I can't feel anything.* I wished I could have experienced the normal thing. I wish I could have pushed him out. People say, "Oh, you really work hard in labor." But not me—it was the easiest part of the whole pregnancy.

All of a sudden it seems, I heard, "Here comes the head!" and I could see the baby. When they took him out, I was really happy. He looked all white, and I was scared for a minute—he seemed too pale. Then they took him over to the little table, wiped him down, and he turned all pink. I thought that they'd give me the baby right away, but they didn't. They put drops in his eyes, measured, and weighed him. He was six pounds, four ounces. I did get to hold him, but he was making these funny noises and had a breathing problem, so they took him to the intensive care unit. I held him for probably less than a minute.

About an hour later, they fixed me up and took me to the nursery. I could see him through the incubator. He was beautiful.

Then, the next morning, no one came in to tell me how my baby was doing. He was still in the intensive care nursery and wasn't being brought in to me. I had to go down myself to find out. But the nurses were very nice. I got to hold him.

Looking back on Ethan's birth, I think everyone did the best they could. They didn't know how to deal with me and didn't know what to expect. I wished that I could have had a more experienced doctor, but Medicaid doesn't pay for that.

Six

WHEN PROBLEMS OCCUR

&

As every expectant mother knows, pregnancy and childbirth may pose risks for both mother and baby. Although most outcomes are good, not all are. In this chapter, we meet strong women who deal with some of the kinds of medical problems associated with pregnancy and childbirth, and who, through faith and/or understanding, have been able to successfully cope with their particular circumstances.

&

Jeannie is a stay-at-home mom living in Storrs, Connecticut, with her husband, David, and three children: John, age six; Daniel, age three; and Katie, age one. Jeannie talked about a miscarriage she had between the births of John and Daniel.

It Felt Like a Death

Before I had John, I was working as a Chapter 1 teacher, helping kids fill in gaps in their lives. When David and I decided to get pregnant that first time, it took us nine months. Then, bingo, I got pregnant. But I got a really bad case of morning sickness, and ended up dehydrated and in the hospital. I lost thirty pounds in three weeks. I was convinced that the baby wasn't going to survive. I had to quit my job. In the hospital they gave me baby magazines to read, but I couldn't even look at them—I thought my own baby wasn't going to live.

Then, around four or five months along, I began to feel better. I could do things again; it was summer and I took it easy. By fall, I decided to enroll part-time in some graduate classes. When John was finally born, he was healthy and everything was fine. I was amazed. Then, after about a year, I began to want another baby.

I must have gotten pregnant even before David and I decided to actually get pregnant—when we were still in the talking stage. I was very excited. I was a full-time mommy and I loved it. I began to look forward to this second baby's coming.

Then I got sick again and needed to have a lot of help. My mother and father-in-law came often, and sometimes my next-door neighbor would come over—I couldn't even swallow water without vomiting.

At about twelve weeks, the doctors decided to do an ultrasound to make sure that the baby was okay. It was the end of the first trimester, and I was beginning to feel better. With John, when the doctors did an ultrasound, I would watch a light pump—which was his heartbeat. When I went in this time, there was no little light. In retrospect, I think I was trying to protect myself because I asked the technician, "Is there something wrong with your machine?" I could see the little blob of baby, but not much else. Later, they said that he must have been about eight weeks along.

I asked the technician again, "Is this a different kind of machine? Shouldn't I see a little light blinking?" The technician just said, "I'm not allowed to evaluate it." I was twenty-seven years old. Some part of me must have been figuring this out. Finally, the technician said, "I think Dr. Larmen's on duty. I'm going to get him." Still, I didn't consciously figure it out—I just lay there.

Dr. Larmen, the obstetrician, came in. He looked at the screen and said to me, "Mrs. Allie, this baby is not viable." He began to go into this long thing: "You know, this baby looks eight weeks' gestation and it should be twelve, according to your medical records."

And I'm thinking, *What is he trying to tell me?* He says, "We should have a heartbeat at twelve weeks. . . ." And I'm thinking, *Yes, that's right. John was only eight weeks and I could see his. . . .* Then I realized what he wanted to say to me. And it wasn't some technical thing like, "This baby isn't viable." I looked at him and said, "You mean that there's no baby anymore."

What I remember next is feeling God's hands under my back, holding me up so I wouldn't fall into a deep, deep pit. I wanted to be left alone. I wanted to go home, be alone and deal with it. The ultrasound equipment is in the hospital, and I needed to leave and get myself out somehow.

I was acting like a child. I didn't ask the doctor, "So what do we do next?" I just lay there on the ultrasound table with my naked belly hanging out. The nurse said to me, "Well, I'd like you to make an appointment at the hospital office to come and have a D and C." I knew what that meant—they'd have to open my cervix and remove the baby—but I barely heard her. I got up and felt God helping me walk. I mean, literally, I felt God carry me down the hallway to the office. I didn't want to cry yet. I was holding it all in. I had to tell the ladies in the office. They were my old pals; they had seen me through my pregnancy with John when I was so sick. I told them that I had to schedule a D and C. Then they knew, and they were immediately sympathetic. One nurse in particular was very professional and yet sympathetic at the same time—she said just the right thing. She said gently, "We're all sorry. I know that John is home probably taking a nap right now, and you'll feel better being with him." I didn't want anyone kissing and hugging me right then.

My mother was taking care of John. When I came in, she had a big smile on her face—she was all excited about having another grandchild. I didn't want to have to tell her first. I wished I could have spoken with my husband.

My mother is Italian and very emotional in either direction—very, very happy, or very, very upset. I just said to her, "I had a miscarriage." She kind of looked at me. It didn't make much sense. Then John woke up. I couldn't wait to see and cuddle him.

When my husband came home, I told him. And the first thing he said was, "Gee, after all that!" It made it harder on me. Really, my husband is a wonderful and sympathetic man; he always tries to understand. He's a great daddy and does all kinds of stuff with the kids. When I've been sick during my pregnancies, he's been great. But to him, the pregnancy isn't real until I get fat and he can feel the baby move with his hand. To him, a baby lost at eight weeks' gestation isn't real. To me, the baby was twelve weeks—I went twelve weeks thinking he was alive. This baby was real to me.

That night I cried and cried. I couldn't sleep. The next day was the D and C. They needed to do it right away because they felt it was dangerous. I kept thinking, *What could I have done differently?* Something had died inside me.

David took off the next day, and we went together to the hospital for the D and C. It was August 23, and that's the day I feel is our baby's birthday. Having an actual birthday helped me to cope. I thought in real life when you lose someone you love, like a friend or family member, it's real, and you can grieve. But here, no one will acknowledge that the baby is a real person. I felt deprived of the gift of grieving. So I thought, *I'm going to let myself grieve. I'm going to let myself handle this. 'Cause if I keep pretending it isn't real like everybody tells me, I'm never going to get over this loss.* I named the baby Laura.

We went to the hospital. It was a one-day thing. We knew everyone on the obstetrics floor because that's where I'd spent so much time during my sickness with the first pregnancy, and that's where I had delivered John. I went there, had the procedure, and then it was over.

My mom made stew—something real homey—to help me feel better. She was babysitting John for us. It was fine.

The hardest part for me was the following year. I spoke with many women friends and it seemed like most of them, if they'd had two babies, eventually experienced a miscarriage. Everyone reacts differently.

I was devastated. After the miscarriage, David decided he didn't want to have another baby right away. I think that contributed to my problem; it made it harder on me because I really did want another baby. It's not a reasonable thing, and I can't explain—only other mothers understand this yearning.

I would see pregnant women and feel jealous of them. I'd have friends get pregnant and become jealous. It was awful. I began to hate myself for having these feelings. I'm mostly a logical person. But when my emotions kick in, and kick my logic out, I get angry at myself. So that following year was really, really difficult for me. It was a very sad, dark, lonely time. My husband didn't understand, and most of my friends couldn't understand. Why couldn't I just get on with my life?

About a month after the miscarriage, I was talking to a friend about it, and I said, "Well, I'm starting to heal. I'm beginning to believe that something might have been wrong with the baby, and God in his mercy decided to take this baby home to him rather than put her through a life of misery." And this friend just said, "God didn't take your baby." Just like that. I nicely ended the conversation, and said, "Goodbye." My friendship with her has never been the same since.

I never knew what somebody else might say. We had recently moved to this neighborhood, and I was still new. Also, I was in a fledgling state of being a mom. I didn't have many stay-at-home-mom friends yet. I had been a teacher, and many of my friends were still teaching.

We lived near a pond. Every night I'd go up and just walk there. I felt God was healing me. I could hear him say, "I'm with you on this. I'm crying too. Have faith." And I did. Faith is like a muscle; it gets stronger as you use it.

David was doing what he could, and John was giving me all the hugs and kisses he possibly could. I'm aware of the clinical signs of depression, and I kind of kept an eye on myself. I never felt like I was *losing it*. I felt that if I could just hold God's hand and give myself time, I would heal.

My due date, March 4, haunted me. I wanted to get pregnant before my due date. I knew that if I wasn't pregnant by that date, I'd feel very empty.

Now, along with all this, I was still in graduate school part-time. By the time I had the D and C in August, I needed to complete one last paper for an independent study. Strangely enough, I was able to. Then I was only six credits away from having my master's degree. And I needed my master's in order to keep my teaching certificate. David said, "You're only two courses away. Take one during the fall and one during the spring. Then we can think about getting pregnant."

So while all this stuff was going on, I was in school part-time. My due date passed. Then I graduated in May. We began to try for a baby in June. In July, we had touchdown.

I was ecstatic. Of course, I went through what many women go through after having a miscarriage—constant nervousness. Then I got sick again. With all four of my pregnancies I had to be hospitalized. But as I got further along, I began to feel better and better, and less and less nervous about losing the baby.

The baby we had was Daniel. He was a special gift. It's just wild. He's the cheerfullest little guy. John is very emotional, but Daniel is cheerful and jokey—our family imp. Doctors say it's impossible, but I swear that he gave me a social smile when he was thirteen days old. On the morning of his first Easter, while John and David were at church, Daniel looked directly into my eyes and smiled. I'll never forget that day.

By the time Daniel was born, we had established ourselves more; we had friends, and our family and marriage were strong. One woman who I became particularly close to, Ingred, also lost a baby through miscarriage. I was able to speak to her. In fact, we became best friends, and she became Daniel's godmother.

Then, last April, Ingred died of cancer. I'm still working through that death. But somehow, it's not as dark as when I lost my baby. Ingred was very faithful, and her illness and death were really a tribute to life. The way in which she handled her death made it easy for me. I still feel her presence, and I imagine her up in heaven with the baby she lost and my little Laura.

I remember that when I was grieving for my baby, so many people would say to me, "Don't worry, you'll have other babies." But that's not the point. It would be like saying after Ingred's death, "Don't worry, you'll have other best friends." Again, that's not the point; people aren't replaceable.

&

Elli was thirty years old and pregnant with her third child when we spoke at her home in Key West, Florida, on a hot and sun-filled April morning. Elli, who has a background in public relations and marketing, discusses the birth of her second child, William Cody, who had died from pregnancy-related complications less than a year before.

With No Warning

My husband and I are both big people, and my first child, Jamie, was nine pounds and nine ounces. Very healthy—scored a perfect ten on his Apgar. In some sense, it was a typical birth. I was in labor about ten hours and delivered in the hospital in Key West. I was the only one giving birth that particular night, and other than my husband, there was only one nurse and my doctor. And even though it was a hospital, I felt that the experience was emotionally intimate—our own private world. Personally, I appreciate hospitals because you never know what can go wrong. My best friend chose to have her babies at home—midwives, the whole natural scene. But I always tell her, "I love impersonal care; I love to have my sheets changed by a nurse I don't know." Many people don't like the rather cold environment of a hospital, but I do. And I like doctors. I mean that I trust them—and that's good, because as you know, my second birth was not so successful. . . .

When Jamie was about a year and a half, we planned our next pregnancy. I had no trouble conceiving and had the illusion, like so many others, that I had life under control. I was very active and kept working. At twenty-five weeks, I went for a sonogram and found out that the baby was a boy. The ultrasound looked great. I remember watching the baby move his little arms and legs about. There was nothing to indicate anything was wrong.

Two days later, however, I was working in my home office, typing away at the computer, when I had the unmistakable feeling that my water had broken. With my first child, that's the way labor began, so I had the immediate sense that something was very wrong. In fact, my husband was in the next room, but I reached for the phone and called the doctor. My husband and I are very close, but I knew something was seriously wrong.

It was 3:15 in the afternoon, on a Thursday. We woke Jamie from his nap and all three of us went to the doctor's office. They did an ultrasound in his office and found a tear in the membrane. Then they ran some blood tests to check for infection. I knew it was bad. I was twenty-five weeks into the pregnancy, and there was a viable child inside me. I couldn't write this off as a miscarriage. This was a baby. And yet I had done enough reading to understand that twenty-five weeks is a really precarious time.

The doctor sent me home for complete bed rest. I was told not to even raise my head. The membrane can't regenerate, but it can seal itself. There wasn't any sign of infection at this point, but, of course, we didn't have all the results of the blood tests, either. I went home to bed. The doctor could have sent me to the mainland, and in retrospect, maybe he should. We're three hours away from the rest of the world in Key West and, to tell you the truth, I wouldn't have wanted to be away from my one-and-a-half-year-old. I wasn't ready to fly anywhere unnecessarily. So I went to bed for the next two days. My friends came over to cook meals and help out. I even began to put ads in the paper for a nanny. I had to lie flat on my back; I could only get up to use the bathroom. But no showers, no sitting up, no working. It was hard for me; I'm a bit of a workaholic.

Two days later, sure enough, I broke out in a high fever. It was an infection, and much worse than we had imagined—a Group B strep infection, sepsis, all throughout my bloodstream. The doctor told us to get on a plane and go to Miami to the large hospital there. This was so frightening. I had to get on a commercial flight and fly to the mainland for special care. The infant was going to have to come out, and here in Key West there's no perinatal care. It was going to be much safer to transport this child in my womb than any other way, so off we went.

I was running 104 and feeling very dizzy. We had to literally go down to the airport, buy tickets and not let anyone know what was really going on. They wouldn't have let me on to the airplane if they had any idea about my condition, but this was quicker than getting some type of medical aircraft down here. So we got on the plane, arrived in Miami, and had to get a taxi to take us to the hospital, which is about an hour away.

And this is all happening on a rainy Saturday night during Memorial Day weekend. Worst-case scenario. Up in the plane, I began to have contractions, and by now I'm fully in labor. But we didn't tell the cab driver; we were afraid he wouldn't want us. I remember sitting in the back of the cab and watching the meter—the contractions were coming *one dollar* apart.

My doctor had phoned ahead and made arrangements. A neonatal specialist and a full crew were waiting for me at the hospital. After I was admitted, the doctor who greeted me was Jamaican. I remember his lovely, lilting voice. Immediately I felt safe. I knew that I had excellent care because this was such a specialized facility. We were going to try a natural labor as I had had with my first. But then, the doctor realized that the baby was breech and that it was best to do a C-section.

I had a lot of emotions. At first, I just wanted to get the birth over with because my husband and I both had accepted that this was the end—the end of my pregnancy. And the end of the baby, as well. But at the hospital I became hopeful and wanted to deliver. Then when the news came that the baby was breech, I just wanted to be done.

During my two days of bed rest, I had read every book imaginable on high-risk pregnancies, so I had given myself a quick education. At that time, I was thinking that I'd be spending the rest of the summer in bed. I imagined myself reading, writing, and having a wonderful nanny to take care of my toddler. But when the fever broke out I was so very ill—nauseous, hot, shaking—and my optimism left me. And now, I just kept going back and forth.

By the time I learned that the baby was breech, I wasn't feeling very optimistic or strong. I was frightened. But I wanted the C-section because the baby would be out quickly. I remember after the decision was made, my husband and I were left together for a few minutes. We have a lot of love, and alone there, all of a sudden, we faced ourselves and decided that we were not the kind of people to go into a situation negatively. We decided to expect the best. Up to this point, we hadn't selected a name for the baby. I don't believe in naming a child after he's born. Children should come into the world named and expected. So we decided to name our son. Our first reaction was

to pick one of our father's names—names we don't really like but feel obli-
gated to honor. That way, if the baby died, we wouldn't have to live long with
the name. But instead, we decided to pick a name that we truly loved. We
named him William Cody.

We had the surgery, and my husband was with me the whole time. I was
awake, and there were about fifteen strangers attending—all specialists of
one sort or another. It was rather beautiful in its own peculiar way. Even in
all the trauma and the uncertainty of not knowing what was going to happen, it was still childbirth. We were given the opportunity to have this second child. I remember thinking, whatever else happens in our lives, I have
given birth twice.

Afterwards, the baby was whisked away. No one reported to us on the
baby's health. I was in a lot of pain that whole first night. I was exhilarated
because at this point the baby was alive, and I really couldn't give myself a
chance to think any more. I allowed myself to take as many painkillers as I
could, and I was on intravenous antibiotics, as well. So I just slept and
thought happy things.

The next morning, a barrage of specialists began pouring in to tell me
that the baby almost didn't make it through the night. They had to do emergency procedures several times, and he was facing this surgery and that
surgery. Then a social worker came in and asked us if we were ready to cope
with the death of a child. We told her to get the hell out. She was so adamant
on trying to sit down and really talk, but we weren't ready to hear the things
that she was saying. We had a few arguments with her during the week
because she kept telling us how we ought to be handling things. We're pretty
confident in ourselves and felt we didn't need her. We needed to trust our
own instincts.

In fact, during this week, against medical advice, I decided to check
myself out of the hospital and go back to Key West for a short visit. I needed
to celebrate being a mother again, to let everyone know and congratulate
me. I wanted to see my toddler. It was the right decision. I went home and
came back to the hospital in a day's time. In our eyes, the social worker was
wrong; this visit was a way for me to take care of myself emotionally.

The baby did die. He was born with many problems and would have
been terribly handicapped, but it was the infection that killed him. We're
somewhat religious, and I think that we would have been perfect parents to
deal with a handicapped child. Who knows what I'll have to deal with in the

future. The baby lived for ten days, and because he was still alive on our last night at the hospital, we were served a steak, lobster, and champagne dinner for new parents. We took two hours to sit and giggle over champagne and just enjoy what we had—however tentative.

Looking back now, I don't blame anyone. When something goes wrong, anywhere in life, we all want to find the reason, or be able to blame someone, find a scapegoat. But I've gone over and over this whole experience, and really searched myself. I don't believe anyone was at fault. In fact, the only question I really have is about whether we kept the baby alive too long.

With this pregnancy right now, I've even gone back to the same doctor. I still trust him. I can take him photocopied material that I've researched about strep infections, and he sometimes teases me and asks, "Who's the doctor here?"

Sometimes I worry about this baby. Ironically, he has *the exact same due date* as William Cody did a year ago. My mother died the first month of this pregnancy, and with all the hormonal changes of early pregnancy, I just couldn't shake the blues. I couldn't even tell people I was pregnant. I was crying in the middle of meals, and feeling very sorry for myself. Then, after about a week of crying, I just woke up one morning, looked at my husband and said, "This is exhausting! Let's call everybody up and tell them I'm pregnant. After all, a new life is coming. . . ."

𝕏𝒪

Lisa and her husband, Keith, live in a small town in Arkansas with their three children: Rebecca, age seven; Noelle, age four; and Emily, age one and a half. Lisa is a stay-at-home mom who home schools, but she had been studying to become a marriage and family counselor before having children. Keith is in food sales. Here Lisa discusses her first pregnancy, which resulted in a full-term stillbirth.

The Experience Was Taken from Me

I became pregnant during my first full-time year in college. Before that I had gone part-time and had taken exams to pass out of some freshman courses.

Keith and I weren't married at the time of conception. I was living in the dorms, and Keith, who is older and had come back to school, had an apartment off campus. It was a scary time. Both Keith and I are from Christian homes and pregnancy wasn't something that I thought would happen to me. I wasn't ignorant, but I was naive.

Keith and I had planned to get married, so we decided to move up the wedding date. We went and talked to my parents—we didn't want to keep anything from them because, sooner or later, the truth always comes out. I knew that everything was going to work out okay because we had a real relationship. I knew that Keith was going to be there, and that added some stability. My parents were very supportive. They went ahead and paid for a wedding 'cause they knew Keith and trusted him. They were really good and there for us. They knew that kids just sometimes mess up. Keith had lived away from home for several years, so whatever he decided to do was fine with his parents. They weren't very involved in his life at that point.

I was still attending classes and going for prenatal checkups at the health department, where all the care is free. We didn't have much money and didn't have health insurance. I don't know if this is true in all states, but in Arkansas the health department can only take you up to the last month. So, at the end, we went to a doctor I'd known almost my whole life.

I was very young and trusted that the doctor would just take care of everything. He would let me know what to expect and would be there to handle things. I think a lot of first-time moms feel that way. We live in a society where that's what you see: the doctor is the person who knows what needs to be done and then gives you your baby.

The people at the health department did as much as they could do to offer good care—they were trying. I remember having a nagging feeling though that there were questions that weren't being asked. But I didn't know what those questions were. When I'd see the doctor, it was very brief—your standard ten minutes. He'd ask how you were feeling and if there was anything going on. Not much rapport there. And I didn't know there were other roads we could take.

I was nauseous for the first three months, but once that passed, physically I was fine. Keith and I married in May when I was four months. And it was five months after we were married that I lost the baby. But throughout the pregnancy we had no indication that there were going to be any problems ahead.

Once Keith and I had a game plan and knew what we were going to do, we were really excited. Of course, I had some ambivalent feelings because I wanted to have a career before I became a mother and had a houseful of children. But once I got through the disappointment of becoming pregnant so soon and under these circumstances, I became very excited.

Keith is a very calm and private person. He's not a man who wears his heart on his sleeve. I think he was kind of scared about the responsibility, but he also was looking forward and was excited about the baby.

I went to the standard hospital class. At that time, the class wasn't so much about birth as it was about what to expect from the hospital. I remember my mom gave me an old copy of *Childbirth without Fear*. That book and the hospital course were the only preparation I had. I finished the school year and got married. We settled into an apartment together, and I went to summer school and took classes part-time that fall. I had a two-day-a-week schedule, and planned to complete the semester even after the baby came in October.

Towards the end, I had a lot of the standard feelings and expectations: the wanting to hurry up and get things ready, the uncertainty about what birth was really like, a sense of *can I do this?* Of course we were very busy. Keith was working full-time and taking a couple of classes, and I was in school. We were constantly getting things ready and doing what had to be done every day.

I went into labor on a Friday night. I had been gone all evening, doing school stuff for a club. When I came in, I went straight to bed. By three in the morning I woke up and knew something was going on. I wasn't having contractions and I wasn't in labor; I was feeling kind of achy. I didn't know what contractions felt like, and I thought that maybe the achiness had something to do with labor. I got up and walked around, but it didn't go away. I was thinking that I had laid down too long and that the walking might help. I wasn't in pain or hurting; it was just a real low, dull ache. After fifteen or twenty minutes of feeling real uncomfortable, I woke Keith up. I just kind of figured that this must be time to go to the hospital.

When we arrived, they hooked me up to a fetal monitor and tried to listen to the baby's heart tones. Nothing was very consistent. They'd hear something and then not. And, at first I thought I could feel the baby moving around a lot, but then there was nothing. Well, the first nurse tried to find the heartbeat, and after a few times said, "I'm not sure what to do. Let me go get my supervisor." The supervisor came, and I remember him saying that he didn't want to make any judgment calls—that it wasn't his place.

I remember lying there and thinking, *They have to be wrong. This kind of thing just doesn't happen anymore.* My doctor came in and couldn't find anything with the Doplar or fetal heart monitor. So he ordered an ultrasound and we went down for that. There was no fetal movement at all. If he had found that the baby was alive, he was going to do an emergency C-section. But there was no fetal movement at all. I remember him looking at us and saying, "I think we're looking at a stillbirth." Of course, he was sorry it was that way, but he also knew that there wasn't anything he could do about it.

This is nothing that anybody plans for—surely, it was the furthest thing from our minds. I think he could tell that we didn't really know what to do, so he just took charge of the situation and made decisions for us as far as how to proceed with the birth and what would be best.

He decided to use Pitocin and induce labor. But he also felt like it would be too much for me to be awake and have those memories, so I don't know what they used, but I was asleep though the whole birth. At the time, I probably would have chosen the exact same thing. But I think now that I wish I had been awake because these are the only memories I have of that baby—memories I could have had but don't have now. I could be wrong, but now that I have experienced birth, I think that these memories would have helped me to feel like not everything was being taken from me. I felt like my baby and the whole experience of her birth was being taken from me.

When I got home from the hospital there were a lot of self-esteem issues for me. It's the same for most women who lose babies. You kind of feel like, theoretically, this is what women are made for; this is what our bodies are designed for. And after you lose a baby, you feel like you're a failure as a woman. I struggled with that feeling until I had other babies. That is what helped me to heal. Since then, I've had two home births, and these were a kind of vindication for losing the first child.

I only have snippets of memory. I remember Keith being there when I woke up for a moment during labor. I remember being taken from a labor room into a delivery room and transferring from one bed to another. When I woke up, I was in the recovery room. My sister and mom were there, and there were cousins, and my aunt from Memphis, who must have driven in. The nurse brought me the baby and asked if I wanted to hold it. But right then I couldn't; it was too much to do. I didn't know if it was a boy or girl—I then found out that it was a girl. We named her Holly Amanda.

Arkansas law required us to have a funeral. Later, when we were at the funeral home—maybe two days after the birth—I did go and hold the baby. I still was just so overwhelmed and sad that even then I couldn't hold her for very long. And that's the one thing I wish I could have done—held her more.

I'm sure that the hospital has a social worker, but we didn't cross paths. Later, I had some women from church who had also lost babies make contact with me. There was one woman who, a week after the birth, came over and sat in my house and waited until I was ready to talk. That was very, very good.

They gave me pills to suppress lactation, which worked for about a week, and then my milk came in anyway. That was a very fresh reminder. I was sore because they had done an episiotomy, and I had stitches. I just had a real difficult postpartum experience. Not that I had a major postpartum depression or anything. We have a lot of friends, mostly college-age, and although they didn't really know what to do, they did come to the graveside service. There were so many people there. Many from the church I had grown up in and still attended. I got lots of support. They brought food, and for a couple of weeks I didn't have to attend classes. No one expected much from me, so I had a period where I didn't have to deal with life on a day-to-day basis. My sister would come and do our laundry. I was really given time to grieve.

It took me a while to enjoy sex again—maybe six months. I was just scared of the possibility of getting pregnant again. There was a lot of ambivalence there. I had this huge ache to have a baby because I lost one. And even though I had gotten pregnant at a time when we didn't plan to have a baby, we had gone through an entire pregnancy, and had those expectations there. Part of me wanted to feel that again. I mean, I knew that we were not going to have *that* baby again, but here I was with the body of a woman who has just had a baby, and I knew what it was like to have life inside me. I just wanted to complete the cycle.

At the same time, I was very scared that it could happen again. The one decision that we were able to make was not to have an autopsy. It had been enough to lose the baby; I couldn't stand the thought of someone cutting on her. Maybe that wasn't the right decision because her death left a lot of questions unanswered. But then again, at the funeral home when I was finally ready to hold her, she looked like an intact baby.

Based on the knowledge that the doctors had, they felt like there were probably some congenital heart problems. They felt that if Holly had lived she would have needed a lot of surgeries. That opened the question of whether her problems were genetic. But our doctor was very reassuring. I remember him saying that he couldn't tell beyond a shadow of a doubt what had happened, but he really wanted us to know that he believed we'd be able to go on and have healthy babies. He said that I had labored well, delivered well, and that there was nothing in us that suggested this would ever happen again. He told us that the statistical chances of this happening again were even lower than before. Early miscarriage does tend to repeat itself, but a late term stillbirth usually doesn't. After about a year, we decided to try to get pregnant. It didn't take us long at all. We tend to be rather fertile.

The doctor never allowed us to pay for his services. They knew that we were hurting financially, and things were tight because we were still in school and the pregnancy had been unexpected. Both the manager of the medical center and the doctor who delivered me were men I had known for most of my life. Under the circumstances, they just forgave us the charges. We owed the hospital about two thousand dollars, and we paid that back over a couple of years. As long as we made the minimum payment every month, they were fine.

As I've gone through the process of having other babies, there were a lot of emotional struggles I went through having to do with issues of self-esteem. Most women who have had problems like mine feel the same way, I believe. As I said before, you kind of feel like having babies is what women's bodies are designed for. After you don't do this successfully, you feel like a failure. Having my other babies helped me to heal. I think that's why I've done two home births; they're a kind of vindication for losing that first baby.

The scariest thing about having my next baby was that I still didn't know what to expect. All I had known during my first experience was that women had their babies in hospitals. There were Lamaze classes, but no Bradley classes offered in my community. There's not a freestanding birthing center. I felt like that my entire first experience was taken from me, and the second time around, I still didn't know what to expect.

There's still a lot of sadness. When October 10 comes, I always remember that that was the day we went to the hospital and thought we were going to have a baby and came home without one.

The loss of the baby was a daily presence for the first year or two. But with time, life does go on. And it doesn't mean that you forget. It doesn't mean that you're not aware that this experience is part of your life. It's hard to explain: the loss of my baby is still there, but it's just not in front of me all the time.

I remember those difficult first years. I would see people with babies about the same age as Holly would have been, and I'd think, *I should have had a baby that age. I should have a child that size with me.* I don't do that anymore. But October is sometimes still a difficult month for us, and every year Keith and I spend time discussing it.

Keith has really been there for me. That whole first year, anytime I needed to cry, he was there. I would ask him, "Okay, tell me again what happened and give me the run of events. What happened after I was asleep?" We'd have entire conversations where he'd just tell me who was there, who came and went.

And then, after that first year, we kind of did a role reversal. There's no real support in our society for men who need to deal with their feelings, so it was my turn to take care of him for a while. He also felt like the baby had been taken from him. But at the time, he had to deal with me and all the practical things as well: he had to make funeral arrangements; he had to find someone to pick out clothes for her to be buried in; he had to go home and put away all the baby things we'd set up. He had to be the strength for so long. It's amazing that neither of us had a major depression. Looking back, I wish I'd been given more choices. That's the major thing. And I also wish that people would not tell grieving parents that their loss is God's will. It really disturbs me to hear that. It's hard enough to deal with death, but to try to figure out why it happened is overwhelming. People need to come to their own conclusions based on their beliefs and on their needs. When death occurs and people need to comfort one another, it's better to say nothing, or even admit that you don't know what to say rather than to say it was God's will.

&

Jeannie has two sons: Logan, age five, and Connor, age three. Jeannie is a Mary Kay representative and this flexible job gives her a sense of independence, yet allows her to remain focused on her children. Jeannie's husband, David, is in the air force. The birth of her second son, Connor, recollected here, took place in Phoenix, Arizona.

Miracle Baby

About six weeks early, I woke at two o'clock in the morning and found myself having contractions. I went to the bathroom, lay down, and an hour later, I nudged my husband and said, "Honey, I'm going to drive over to the clinic. I must be dehydrated." That had happened with my first son, and once they rehydrated me, labor stopped.

We were living in Arizona, at Williams Air Force Base, and there was a tiny clinic on the base where I was scheduled to have the baby. When I arrived, they hooked me up to the monitor and said, "Oh, my gosh! You're in labor—we don't have the facilities to handle a baby this early." So they tried to rehydrate me, but as soon as they put the IV in, I started to go to the bathroom. I wasn't dehydrated. Then, my water broke. And, of course, they panicked. My husband was still at home because Logan was sleeping. But when this happened, we got him on the phone and said, "Get up here!" They put me on a drug to stop labor. It works great, but it makes you vomit like crazy. They stuck me on an ambulance. I threw up the whole hour's trip to Good Samaritan Hospital in Phoenix, which is also Phoenix Children's Hospital. It's an excellent facility. They had a team of high-risk doctors waiting for me. Immediately, they did an ultrasound and said, "There's very little fluid, you've definitely lost your sack." I was dilated to seven centimeters already. They told me, "We're going to have to let you deliver. The bad news is that the baby is small—only about four pounds. The good news is that we have a level-three nursery. There's very few of them in the country. We can handle this. Don't worry." So they took me off the medicine that stopped labor. It was very frightening. I felt guilty that I hadn't gained enough weight, and somehow felt responsible for this early labor.

Off the medicine, we all expected labor to hit hard again. But it never came back. They sent me up to a room to wait it out. Five days later, the tear in my sack had resealed and my water had regenerated. I was sent home. While I was still there, I talked to the doctor and asked, "How often have you seen this happen?" And he said, "I've been in high-risk obstetrics for thirty years, and I've never seen it happen." There was no infection; everything seemed magically alright again. But in the process, I was transferred to the high-risk team for the remainder of my pregnancy.

At a certain point, they sent me to have an ultrasound, and they found a heart defect in the baby. They didn't know exactly what was wrong, but they diagnosed it as Ebstein's anomaly, which is serious, but normally doesn't require surgery immediately after birth. Usually, these babies will be okay for days or even months before requiring surgery. Ebstein's anomaly is a malformation of the tricuspid valve in the heart. We were both very scared. I prayed a lot. We were very confident in the facility, and we put our faith in God and then plunged forward. They did amniocentesis before they let me leave the hospital to see if the baby's lungs were ready. They were not. After that, every few days to a week they would do amniocentesis again to check if the baby's lungs were ready; with a small baby, it is essential that the lungs be strong.

After I was released, I had to return to the hospital every week—the trip was over an hour in traffic. Amniocentesis is very uncomfortable, more so psychologically than physically. We had to check the numbers on the amnio that indicate lung maturity. They kept getting better. They were planning to induce me because I was now such a high risk that they wanted to have a whole team present at the birth. When I was about three weeks from my due date the doctor said, "I think we'll be good to go in a few days. Let's do it on Wednesday. I don't think we need another amnio."

But I felt funny about being this early. I told the doctor, "I just feel that we need to have a positive lung study before we induce. Would you mind if we did one more?" And he said, "No, that would be just fine." So we did one more, and it wasn't good. We weren't ready. The doctor said, "Oops, I guess you were right!"

So we waited a few more days and finally got a positive lung study. And as it turned out, because Connor was born with a defect, it really did prove essential that his lungs were strong. He had to go right to surgery after birth and if his lungs had been weak, he wouldn't have made it. Looking back, I feel that I was cared for very well—by God and by everyone. I believe that this entire experience was in some sense miraculous. My belief is that God was looking out for us and that, for some reason, he saw to it that Connor is here. I can't say why babies die. I can't say why some children go to be with him when they're infants and some go to be with him at ninety. I don't have anything to say to people who have miscarriages or experience other forms of seemingly irrational losses, but I believe that there's a reason why Connor is here. I don't know why my water sack resealed, or why intuitively I knew that we needed another lung study, but I can't help but believing that God's hand was at work.

Connor didn't have Ebstein's anomaly as they first suspected. If he did have that problem, being born without lung maturity wouldn't have really mattered. But he had another problem which required immediate surgery after birth. And he wouldn't have made it through surgery without properly developed lungs. I just think that's amazing.

At any rate, we went in to be induced. We went to the birthing room with the understanding that when the baby crowned I'd have to move to an operating room. The birthing room didn't have the equipment to deliver a high-risk baby. By the time I got to the birthing room, my sack of water was bulging so bad that they couldn't believe it hadn't broken. The doctor decided to break it and see what would happen. It was 11:00 A.M. At 2:00 that afternoon, he came in and said, "This isn't going well; you're not progressing." I said, "I'm having contractions." And the doctor said, "Look, you're playing cards with your husband; you're not progressing!" He told me that we were going to have to begin a Pitocin drip. For some reason, I was terrified of Pitocin. I pleaded with him to let me go a while longer, but he said no. David and I joked that he wanted to get off to the golf course. When he left the room, I started to cry. David held me. I kept saying, "I don't want Pitocin!" And I prayed about it. Literally, "Please God, please, let my body do something so I don't have to have this Pitocin." Then amen, wham! I had a contraction that knocked me back on the bed. And David, goes, "No—you're kidding!" Connor was born just twenty-eight minutes from that first big contraction. Later, we realized that the baby couldn't have tolerated a long labor. But we didn't know that at the time.

Connor was born directly into the hands of the neonatologist. The first thing I heard was, "Come on, baby, come on baby!" I just lay there. They were trying to get me to deliver the afterbirth, but I just kept thinking, he's gonna die, he's gonna die—yet all I heard were these voices trying to get him to live.

He was dark blue when he came out. As soon as they got him breathing, they ran him over and stuck him by my face. The neonatologist said, "Kiss him, mom, I've got to go." I kissed him, and they ran out of the room.

I got the afterbirth delivered and went to recovery. David went to the nursery, and I thought, *Oh God, something's wrong.* When David came back, he told me that the baby was okay. I told him something was wrong. David said, "Yes, he has a heart defect, but he's doing okay."

When I left recovery, they wheeled me by the intensive care nursery, and he was right near the door. I met the neonatologist, a woman, and she told me that he was breathing on his own, but oxygenating only 70 percent of his blood. She wanted to intubate him.

They wheeled me up to my room. We began to call everybody to tell them I had delivered, and the baby was on air, but okay. Then at 6:00, the neonatologist came, clasped her hands behind her back and said, "We're losing him. We don't know what's wrong. . . ."

I didn't hear another word she said. I grabbed the phone and started calling members of my family. "Jenny, the baby's dying, pray. . . . Dad, the baby's dying, pray. . . ." One after another—everyone I could think of.

As it turned out, what had happened was they thought the pulmonary artery that leads to the lungs had clamped down. They were giving him drugs to relax it, and he wasn't responding. There was very little blood getting to his lungs. And he kept getting worse. Less and less blood was getting through. The pediatric heart is tremendously different than the adult heart in that there's a lot of holes and passageways. In the womb the baby's blood doesn't have to go to the lungs because the mother oxygenates it. There are passageways that allow the blood to escape or bypass the lungs. Soon after birth, those passageways close down because the baby has to oxygenate his own blood. Well, with my son, as those passageways closed down, he got less and less blood. What we later discovered was that his pulmonary valve was sealed shut. The only significant amount of blood getting to his lungs was escaping backwards through a connection off the aorta. It was a fluke that he was getting any blood. As nature took its course, this passageway, the ductus arteriosis, began to close, and the baby began to fail more and more.

They couldn't see the blocked valve. All they knew was that nothing was going through the tricuspid artery. That was at about 6:00. We went downstairs and the doctor talked to us and she told us that she had tried different drugs to relax his artery, but nothing was working. "The cardiologists," she said, "are looking at it. The bottom line is that we can't figure out what's going on and he's dying."

Immediately, I asked to speak with the psychologist and told her, "I'm losing a baby and I need to know how to do this right." I needed to know if I should hold him while he's still living or wait until he's gone. She said that most people want to hold their baby while the baby is still alive and then again after it's gone.

And so we planned it. They told us our baby was dying. And as I prayed with all my might that he wouldn't, the logical, practical part of me had to cope with the reality. And coping involved figuring out how we were going to deal with this death. I called my father. My mother had passed away when I was young. And we talked about a burial plot and if there was room out where Mom is.

Meanwhile, the doctor came up to explain a new experimental treatment called ECMO—extracorporeal membrane oxygenation—in which they remove one carotid artery to take the blood out of the baby, put it through a machine which cleans it, oxygenates it, and put it back in. This can cut off the blood supply to one side of the brain, affecting the motor skills. There are interconnections with blood flow between the left and right sides of the brain. Most children do well, but in a small percentage, the interconnection is incomplete and this can lead to a loss of blood flow and brain damage similar to a stroke. It's impossible to tell which children might have problems. Some babies come through fine; others go deaf or are unable to control parts of their bodies. The neonatologist said, "I don't know what's wrong with your baby. We're trying desperately to figure it out. This procedure is experimental. We don't have any beds here for this; our ECMO machines are full. But we could get you in Texas. Walter Reed Hospital will come with a team. They have the only mobile ECMO team, and they'll hook the baby up and fly out there."

My husband looked at me, and the doctor added, "This kind of treatment tears your family apart. And it might just be prolonging the inevitable because we don't know what's wrong. This decision has to be yours."

She also told us that about 80 percent of all couples that go through experiences like this wind up in divorce as a direct result—because of what they saw in each other during a moment of crisis. She told us that it's really important for us to be a family right now. She said, "This baby may make it, or this baby may not, but you guys were here first. And you have to think of your other son. He matters." She added, "I can't tell you what to do."

It was the hardest decision we ever had to make. And we decided against it. We felt he needed to go peacefully if he was going to die.

The doctor was very supportive. And so at about 11:00 at night, she said, "You guys need to get some sleep. I'll call you if anything changes." We were given a private room.

We cried and cried. And we prayed and prayed, but finally, I didn't know what to pray for. Do I pray for healing? What if it's not God's will? What if He has something else in mind? So, I came to the conclusion that I needed to pray for God's will to be done.

The most miraculous thing of this entire ordeal was the incredible peace we felt that night. We slept all night. After praying, we both had this tremendous sense that whatever happened, our baby would be alright. If he went to heaven, he'd be in the loving arms of God. Can you ask anything better for somebody? This night changed our perspective on death. We were given such a clear vision of Connor in God's arms.

We got a call at about 6:00 A.M. the next morning. The doctor said that Connor had made it through the night, but was going fast. We ran down to be with him. She said that his pressure was falling, and that I needed to hold him. She said, "I've done everything I can do." Then she added, "Cardiology wants to take one last look." And I brightened. But she said, "Jeannie, they've already done three echocardiograms. We're out of time. We're losing him." I hesitated. She said, "You told me that you wanted to hold this baby alive. Here's your last chance." I asked, "Could my holding him kill him in his condition right now?" She said, "I can't tell you it won't. He's so fragile; he's barely here." And I told her, "I'm sorry, but as long as one more person wants to look, I can't take the risk of killing him." Then, she got up real close to me and said, "Do you realize that you've giving up what is probably your last chance to hold this baby alive?" And I said, "I know, I know." She said, "Well, okay. I'll call you when cardiology is done or when he's gone. Go to your room."

David and I got a cup filled with water and baptized him. We made the sign of the cross over his forehead and prayed over him. I kissed him. Then we went up to our room to wait. We were quietly sobbing.

Then the next thing we knew, the door to my room flew open so hard that it hit the wall. The neonatologist and the cardiologist ran into the room yelling, "We figured out what's wrong, and we think we can fix it."

It was a roller coaster. After surgery, first the cardiologist came up to tell us the good news that Connor had made it off the heart-and-lung machine. And then the surgeon came in and said, "Your baby is very sick. I don't know if he's going to make it." Naively, David and I thought that once the surgery was over, everything would be fine.

But it wasn't. Connor's medical problems continued. We stayed at the Ronald McDonald House and had a beeper. We lived there for about two weeks. Then, about four weeks after his birth, they released him. He wasn't gaining weight in the hospital, so they let me take him home.

He went home without any monitors—only two medicines, a diuretic and a heart medication. I had started pumping breast milk in the hospital after he was born. They were telling me that he was dying, and I'd be sitting there with a breast pump. I kept telling my husband that if this baby makes it, I want to be ready.

At about four months, his heart muscle had softened to the point where he was able to oxygenate 99 percent of his blood. The doctors were astounded. Now, his heart is so close to a normal heart that only an expert could tell there had been a problem. Connor is three years old. He does everything. He's "supposed" to be mentally retarded. He's not. His doctor says that he'll live to be eighty or ninety with the heart that he has. He might, they say, end up with a learning disability, but somehow I don't think so. He says his ABCs.

Seven

TWO OR MORE

ॐ

WITH THE INCREASED AVAILABILITY of fertilization treatments, more women are giving birth to multiples—two or more babies. In this section, we'll meet three women—two who deliver twins, and one who delivers triplets—as they respond to the challenges associated with the special "gift" of preparing for and giving birth to multiples.

ॐ

Rachel is a stay-at-home mother who lives with her husband, Bob, and their three children: Christopher, age three years, and fraternal twins, Callie and Jeremy, age nine months. Originally from Sacramento, California, the family moved to Memphis, Tennessee, where Bob works as a restaurant manager. The twins, whose births are described here, were born in Memphis.

Chosen for Twins

My husband, Bob, came out here to Memphis to train for his present job as a restaurant manager. He had to live away from Christopher and me for almost three months. We decided over the phone that as soon as we were able to come out here and join him, we'd try to get pregnant. It didn't happen the first month, but it did the second. We didn't have any problems conceiving.

With Christopher, I had gone to a doctor, but I was upset with the lack of personal care. There was never really any way for me to talk to this doctor about how I felt—it was all about the physical pregnancy. This second time around, I decided to go to a nurse-midwife—I wanted something different. Also, I objected to the atmosphere in the hospital and everything that "had" to be done—the lack of choices.

I went out looking for a midwife even before I knew I was pregnant. It was very difficult; I had to actually call the Board of Nurse-Midwifery, the association that certifies them in Washington, D.C., to get a name, because there are only two who practice in the entire Memphis area, and I found that they practice together.

I was pretty dedicated to the idea, and Bob wanted whatever I wanted. He left this decision mostly up to me. But as the pregnancy went on, he really got close to the midwives because they included him—which was very different from our first experience.

In the beginning of my pregnancy I was very sick and lost about twenty-two pounds. Everybody said, "It's because it's a girl." We never had any reason to think I was having twins. There's often a hereditary factor in fraternal twins, but this is the first set on either side of the family for at least eight or ten generations. Before that, we don't have any record. Also, I'm only twenty-five; if I were older or taking fertility drugs, that would up my chances. So it was definitely unusual and unexpected.

My nausea lasted from about the third or fourth week of my pregnancy to the end of my first trimester. It was a hard time for me. Thankfully, my toddler could entertain himself, but being so sick I couldn't get out a lot to develop relationships. We were very new in the community. Once the nausea let up, I got involved with LaLeche League because I wanted to nurse this next baby and had had difficulty with my first. This helped me to connect.

So, from three months to six—before I learned I was having twins—was trouble-free. I remember the day that we found out. My husband didn't have to go in to work until late, so he was able to come with me on this appointment. When they measured me, I had grown eight centimeters—I was only supposed to have grown four. They decided to do an ultrasound because they thought I might be further along than originally thought. The midwife said, kind of joking, "Or it could be twins." I laughed and was like, *Yeah, right! Whatever!*

I went to a separate clinic that does just ultrasounds. My husband went in with me but had to leave because he was going to be late for work. I ended up having the ultrasound by myself—as he left, they took me in.

When the technician started, she began scanning me and said, "Wow, you have a really large placenta." And I said, "That's good, as long as there's only one baby attached." She said, "Oh, yeah, there's only one." Then she moved to the other side and said, "Nope, there's two." Every hair stood up on my body, and I said, "You have to stop!" If I'd not been lying on that table, there's no doubt I would have passed out right on the floor! It had never crossed my mind that I could be having twins. But there they were—it was so amazing.

My husband was supposed to pick me up, so I was sitting in the waiting room. Everybody knew what had happened, and as soon as Bob walked in, they all looked at him and started smiling. He just looked at me and said, "It's twins." I said, "Yup!" Bob sat down in a chair and kind of went, "Whoa." That morning will certainly go down in the history books for us.

Our lives changed drastically after that. I mean, we were prepared to have *a baby,* and were planning on using Christopher's baby things. We weren't ready for the financial impact. Also, I'm the kind of person who likes to read about everything, so that day I went to the library and checked out every book that had the word "twins" in it. I read and I read, which was good in a way, but it scared me. I mean, the first thing you always read about when you're having twins is that they're often premature. It scared me for a long time. And I did have bouts of preterm labor, so it was a very real thing. That imminent fear definitely changed the way we looked at things and how we did things. And it changed what I was able to do physically.

First off, I couldn't lift, and my three-year-old didn't like that. Then, I had to take it easy, and I don't take restrictions very well. I was constantly feeling ambivalent. On one hand, I felt lucky to be part of this small group of women who have twins—it's just such a neat thing. But on the other hand, it was taking over my life.

Bob has a very high-stress job, and he was concerned about the financial impact of twins and concerned about my health. This was a lot of stress on him. We didn't know what the future was going to hold. For a long time, we'd go very up and then very down.

Thankfully, I became involved with a twins group here in Memphis right after that first ultrasound. My nurse-midwife hooked me up with them. I went to their next meeting, which was just a few days after I found out. And

I still go. They're a big inspiration and have helped me to deal with a lot. Many of the women there had the same ambivalent feelings, and it's nice to know that you're not alone.

As I got further along, I began to think about birth plans. The midwives brought in a doctor who was, like, automatically wanting me to have an epidural and IV. He felt that if I went into labor and ended up needing a C-section, he wouldn't have to put me under general anesthesia. Or if one of the babies became lodged and they needed forceps, they'd already have the epidural in place.

We came to a lot of compromises. We left the decision about the epidural up to me. I didn't have one with Christopher and didn't want one now. They asked that I deliver in the operating room rather than the birthing room. I said, "Okay, as long as I can have the birthing-room bed there." They agreed. The doctor said that he didn't like having to do a C-section on the birthing bed because it's so low, but he'd do it. I still felt really in control. Even though I was making compromises, they were making compromises, too. They never made me feel like *I had to do anything*.

With Christopher, I attended Lamaze classes. I used some of the breathing but not the external focus they suggest. Instead, I used an internal focus— that just worked better for me. I didn't take another childbirth class, but I did take a breast-feeding class and an epidural class, which covered C-sections. After that, I was even more determined not to have an epidural. My midwives and I agreed to focus on having the twins vaginally and naturally. Both twins had their heads down, so fortunately, they were cooperative, too.

Between my seventh and ninth month I ended up in the hospital four separate times with preterm labor. They gave me Terbutaline shots and put me on anti-labor medicine until I was thirty-seven weeks—which they considered full-term. They expected me to go into labor as soon as they took me off those pills, but I actually went another two weeks.

On January 23, which was my birthday, and about a week and a half after I stopped the medication, I went to the hospital. I was having contractions, not sleeping, and getting very uncomfortable with my size. They gave me a choice: I could either have them that day or go back home to wait. I didn't want to have them on my birthday, so I chose to try to wait a bit longer.

On January 27, just four days later, I came back and they broke my water. It was morning, and they said that I'd probably not have my babies until late afternoon or evening. They said that with twins, it takes a lot longer because of the uterus being so stretched. I tried to tell them that my labor doesn't work that way.

I had my babies two and a half hours later. And it was a fiasco. They broke my water at 10:40, and my first was born at 1:21. Christopher was born fast, too. People are always saying, "Wow, you're so lucky to have had such a fast labor." But I have mixed feelings about it. I knew that this was my last pregnancy, that we weren't going to have any more kids. We only wanted three, and we got our girl. For me, I almost wish it had been a little longer so I'd have more to remember. Maybe that sounds kind of strange. It felt like it went so quickly that it turned into a blur. I'm usually a very outspoken person, but for labor, I get very concentrated and quiet. The screaming and swearing—well, that's not for me. I was still. I had my eyes closed and stayed focused.

They had an external monitor on me and an internal one on the first baby. I was lying down. When they checked me forty minutes after they had broken my water, I was only about three centimeters dilated—which was really not any progress at all because I'd been dilated two for months. But I had effaced. They still thought, *Oh, this is going to take a while!* After an hour, they checked me again—this time I was only at five. But I was starting to feel the contractions more strongly, although they weren't showing up strongly on the monitor. A nurse asked, "Do you want an epidural?" And I said, "Why don't you send the anesthesiologist in, and I'll talk to him." And so she went outside, called him, and he said, "I'll be there in a second." She came back and said, "Let me check you one more time." She reached in and I was fully dilated. She rushed into the hall and yelled, "We'd better get somebody down here right now!"

I was so focused on maintaining control and getting over each contraction that I don't think I really knew how fast they were coming or how strong they were. My doctor was at another hospital delivering, but both midwives from the practice were there with me. I had seen them each during my pregnancy, and I really did get a lot of special attention.

They threw scrubs at Bob and unhooked all the IVs and stuff so they could get me into the OR. And that's when I started feeling the urge to push. I said, "I have to push!" And one midwife said, "Don't push!" Thankfully, they'd put me into the birthing room closest to the OR, so we didn't have a long way to go. Nobody was ready. No doctor was there, no nurses, no anesthesiologist. They were calling on the intercoms: *Any doctor on this floor, get here!*

I said, "Either get me to OR or get me back to the birthing room—this baby's coming!" One of the midwives said, "Push!" meaning for the other midwife to push the bed. And I made a joke, "I thought you said not to push." She said, "I'm not talking to you!" I said, "It's a joke!" She just looked dumbfounded.

They got me into the OR and situated on the bed so I was in a sitting position. They took the bottom half of the bed off and raised the back. The midwife had one glove on, I pushed twice, and that was it for the first baby.

The only people in the room were my husband, the midwives, and one hospital nurse. Callie came first. They let Bob cut the cord, but then whisked her away. That was one of the things I didn't like—I didn't get to hold her. But I understand it was because I still had another baby to deliver. Then, a doctor showed up. He was just doing his rounds and was like, "What's going on?" Then, another doctor showed up, and they just kind of stood around and let the midwives deliver.

They waited for Jeremy to come into the birth canal and then broke my second water. They let him come naturally—they didn't try to force him. About fifteen minutes later, I started to feel that urge to push again. I pushed only once, and out he came! The only problem was that Jeremy had his hands up by his face, so I tore when he came out. I hadn't torn with Callie.

They whisked Jeremy away, too. I didn't get to hold him either. Things were still pretty hectic. With Callie, they originally thought that she was very small and would need medical attention—that why they took her away. Actually, she was six pounds, four ounces and there were no problems. But Jeremy was seven pounds, and they took him away—I don't know why. As soon as the second baby was born, my doctor showed up. We're like, "You're a little late."

They took me back to the birthing room and brought my babies to me there. It was about thirty minutes later. I remember looking at them and thinking how big they were, and wondering how they could fit inside me. I mean, having one baby is a miracle, but twins . . . it's just overwhelming.

I'm a religious person and to see what God can do—bring two lives into the world at the same time—it's very breathtaking. I prayed a lot during my preterm labors. I'd say, "God, I'm not ready for this. Please don't give me these babies right now. If this is what you want, I'll do my best, but I'd really appreciate it if you don't do this now."

I've always believed—and I said this to myself often during my pregnancy—"God never gives you more than you can handle." And I always wondered why he thought I could handle this. I always saw the twins as a blessing, a special gift, and I thought, *What is it about me that makes me so special that I deserve this?*

I don't know if I really ever got an answer. I just became more and more comfortable with the idea of having twins. I think I began to realize what a strong person I could be.

During my pregnancy, I was just focused on bringing the babies to term. I never thought about what it was going to be like afterwards. That was a whole other shock altogether because, all of a sudden, I looked at my husband and these babies were here. I remember saying to Bob, "We've got to take these home."

The initial adjustment was difficult. I tried to breastfeed both of them—it was no fun at all. I never did it exclusively and finally stopped completely after three months. Also, it was very hard at first to think of the babies as individuals and make connections with each. I bonded more easily with Callie than with Jeremy. Perhaps because she's a girl, and Bob and I had been looking forward to having a girl. Also, she had a more easygoing personality. My boy cried more and demanded more attention. This is no longer the case. Now, they take turns. One will be asleep and the other will scream. The next day, it's the opposite.

But it gets easier as they get older. And I still feel very lucky, very blessed. Although it continues to be a learning experience, I feel like I was chosen to be the mother of twins because God thought I could do a good job.

Lisa lives in Spotswood, New Jersey, with her husband, Jeffrey, and their fraternal twins, Joshua and Emily, age five months, and Howard, age five years. Lisa is a stay-at-home mother who used to work as a music therapist before her first pregnancy and then briefly sold Tupperware before the twins came along. Jeffrey is an electrical technician.

Twins—One Vaginal, One by C-Section

For both my pregnancies I had to be on fertility drugs—Clomid and Pergonal. I was going to the fertility clinic at Robert Johnson University

Hospital. When I wanted to get pregnant the second time, I had to wait until I weaned Howard—I couldn't be on these drugs and nurse safely. I got pregnant both times through IUI—interuterine insemination, which is also called artificial insemination.

These drugs are very expensive—thousands of dollars. I agreed to a series of three cycles of fertility treatment. Our insurance didn't cover it all. Also, they involved Jeff giving me injections. It's all very difficult. And now they're even saying that these drugs are linked with ovarian cancer.

During my last cycle with these drugs, I got pregnant. Howard kept saying that he wanted twins—a brother and a sister. But I kept telling him that there might not be any baby, that it might not even happen. Going into this last cycle, this last IUI, the doctors told me that there were three or four eggs that were ready. We hoped for the best. Right after the insemination, they put me on progesterone suppositories—with the idea that I'd be pregnant. I was already on maternal vitamins, and had been for five years.

When I first learned I was pregnant, Howard was with me. And later, at seven and a half weeks, when I learned I was carrying twins, Howard was with me holding my hand! I was kind of prepared, 'cause I knew it was a possibility, but I don't think you're ever really prepared. I was like, *Oh, my God!*

During the two weeks after the IUI procedure, I began to feel a lot of pain. I couldn't stand, couldn't bend, and they were ignoring me. Finally, I went in for a third pregnancy test—I had three tests in a period of a week and a half to make sure that my hormone levels were going up—and the coordinator of the program, a nurse practitioner, said I should be checked. The doctor examined me and found I had major ovarian cysts that were huge. I had to be off my feet so that they wouldn't burst. After a short time, pregnancy hormones level out and the cysts go away, so it's self-correcting. I'd had a little of this when I was pregnant with Howard, but there weren't multiple cysts on both sides. If they had burst, I would have had to have surgery.

Then at eight weeks, I started bleeding very bad. They thought I had a subcorianic hemorrhage, where the placenta began attaching to the uterine wall, and then breaks free. Fortunately, it was on the end of the placenta, so it didn't interfere with the babies' nutrition. But I had to stay off my feet again. I was just starting to feel better from the cysts and then I started bleeding.

Actually, they weren't quite sure early on about what was causing the bleeding. When it began, they thought that one of the babies could be absorbing—like when you lose a baby and it gets reabsorbed. It wasn't that, thankfully.

I was basically on bed rest for my first trimester—three months. I never had much help. I have a very dear friend who would take Howard out for the day on occasion and would bring me things I needed, but that was all. Howard was three and a half. We'd play some games where I'd be lying down, but he went through a period of acting out—tantrums and stuff. It was hard. Jeff, though, was very supportive and sympathetic about what I was going through. He was also worried.

Anyway, after going to the fertility clinic, I began seeing a high-risk obstetrician. We went to the same doctor that delivered Howard. I was up from bed rest in November, and, although I didn't realize it at the time, began to get Braxton-Hicks contractions. The doctor told me that it was too early for them, but that tightening of my abdomen told me otherwise.

By January, I was feeling them so strongly that I'd have to stop in order to breathe. The doctor really started monitoring me, and I had sonograms first every month, then every three weeks. I was much bigger with this pregnancy. With Howard, I didn't need maternity clothes until I was in my eighth month. With the twins, I was big very early.

I also had other discomforts. The babies were hitting my nerves in such a way that I often couldn't feel my legs. Or they were tingling. I had varicose veins that popped up really bad in one leg. I had to keep my legs up for a while, and sometimes the pain would be so bad I couldn't stand it.

With my first pregnancy, with Howard, I loved being pregnant—I loved feeling him and didn't even want him to come out. But these two were so active that I was almost always uncomfortable. And they were always to one side—which we later found the reason for. The nights were especially horrible. I couldn't even turn to move over from side to side. The pain was like ripping paper, like this tearing pain. I dreaded sleeping, and I'd have to get up to pee all the time. I felt like I was walled in.

With Howard, we had used Lamaze, which was awful. This time we used Bradley. I definitely wanted to have a vaginal delivery. I had drugs during Howard's delivery. For these guys, I didn't want to be medicated. The doctor agreed to do a vaginal delivery with the twins because Howard was a vaginal birth—even if one was breech, he said he'd deliver. I wrote out a birth plan: I wanted a vaginal delivery; I didn't want medication; and I didn't want an episiotomy. The doctor who delivered the twins was a female OB; she was aware of my birthing plan and had discussed it with others.

I delivered at Robert Johnson. They have a birthing room, but because I was having twins, I had to use the OR. It's a bigger area, and they needed the room as they had to be double-staffed for two babies. I wasn't comfortable with this, but I didn't have much choice. And the way things ended up happening, I needed to be there.

Based on my last menstrual period, the due date that the doctors originally came up with was May 2. But based on my knowing when I conceived, it was like April 30.

I carried the babies to almost thirty-seven weeks. On a Monday, I had the bloody show—the mucus plug came out on the Monday. I had a sonogram and a non-stress test already planned for that Wednesday, and a doctor was going to do an internal. It was the weekend before Easter and Passover, and I was afraid that the internal would stir things up and I'd go into labor on a holiday weekend. (We were invited to dinner on that Saturday.) I had the tests and the internal, and afterwards the doctor said that I wasn't dilated. The doctor told me I'd probably make it to our Saturday night dinner and through the weekend, but I shouldn't hold him to that.

Emily, they found, was head-down, and Joshua was transverse—lying across. He was on top of her, mostly to one side—and that's why I always felt them there. They were going to be around six pounds each. I had gained about fifty.

Okay, now it's Friday, and I'm in the kitchen, cooking food for Passover. It was going to be a small dinner—no guests. I was really achy, and I just had a feeling. I'd been wanting to get my music out, the music I wanted to listen to during labor. I had two tapes of piano music, written by a music therapist, and I wasn't sure which of these I wanted to bring with me to the hospital. I went to bed on Friday to listen to them both in order to decide. Jeff played computers that night and came to bed around midnight. I wasn't feeling great.

At one in the morning, all of a sudden, my water broke. It began spurting. And the Braxton-Hicks contractions changed pretty quickly—they'd been around my abdomen but now felt much lower.

I didn't want to have to sit around the hospital, so I decided to wait a bit. I called my parents, who live out in Long Island. They were going to drive the hour and a half to come. And I called my friend Sharon who lives about fifteen minutes away; we had planned that she'd come over or I'd bring Howard to her—depending on the time of day. She came over with her husband.

I was flooding the bed. I woke Jeff up and said, "Get up, get up, get some towels!" So he got up and began to get ready. My bag had been packed—they'd told me to have it packed at thirty-two weeks. Just that day, I'd thrown in the camera. And I made sure I had my music.

My friends arrived at about 2:00 in the morning. Sharon asked if I had called the hospital. I said no. Jeff kept timing my contractions. They were lasting like ninety seconds and coming like every three minutes. But I didn't quite realize this—I thought I had all the time in the world.

I called the doctor. The one on call was the woman OB—she wasn't my primary doctor, but of all the others in the group, she's the next I would have wanted. She said, "You're having twins, right?" I said, "Yeah." She said, "I think you'd better come in now."

By the time we got there, it was about 3:30. The contractions were pretty heavy and strong, but I didn't want drugs. I had my music going. The doctor came in at 6:30 to check me—I was only two centimeters. She said, "It could be a few more hours."

I was having contractions that would not stop. One would start and the next one just came—wave on wave. No breaks. The music was so in time with them. Jeff was massaging my feet and couldn't believe how well I was dealing with the pain. Really it was horrible. I just closed my eyes—I had the music on, wanting it louder and louder.

At one point, I went to the bathroom, and I said to Jeff, "I feel like I have to push already." The doctor came in and checked me—I was at five. She said, "It still could be a few more hours."

It was the same thing that happened with Howard—I wasn't dilating, I wasn't dilating, but when I finally did, it went fast. I told Jeff, "I don't think I can last a few more hours; I think I need to have an epidural or I'm not going to have any energy at the end."

So we agreed. And an anesthesiologist questioner-person came up to get my history. But it turned out that there was some emergency in the hospital and no anesthesiologists were available. They kept saying, "You're going to get it, you're going to get it, just a few minutes more . . . ." But I never got my epidural.

At 7:00, I'm like, "Jeff, I have to push." At 7:30, I'm like, "Jeffrey, the babies are coming!" The doctor came in, and I was at nine centimeters. I asked, "Can I push now?" And she said, "No, we have to take you to the OR and it's not ready yet." So, I'm there dying and breathing and all this stuff. I was stretched across this long body pillow I'd brought.

Finally, at ten minutes after 8:00, they start bumping me down the hallway to OR. I'm dying 'cause I have to push these babies out!

I stayed on my birthing bed. They did a quick sonogram to see if Joshua was still transverse. He was. The contractions would not stop, and I needed to catch my breath. But I just kept pushing Emily out. At some point, I had a catheter cause my bladder was really full. I thought the doctor had her hand up me, but it was Emily. I was going to have an episiotomy to make her come out faster—the pain was so intense, but the doctor didn't have time to give me an injection—Emily was out. She was born about 8:32. I tore just a little.

Right after, they whisked her away—they didn't even put her on my belly. Then, they had to try to turn Joshua. I had no drugs, so it was very painful. I can't even describe my agony; I get chills now just thinking about it.

They were monitoring his heart. And suddenly it dropped—fifty, forty, thirty. I heard, "Okay, emergency C-section!" They whisked Jeff out of the room and tried to get me onto the operating table. There's blood all over the place. They took my glasses, and all I remember is that as they began to scrub my belly, the doctor yelled, "Just pour it on, pour it on!" They put a mask on me to administer general anesthesia. I didn't realize it until I woke up and found my throat sore from having a tube down it. I couldn't take the pain. I breathed into the mask—*just knock me out*, I thought. *I can't take the pain. I'm ready.*

I don't remember anything. I had a vaginal delivery and an emergency C-section. Later, Jeff told me that he just sat at the nurses' station with his heart in his mouth, waiting to hear what was going to happen. He couldn't even go see Emily. When he finally heard that everything was okay, he went and held Emily.

If they had administered the epidural like I had asked, I believe that Jeff would have been able to be there with me the whole time. But I had nothing, so they had to knock me out. With general anesthesia, the husband can't stay. I feel like I lost something because I can't remember much.

When I woke up, I asked, "Are the babies okay? Tell me about the babies! How much do they weigh?" Jeff was with me when I woke, and he made sure that I had my glasses right away. I was shivering. My throat was dry and hurt.

I kept putting ice in my mouth. I was still in pain. They had to cover me with five blankets. And they gave me Demerol, so I fell right back to sleep.

When I woke up, they wheeled me into my room. It must have been 12:00 or 1:00 in the afternoon. I was in terrible, terrible pain, but I didn't want to take anything—I just wanted to see my babies.

I was very groggy, still dopey from the drugs. These next few hours are foggy to me. I saw the babies, held them, and tried to nurse. I remember that my sister called from California. I was like, "I can't talk; I'll have to speak with you another time."

The babies were fine. Josh was about five-one, and Emily was about five-four. Later I was told that my uterus was kind of heart-shaped, with like a little protrusion down there—and probably while they were trying to turn Josh, they compressed the cord. He was getting hung up. Even with Howard, they had trouble turning him, and he was always on my right side.

I didn't want to stay in the hospital. I was crying and felt like I was still in labor. That night they took the catheter out and made me try to go to the bathroom. I was in a lot of pain. They didn't check my stitches where I had torn with Emily; they were only concerned with the C-section. After a general, you have to pass gas and all this stuff. They gave me gas pills. They wouldn't really give me anything to eat. I was like, "Could I get some yogurt, could I get some fruit, please?" I was only given one cup of chicken broth—I mean, I was starving!

I had my babies room in with me—it was instant love! I mean, you think that you love your husband and that you know love—but when you have children you can't believe that there's so much love in you. I was in a lot of pain, but this love was really a miraculous thing.

My parents were staying with Howard at our home. Jeff was coming back and forth. I saw Howard on Saturday night and my parents on Sunday. Monday afternoon, around 5:00, I came home. It was great to be there, but by Wednesday, I started having problems. I developed a breast infection. And when I came back to the doctors' to get checked, I had blisters on my C-section wound where they had taped me. It was horrible. They gave me some stuff for it. The doctor who delivered me said, "I've never, never seen anyone with a pain threshold like you have, and I've delivered a lot of babies. I don't know how you do it—you're so great."

My mom took off from work for a week and helped me. When I took Howard to school for the first time, she made me carry the babies with me.

I asked her, "Mom, couldn't you let them stay in the car with you?" I felt terrible that she made me do this, but I guess I needed to learn how. I had some postpartum depression when my hormones clicked in—crying at the drop of a pin. And I ended up having three breast infections during my first six weeks. I was doing too much. At one point, I even mowed the lawn. Also, it was hard and stressful having to nurse two babies.

Throughout all this, Jeff was very supportive, and that helped. He's a great husband and really a wonderful father. We made it through this difficult time. And overall, I feel that, as much as I could, I was able to take charge—of my pregnancy, my birth plan, my diet, and even at the hospital. I always read and read. Things don't always go as planned, but I believe that the more educated you are, the more power you have.

$$\mathcal{RO}$$

Millie and her husband, Jeff, live in Charlotte, North Carolina. Millie works as a hospice grief counselor, and Jeff is the owner of a family-run furniture store. Here, Millie recounts the birth of their triplets: Giles Taylor, Mary Margaret, and Abigail Jane—who were born by C-section.

All Beautiful and Healthy, Just Small

Jeff and I were married in 1990. I came off birth control pills after a year, and then we tried to get pregnant for two years after that. I suspected that I might have some trouble because in 1986 I found out that I had cervical cancer.

I was living in Chattanooga, Tennessee—it was after I graduated from college, and I just went in for a routine pap smear. They found out I had cervical cancer—they caught it very early. When they first told me and discussed all my options, the doctor said that they might need to do a partial hysterectomy. I became unglued because I knew I wanted children—I've wanted them all my life. I just said, "You're not going to give me a partial hysterectomy." And they didn't. First, I had cryosurgery where they freeze the cervix, but that didn't take it away. Then I had to have laser surgery, where they burn it. Afterwards, I had follow-up treatments of chemotherapy for three weeks.

It wasn't the intravenous kind; it was called a 5-FU suppository, and I used that twice a week at night.

It was really scary because, at the time, my mother was dying with lymphoma. And right before this happened to me, my father had just found out that he had prostate and bladder cancer. So, my whole family was in huge turmoil. When I called home from Chattanooga to tell my mom I had cervical cancer, she almost fell apart 'cause I'm the baby of five children. I was very attached to my mother, and when I became ill I wanted to go home. But I didn't. I stayed there and got wonderful care. But after the chemotherapy, during the healing process, my cervix closed off. So this illness led to my having problems getting pregnant.

When Jeff and I would try to get pregnant the typical way, my cervix was too closed to allow much sperm through. Usually, sperm enters the vagina, and some are killed off. Then, as they travel up the vagina, more are killed. By the time sperm reaches the cervix, there aren't many left, and, in my case, I began killing off more than most women would simply because the passage from my cervix into my uterus was barely open.

Anyway, after my illness I continued to live in Chattanooga and worked as a marketing rep. I was always traveling—either in a car or an airplane. For three years, it was great. I was young, and it was exciting. But I was growing quite weary of it by the end of 1988 when my mother became ill. I was really getting unhappy and decided to move home to Charlotte.

I'd been living here for about a month, and I went out to dinner and drinks with a friend of mine. I ran into Jeff, who was out with a couple of friends and whom I'd known since first grade. We're all from the same town and had a couple of glasses of wine and talked. About a week later, Jeff called me and asked me out. We started dating, and a year later we were married.

We were married in February of 1990. At first, we planned on a June wedding, but the doctor said that my mother wouldn't live until June, so we backed the wedding up from June to February 10. My mother lived for a year and a half after we were married. She had a very strong will to live and a huge amount of faith—she always said that she would die when the Lord was ready for her to die.

When she died, Jeff and I and other family members thought it wouldn't be such a good idea if I turned right around and got pregnant after my mother's death. So we waited. Mom died in July. About four months later, I went to work for the hospice where she'd received care. Soon, Jeff and I decided to try to become pregnant, and about six months later, after trying on a regular basis, I went to my gynecologist to get checked out. I know my body pretty well. He put me on prenatal vitamins, but after six months I knew that something was really wrong. At first, he gave me the old song and dance about my biological clock ticking, and that I should just give nature a bit more time . . . that I was just nervous. We tried for one more month, then I went into his office and demanded that he do something. I have a very strong personality and I can be quite abrasive sometimes—which is not a wonderful trait to have, but it gets me what I want sometimes. I told him, "If you don't get me some help, I'm going to find someone who will."

They did an endometrial biopsy, and it came back normal. They did a hysterosalpingogram, a procedure where they inject dye into the uterus, but that didn't work. Finally, I said, "Okay, I've had enough. Find me a doctor; I want a specialist." So he sent me to the Nalle Clinic in Charlotte.

I saw a man by the name of Dr. Daniel Whiteside, whom I adore. He ran some more tests and said, "You don't have any problems except you have this little teeny-tiny cervix. I'm going to make an instrument for you and put you on fertility drugs."

Basically, what he did was draw a roadmap of what I looked like on the inside from the top of my vagina into my uterus. Then they stuck a very thin wire up into my body and molded it. From this mold they constructed an instrument that was hollow and shaped to fit exactly inside me. All they did was put my husband's sperm in that tube and inject it straight into my uterus. At the same time, they had me on a very low dosage of Clomid. Ovulation was not my problem, but they say that your body tends to reject stuff, and a lot of times it won't release an egg, so they cause you to super-ovulate. We tried artificial insemination in April, and it didn't work this first time—that's not unusual. But in May, it finally worked.

I had been a nervous wreck the whole time, since we went to the clinic. Jeff was very anxious, too. He's a much calmer person than I am—I live on a lot of highs and lows, up and down a lot. Jeff is very even-keeled, and he had a very calming effect on me. He's a wonderful husband. This was a very try-ing experience for both of us.

I must say that we have a lot of faith in God. I'm not a pew-jumper, and I don't handle snakes, but we both prayed about becoming pregnant all the time. Jeff kept saying that he knew it was going to happen, and my sister kept telling me that as well. My doctor at the clinic was a Christian, and after they inseminated me in May, he said the funniest thing to me when he left that day. They had done all the processing, and I had to lie on the table for twenty minutes so that the sperm didn't run out. He looked at me and said, "Well, Millie, it's out of my hands now. Only one man can make the decision." And that's the day I got pregnant—May 15.

Around May 29 or 30, I had a blood test and found out that I was pregnant. My doctor called me at 7:00 that night from Charlotte. I'll never forget. Jeff had to work late cause they were having a sale. The doctor said, "Millie, this is Dan." And I said, "Dan who?" 'cause I always called him Dr. Whiteside. He said, "This is Dan Whiteside; you don't have to call me Dr. Whiteside." He's a huge jokester and said, "Well, I have the results of your pregnancy test." And I just sat there and said, "I'm not pregnant, am I?" He said, "Yeah, you are!" I started crying and he started crying. I told him I was cramping and felt like I was going to get my period, but he said, "Millie, you're not going to get your period, you're pregnant!"

I went in the next day to have the HCG level in my blood checked. It was high. I came in again two more times, and it was skyrocketing. Finally, they did an ultrasound and found that I was having twins. We were thrilled, and I said, "Oh thank you, Lord. You answered my prayers; now I won't have to go through this again." I'd always wanted three children, but Jeff had wanted two, and I had resigned myself that two would be fine.

About three weeks went by and they ran another blood test for something else, and my HCG level had climbed even higher. They decided to do another ultrasound. The day I went in for this ultrasound, Dr. Whiteside had been in a car wreck, and I had to see a guy named Dr. Wing, who is also very well known for being a wonderful fertility specialist. He's Chinese.

This early along, they do an internal ultrasound. My husband and sister were with me. They could see the screen, but I couldn't. And suddenly, they both had this really strange look on their faces. Dr. Wing pulled the instrument and looked at me with a kind of puzzled expression, "Dr. Whiteside say you have two babies?" And I said, "Yes, Sir." And he said, "Ms. Horne, you don't have two babies . . . ." Well, my heart just sank; I thought I'd lost one. Dr. Wing said, "Oh no, Ms. Horne, don't be sad. You have three babies!"

My husband turned sheet-white. My sister immediately burst into tears of joy. She thought it was the most wonderful thing she'd ever heard. I really am not quite sure what to tell you I felt at that moment. I was shocked. I was excited. I was scared to death.

One of my best friends had triplets nine months before I found out I was pregnant. She'd been on fertility drugs. She's a year younger than I am and lives in Greenville, South Carolina. And in February before I got pregnant in May, we buried one of her triplet daughters. I had sat there and watched my twenty-eight-year-old friend bury her nine-month-old child. So when I found out I was having triplets, that was the first thing that came to mind.

So, by the end of June I knew that I was having triplets. But I felt wonderful. I had great hair, fingernails, and my skin was radiant—I felt like a million dollars. At one point I threw up looking at some raw chicken breasts, but that was only one time.

I quit working at the end of August. Part of the reason I quit was that I worked with AIDS patients, who can carry the cytomegalovirus and tuberculosis. That can be detrimental to developing fetuses.

I was a high-risk pregnancy and went to the doctor every week. For the first trimester the Nalle Clinic kept me—I was three months pregnant when they recommended Dr. Philip Jones, a high-risk OB/GYN in Charlotte. I love this guy, and I tease my husband that if he ever leaves me, I'm going to run after Dr. Jones.

I chose to have the birth at Carolina Medical Center—it's a thirty-five minute drive. They have great equipment there. At twenty-four weeks I went on a home-monitoring system—which is a computer thing that you wrap about your middle and it measures your contractions. You wear it an hour. I had to do it twice a day from 6:00 to 7:00 in the morning and again from 5:00 to 6:00 in the afternoon. Then I called this number in Greenville, South Carolina—it's a nurse's office. You put the receiver of the phone down on your little computer, and it feeds the strip down to Greenville, where they read it. Then, they call back and say something like, "Okay Millie, you've had fifteen minutes of irritability," which meant that I was trying to have a contraction but never did. "And then you had six contractions." My doctor would give me a baseline like five, which means that I can't have more than five contractions in an hour. If I went over my baseline, I'd have to go to the hospital. But that only happened once, and they had me drink eight ounces of water, lie on my left side and repeat the strip. The contractions stopped, and I didn't have to go to the hospital.

I went to Carolina Medical Center, and we took Lamaze classes just 'cause I wanted to. I knew I wasn't going to deliver vaginally, but this was what my husband and I had wanted all of our lives. So we went and did it just like everybody else. They had a class on C-sections and that helped me. Then we took a class on infant CPR—that was wonderful. Then I had to be hospitalized twice during my pregnancy—once in August, when I was dehydrated, and once the day before my thirty-first birthday, when they thought that "Baby C," who was Abagail, had IUGR—intrauterine growth retardation. That time, they kept me flat on my back in the hospital and fed me 3,300 calories a day. I thought I would die! In a week's time, she gained a pound and was fine, but that was a very hellacious week.

That was around week twenty-nine or thirty. I had the babies at thirty-four weeks. I remember the Tuesday a couple of weeks before, I went to the doctor's. I was very large—measuring forty-six centimeters. In fact, they didn't really measure me anymore cause I'd get too depressed. The doctor teased me; he said, "Okay, two more weeks and we'll take them." Then at thirty-two weeks, he said, "Okay, at thirty-three weeks we'll think about it." At thirty-three weeks I went in and said, "I want them out! I'm scratching myself to death." I was itching cause my body was growing so fast. I had stretch marks all over the place. He told me I wasn't dilated and not ready.

The next morning I woke up ravenously hungry. I called my husband at work and told him that I wanted a McDonald's breakfast. He said, "Well, Millie, I can't leave now." And I said, "Well, too bad. You've got to get somebody that can bring me to McDonald's." Our best friend, Dickie, happened to walk into the store, and he agreed to come get me.

We got McDonald's and came back to watch Phil Donahue and curl up together on my king-size bed. It was time to do my strip. I did it and the lady called right back. She seemed wigged out and said, "Millie, you're having eighteen contractions. You need to lie on your left side and drink your water—don't talk, just lie there." I didn't feel any of this and wasn't worried. To be honest, I knew what was going to happen: I was going to drink the water, lie on my side, and be fine. But the second time, I had thirteen contractions, so she said, "You have to go to the hospital!" She called my doctor, and he called me. He told me not to worry and that they'd stop the contractions at the hospital. I got up and told Dickie to call Jeff for me and tell him to come home. I asked him to begin packing my bags—I was going to take a shower. Dickie started flipping out, "You're not going to take a shower now!" But I said, "Dickie, I'm not delivering these babies with dirty hair and unshaved legs. I'm taking a shower!" He made me crack the bathroom door.

Usually it takes Jeff fifteen minutes to get home from the store. That day he was home in five. So he and Dickie are going banana-bean. My sister is over too—I don't know who called her. They're all standing outside the bathroom door screaming at me to get out of the shower—I guess they thought my babies were going to fall out. Needless to say, they didn't; I took my nice long shower, got dressed, dried my hair, and we went over to the doctor's office.

By the time we got there, the contractions had stopped on their own. They did an ultrasound and they couldn't get the babies to move at all. That gave reason for concern. They made me drink Coca-Cola, thinking the sugar would hype them up—but it didn't. They wiggled me, mashed on me, shook noisy things at me—nothing worked.

They took me to Carolina Medical Center and did a level-three ultrasound, where they could see the chambers of the heart and the hemispheres of the brain. The babies were fine, but they were in distress simply because there was no room for them anymore. They came to us and asked everybody to leave except for Jeff and me, then told us that we had to make a decision. They could either (a) leave the babies in there for four or five more days, and we'd run the risk of possibly one of them being stillborn, or (b) take them out now and run the risk that they'd be small and possibly have problems. I said, "I don't want to be the one to make that decision. Why can't y'all decide 'cause I don't know."

They left the room to discuss it. I'd been having betamethazone shots, which help fetal lung development, and had just had the last of eleven shots the day before. The doctors decided to go ahead and take the babies that day, primarily because they felt really good about the lung development.

I had gotten to Carolina Medical Center at around 1:30, 2:00. At 4:00 they started prepping me for surgery. It was December 22 and snowing outside. They hooked me up to an IV and fed me several bags of fluids. My brother, my dad, my stepmom, brother-in-law, and minister were in the room. It was a peaceful Wednesday afternoon, and I was in a labor-delivery suite.

At about 5:00, a nurse came in and said "We're ready to take you into OR." She asked if I wanted a wheelchair, and I said, "No, I can walk." So I got up and walked to the operating room. And when we went into OR, it was really neat. I've had surgery on my knee before and my wisdom teeth taken out, but I'd never seen anything like this.

It was freezing cold. They made my husband wait outside for a few minutes. They took me on in and got me kind of prepped and gave me an epidural. After the epidural was started, they let him come in. He had the video camera with him. We were all talking. Dr. Jones came in and was telling me jokes. His assistant, a doctor about my age, also came in to help. The first time I met him and he tried to examine me, I said, "Don't look under there! You're as young as I am!"

They cut me open and were telling me where they were located. They said, "The first one is breech, and he's a boy!" I said, "That's Giles!" And then they said, "Millie, we're pulling on your right side, and this is a butt-breech little girl!" And I said, "That's Maggie!" Then they went in and said, "I'm on your left side now, and this girl is head-first!" I said, "That's Abby!" They held them all up for me to see. At first, they couldn't get Abby to cry and I got real frightened. But they sucked her out pretty good and she started crying. They were born at 5:25, 5:26, and 5:27. Giles weighed four pounds, nine ounces; Maggie weighed three pounds, three ounces; and Abby weighed three pounds, thirteen ounces. I just sobbed my heart out. Jeff was crying, and my doctor was crying.

They took the babies to neonatal intensive care—basically they just had to grow. I started pumping my breasts that night. By 8:30, they put me a wheelchair and took me up to see my children.

After five days, the babies were transferred to Gastonia Memorial Hospital so we wouldn't have to travel so far back and forth. Giles was at Gastonia Memorial for five days; Maggie came home next on January 17; and Abby came home January 29 or 30.

I had a full ten days to recuperate from my C-section. I didn't have a hard time. My epidural was wonderful, and I didn't have any problems. The only thing that was really painful was the next day—and this is really gross—but I'm going to be honest. They tell you that you have to try to go to the bathroom—have to have a BM or pass gas—and I thought I was going to die! Jeff never left the hospital except to run home one time to get clean clothes, and when he came back he found me in the bathroom, sitting on the potty, sobbing. And when I got in the shower to wash my hair, it hurt to raise my hands above my head. But, after two days, I felt fine.

I came home on a Sunday, Christmas Day. But we spent every minute we could up there in the nursery, and I nursed in front of God and everybody— I'd lost absolutely all modesty. After people poking and prodding on you for twelve or ten months even before you get pregnant, you start to not really care. I will never live through anything like that again. And, to be quite honest, I don't want any more children, but I'll miss being pregnant. At one point, I even considered becoming a surrogate. But I decided not to—also, I wouldn't want to carry triplets again. I can't carry triplets and be a mother to three two-year-olds.

For the first five months they were here, I didn't know who I was; I didn't know where I was. There were days I wasn't sure I'd had a shower. And I felt like a milk machine. We didn't get any sleep—it was very difficult. I think that the Lord cured me. I always thought that I'd want to be pregnant more than once, that I would want another child and would be sad because I'd never be pregnant again. The Lord cured me, though. Those first five months were so hard that I don't ever want an infant in my home again. I'm being honest—I wasn't crazy about the first five months. I felt real guilty for a while—and we'd spent thousands and thousands of dollars getting pregnant. The insurance didn't cover infertility work.

After those first months, though, things got easier. Jeff and I went through hell. First getting pregnant, then getting up all those nights. There has not been a night that he doesn't get up with me—even though he has to wake up early and go to a job every day. Even still. He changes diapers, he bathes them, and this week I'm going to the beach with five other women, and Jeff will keep the babies by himself. Sure, we fight about financial things—we were used to two incomes and now we've gone down to one. We've had to learn to live a very different life. But that's okay. We love our children dearly, and love where we are in life, right now.

AFTERWORD

Grey Brown

&

As women giving birth, we are connected through time and space to all other women who have ever given birth. Rather than being ordinary, it is a profound experience, worthy of respect. That the process of labor and delivery is universal to all mothers, everywhere and at all time, dignifies our experience even further.

The Boston Women's Health Book Collective, *Our Bodies, Our Selves*

THREE AND A HALF YEARS ago, on the fourth of July, my daughter, Jessie, sprang into our lives by an unplanned C-section. It was a fast-paced evening from the moment my water broke to the pelvic exam and my doctor's disturbing perplexity as she muttered, "I just can't find a baby; there's nothing in line for the birth canal." An ultrasound followed, revealing my daughter diagonally wedged between my left rib and my right hipbone, nearly sideways in my womb. My water had already broken; there was no hope to turn her. The surgeon on call admitted he was known for his radical vaginal deliveries of breech births, but my daughter's particular position placed her in danger. With no part of her in line for the birth canal, the chance of a serious problem increased dramatically.

We made a call to our doula, a woman adamant in her pursuit of natural birth, who had warned us against unnecessary cesareans. I put the surgeon on the phone to give her the details. When the surgeon handed the phone to me, all our doula could say was, "It's a bad situation. You get a C-section as fast as you can. I'm so sorry."

I felt myself falling. Only an hour ago, I had felt empowered with birth. The first few contractions had left me giddy with excitement. I had felt open, expansive, so ready for the experience. Now I slumped on a metal exam room stool and quietly accepted the hospital gown they gave me. I felt like an invalid, no longer in control. Time stopped as my husband and I accepted the inevitable. Then, suddenly, time lurched into fast-forward as the crew and the room flew into preparation for surgery. It seemed that every orifice in my body was being poked and prodded as I lay flat on my back with my arms outstretched for IVs and blood pressure gauges.

My daughter was "born" one short hour later, with a lusty cry and a full head of dark hair. They gave her a quick check, bundled her in a blanket, and placed her in my husband's arms. I vividly remember clutching at the empty air around my head, and crying, "Where's my baby, where's my baby?" I had so often imagined my warm, wet, naked baby resting on my belly and then the moment when I cradled her to my breast for the first time. Instead, there she was wailing, so beautiful, but her fine skin swaddled beyond contact, her tiny face nearly beyond my reach. I stretched out and stroked her brow and for one moment, she seemed to come to and be calmed. The team stitched me up quickly, and as soon as we were in the recovery room, my doctor helped me into a position for nursing and we began.

I remember pacing the floors of the maternity unit during the four days of hospitalization that followed my cesarean, as I had been instructed to walk to relieve complications from surgery and to regain my strength. With my daughter safe under the watchful gaze of my husband, I allowed myself to begin my initial investigation into the loss of our perfect birth. I inevitably found myself drawn to the birthing rooms with their inviting rockers and birthing tubs. I hovered at those thresholds, which I myself had been unable to cross. It was painful, even when I clung to the gratitude I felt for the health of my baby. My baby was here, beautiful, strong, and wise in that wonderful newborn way. I was well aware that in another day and age, she or I or perhaps both of us might have died due to the complications of her positioning. Still, without my attention absorbed by her wonder, I leaned against a wall and cried. I gazed in the birthing rooms as though by some miracle my first daughter's birth and all of our hope for that experience still lay ahead. But I could not fool myself. I knew that, at least in this birth, I would remain in the world of the uninitiated. I had just barely tasted the power of birth, the spirituality of it, in those first few contractions, and that was as close as I would come for now.

A month later, at our birthing class reunion, it turned out I was the only one in a class of ten who had had a cesarean. Some of the births had been completely natural by choice, others had involved unwanted intervention, and others the medication of the mothers' choice. As we shared our stories, I again felt the pang of being left out of what I valued as one of life's most heightened experiences. Each of these women had found their own way with labor; each had had their say. I alone, and I couldn't imagine a time when I had felt more alone, had not had the chance to labor and deliver a baby vaginally. I felt untethered, disconnected from a group of women I had felt so bound to during the hopeful and giddy final weeks of our pregnancies.

In an attempt to deal with my loss, I began to read and talk and read and talk. But the manuals and guidebooks glossed over the emotions that often rise in the wake of a cesarean. They discussed recovery from surgery and gave pep talks about gratitude for the health of the baby, but nothing seemed to help me cope. I began to wonder if I was not just being selfish and ungrateful; I began to feel guilty for my own feelings.

Talking to the women in my birthing class and to others who had delivered vaginally left me feeling ashamed and disheartened. I knew no one was judging me. Still, there was always an uncomfortable silence when I finished my story as my friends searched for something to say. How could they relate? How could I expect them to?

As time went on, I talked to more women who had had C-sections. These conversations helped somewhat, but still, all of the women I spoke with had had the opportunity to experience labor before their surgery. This difference still left me feeling isolated. For me, my water had broken, and within an hour I had found myself in the operating room. In some ways I envied the women who had at least labored for some period of time before their cesarean. I felt even they had some knowledge of the birthing process that I continued to feel so excluded from.

I realize there are many women who would throw up their hands and dismiss me as crazy for my need to experience a labor that they themselves view as only painful and frightening. And I have often been reminded that the birth itself is irrelevant when you consider the final outcome of having a healthy child. I will always be grateful for my child and for her safe entry into this world, but I still could not deny my sense of loss, one that has continued over the years, even as my child grows and her birth becomes only one moment in our years together.

When I was asked to write the afterword for this book, I felt not only honored and excited to do so but also grateful for the chance to continue my investigation into the experience of birth and in particular my own understanding of my C-section. Here was a collection of thirty-six birthing stories that reflected a wide array of experiences, from women who had chosen a birth with a high level of medical intervention to those who had opted for home births. I was always ready to read more about birth, and this was a storehouse of experience from those who knew it firsthand.

I was immediately drawn to the chapter including cesarean births, and as I am now six months pregnant with our second child, was encouraged by the titles mentioning V-BACs. As I pored over the collection, my head swimming with one birthing story after another, I kept circling back to Sue's account, "C-Section Again," reading her story over and over.

It was almost eerie as I noted the similarities between my daughter Jessie's birth and the birth of Sue's first daughter. Reading her account, I was comforted by what I felt to be a kindred spirit in the similarities of our stories. At the same time, it forced me to face a fear I had harbored in the back of my mind: what if my second child was also discovered to be riding high in the uterus, and what if she too failed to engage in the pelvis before my labor? I have always believed that given the chance to labor, I would succeed, that I had the capacity to find my own way with the pain and that for me, birth would be an empowering experience, a rite of passage. Perhaps my darkest fear in facing a V-BAC was not laboring and failing, not even a repeat C-section, but in, once again, not having the chance to attempt labor. Ironically, as I read Sue's story again and again, this fear slowly transformed into my own sense of resolution. I came to realize, with the help of Sue's experience, that if my second baby was also unable to engage, if there was indeed something in my physical structure that precluded vaginal birth, then all I could do was embrace that fact and be even more grateful for the option of surgery.

For three years I had heard a nagging voice in my head, one that questioned the rightness of my first daughter's cesarean birth. Had I given in too quickly to the medical specialists? Thanks to Sue's story, I confronted this voice again. I began perusing my birthing manuals searching for details of complications due to positioning. Finally, in a book that I trusted for its endorsement of natural births, I found a paragraph printed in boldface. This paragraph outlined the obstetrical emergency presented by something called a prolapsed cord. In this situation, the cord exits the birth canal before the baby and there is the chance the cord will be pinched closed by the pressure of contractions or by the baby itself. If the cord is cut off, the baby cannot receive oxygen and will have about two minutes to live. The manual then outlined the conditions most likely to lead to cord prolapse: a baby riding high in the uterus combined with a total loss of amniotic fluid—a description of my prelabor in a nutshell. I read and reread that paragraph as my daughter sat beside me eating her breakfast. I had never before realized just how much danger she had been in at the time of her birth. I showed my husband the passage and kept turning to it again and again throughout the day. In the week that followed, I began to view my C-section differently, that nagging voice in my head began to silence and I, at last, felt more at peace with the birth of my first daughter.

I feel most grateful to have had the opportunity to read *Real Birth* as I continue to work through this first birth experience and as I look forward to my second. In addition to helping me heal emotionally from the cesarean, these stories are also helping me to prepare for what I hope will be a successful, safe, and rewarding V-BAC. When I think back over the stories, there are many voices that I hope to recall during my upcoming birth, conjuring their words as my own private, little cheering section. I applauded Elly's spunk and forthright courage in "Fighting All the Way." Like me, Elly knew she wanted a V-BAC even before she was pregnant a second time. Undaunted by a physician dedicated to a high level of intervention and control, she succeeded in her V-BAC even against high odds. I have Elly's bravado tucked into my bag in case I find myself at similar odds against standard hospital procedure. And I will hold close to Jennifer's account in "V-BAC, I Did It," reliving her pride and excitement in those first few moments after birth.

For me personally and I also believe for its future readers, the power in *Real Birth* will rest in its open acceptance of a diverse range of birthing experiences. This collection could have been filled only with the most joyous, empowering tales of natural childbirth. Or the stories might have been confined to a genre that exclusively illustrates the impact of medical intervention and the ability of technology to save us from complications and emergencies. But if *Real Birth* had been polarized along the lines of one birthing philosophy or another, then I would never have found the story of Sue's birth and the voice that led me to a better understanding of my own experience and helped me find a context for that experience. In actuality, our birthing processes and our methods for coping with them are rarely confined to one philosophy or method. In the end, the birthing process leaves us and our babies open to possibility. Perhaps our best preparation is to be ready for anything. We make our birthing plans, take our Bradley or Lamaze classes, and while these steps help us visualize what is to come and give us a structure for that visualization, we will be lost if we cannot move beyond that imagined structure if the actual birthing process demands we regroup and reassess our strategies. Reading *Real Birth* has helped me broaden my preparation for my V-BAC and perhaps to realize that in many ways I will never be prepared, as I still will need to face this birth on its own terms as the singular experience it will be.

All my mother had ever said about my own birth was that I was also a breech baby and that the doctor had knocked her completely out. I was then turned inside my mother and delivered with forceps. At the time she was giving birth, most women had their babies in hospital with a high level of intervention. They were heavily medicated, and often these drugs left them without any sense of control or participation in the birth of their own child. As a result, many women either could not remember many details from their birthing experiences or fought hard to forget. Even my sister, who thirty-two years ago delivered her first child, gave only a brief, stereotypical account of her experience. Asked about this birth, she would only conjure up the image of her own fingernails digging into her palms as she waited for the drugs, and then she wagged her finger, admonishing me to "just wait and see."

Real Birth reminds me again and again how fortunate we are to live in a time that allows for greater choices in our births. I see this collection as a celebration for this empowerment through choice and as a chance to educate ourselves to be better prepared to make these choices. For me, the collection has also provided a chance to heal from one birth and in that healing be better prepared for the birth of my future. I thank Sue in particular for sharing her story and providing just the voice I needed to hear, I thank all thirty-six women for their openness, their honesty and their courage in sharing their stories, and I thank Robin Greene for bringing these stories to us all.

GLOSSARY

afterbirth: the placenta when it is expelled after the birth of the baby.

amniocentesis: a procedure in which a small amount of amniotic fluid is withdrawn from the amniotic sac in order to test for the baby's lung maturity or potential problems, the most common of which are Tay-Sachs disease and Down syndrome. The procedure is usually done when the mother is between weeks 16 and 18 of her pregnancy or when delivery is anticipated. The test carries a small amount of risk.

amniotic fluid: the liquid inside the amniotic sac.

amniotic sac: the envelope-like sac that encloses the developing baby and placenta.

Apgar (score): a number that measures a newborn baby's vital functions at one minute after birth and then again at five minutes after birth. Included in this score are the baby's heart-rate, respiration, muscle tone, color, and reflex response. Zero is the lowest score; ten is the highest.

arrhythmia: an irregularity of heartbeat.

bag of waters (*see* amniotic sac).

bed rest: sometimes prescribed by health care providers for patients who need to remain in bed for a time, usually to prevent the onset of early labor.

bilirubin: a substance made from broken-down red blood cells. Too much bilirubin in the newborn's blood will cause jaundice. A simple blood test can be done to check bilirubin levels.

birth canal: during childbirth, the vagina is often referred to as the birth canal.

birthing center: a place, either free-standing or located in a hospital, especially dedicated to providing care for women during birth. Some birthing centers also offer gynecological services.

birth monitor (*see* fetal monitors).

birthing plan: in order to take charge of their births, many women develop birthing plans which outline their wishes for their childbirth experience. Often, they will discuss their wishes and have their health care provider sign a written agreement.

birth positions: the positions that a woman assumes in order to labor and deliver her baby. Although traditionally in America women were advised to remain on their backs during both labor and delivery, they are now often encouraged to try other positions, especially more upright ones that use the force of gravity to help speed up labor and facilitate birth.

birthing room: a room, sometimes located in a hospital or birthing center, equipped for a more "home-like" birthing experience. Typically, a hospital bed is replaced by a regular bed and there is comfortable furniture for others wishing to be present at the birth.

birthing stool (or chair): one of a variety of types of stools and chairs designed to help accommodate women during labor and delivery.

birthing tub: some women prefer to give birth in a tub of water, using their own bathtubs or hot tubs (if the heat is lowered to body temperature) or a tub designed for this purpose. Some birthing centers will have these tubs available; others will allow women to rent them for home births.

bloody show: a discharge that occurs sometimes during the onset of labor when the mucus plug that blocks the cervix is expelled through the vagina along with a certain amount of blood.

Bradley Method: a method of natural childbirth, developed Dr. Robert Bradley, which stresses the use of relaxation, working with labor's contractions, and yielding to the process of labor rather than resisting it or finding an external focus to manage pain. Sometimes this method is referred to as "husband-coached childbirth" because it also stresses the role of the father, a labor coach, or partner during birth.

Braxton-Hicks contractions: contractions, sometimes called "false labor," that are usually felt by women later in their pregnancies. They are usually irregular and sometimes uncomfortable.

breech (or breech birth): when a baby is positioned so that he or she is born bottom first

bulging: term used when the amniotic sac doesn't break early in labor and instead bulges, so that it extends past the cervix.

C-section (cesarean section): the procedure whereby a baby is delivered through a surgical incision through the mother's abdominal wall and uterus.

catheter: a flexible rubber or plastic tube, used for many medical purposes. In childbirth procedures, catheters are sometimes inserted through the urethra into the bladder in order to withdraw urine.

centimeters: the unit used to measure the opening of the cervix during labor. A measurement of "one" denotes a closed cervix; a measurement of "ten" denotes a fully opened cervix and a readiness for delivery.

cesarean (short for cesarean section, *see* C-section).

cervix: the lower portion of the uterus, sometimes called the mouth of the womb, which is a neck-like structure. The cervix opens (dilates) and effaces (shortens) in order to allow a baby to pass through into the birth canal for a vaginal delivery.

circumcision: a medical procedure in which the foreskin of the penis is surgically removed. Although for years circumcision was performed routinely at most hospitals, the health care profession is now questioning the medical benefits of this procedure.

Clomid: a drug used to stimulate ovulation in women.

colostrum: a thin, yellow-tinted fluid secreted by the mammary glands after birth. This fluid contains important antibodies and minerals, and precedes the production of milk.

contractions: the tightening and relaxing of the uterine walls during labor. In labor, these contractions occur at regular intervals with increasing intensity and frequency; in "false labor" they tend to be irregular and don't increase in intensity or frequency.

cord (*see* umbilical cord).

Crohn's disease: an inflammatory disease of the colon and intestines characterized by abdominal pain, poor absorption of food, and other complications.

crowning: the appearance of the baby's head at the opening of the vagina during childbirth.

cryosurgery: a kind of surgery that involves the freezing of tissue or cells.

cytomegalovirus (CMV): a group of viruses that can cause various human diseases, for instance, hepatitis or jaundice in newborns, swollen glands, fever, fatigue, or brain damage.

D and C (dilation and curettage): a procedure in which the cervix is dilated and the lining of the uterus is scraped. This procedure is usually performed after a miscarriage occurs.

Demerol: a synthetic pain-killer that has similar effects and uses as morphine. Some common side effects of this drug include drowsiness, sweating, nausea, vomiting, and dry mouth.

dilation: the term used to describe the opening of the cervix during labor (*see* cervix).

diuretic: a drug that acts on the kidneys to produce urination. Some diuretics are natural, such as coffee and tea; some are medicines that must be prescribed by a physician.

doula: a lay person specially trained to assist in childbirth. This person is sometimes a staff member at a birthing center or hospital, or sometimes an independent doula can be hired to work with a pregnant woman during her childbirth experience.

Ebstein's anomaly: a very rare heart defect that can be found in newborn infants.

echocardiograms: visual images of the heart that are used for diagnostic purposes and made with ultrasound technology.

echoes (*short for* echocardiograms: *see* echocardiograms).

ECMO (extracorporeal membrane oxygenation): a specialized type of heart-lung bypass that assists babies who are having difficulty breathing due to poor absorption of oxygen caused by either lung or heart problems.

effacing: the process whereby the cervix gradually shortens by being incorporated into the lower uterus (like the stem on a balloon when you blow it up) to allow the baby to leave the womb and enter the birth canal.

epidural: a form of anesthetic that numbs the lower portion of the body during labor. It is administered with a needle or catheter placed into the spinal canal through which pain medication is delivered.

episiotomy: a cut made in the perineum that allows the vaginal opening to widen and thereby ease birth. This procedure also prevents vaginal tearing.

external monitor (*see* fetal monitors).

fallopian tubes: the tubes that connect the ovaries to the uterus and convey the egg and embryo to the uterus for implantation.

fetal monitor: one of two kinds of fetal monitors generally used by the medical profession. The external monitor is belt-like, attached across the pregnant woman's middle, and used to gauge the frequency of contractions and to monitor the baby's heartbeat pattern. The internal monitor is attached through a wire directly onto the unborn baby's head through the expectant mother's vagina and is used to check the unborn baby's heartbeat. Simultaneously a pressure monitor is inserted alongside the baby into the uterine cavity to document the frequency and intensity of the mother's contractions.

fetal positions: The baby sometimes changes position as it develops inside the mother's womb. Some of these positions are associated with an easier birthing experience for the mother and infant; others are associated with longer and more difficult birthing experiences. Sometimes it is possible for a midwife or physician to turn the baby so it settles in a more advantageous position.

fetoscope: an instrument placed on the expectant mother's abdomen that is used to detect the fetal heartbeat.

fetus: the term used for the developing baby.

forewaters: a fold in the bag of amniotic fluid that is occasionally closed off by the pressure of the baby's head on the cervix. This process sometimes causes amniotic fluid to leak.

genital herpes: a virus that infects the skin on and around the genitals. Genital herpes is contagious immediately before and during the period when lesions appear on the skin. If a pregnant woman has an active outbreak of herpes when she is in labor, she is advised not to deliver vaginally so as not to infect her newborn.

gestation: the period in which a developing baby remains in the uterus. Human gestation is usually thought to be 40 weeks, but a range of 37–42 weeks is considered normal.

gynecologist: a physician who has received specialized training in the care of women. Most gynecologists pair this specialty with training in obstetrics, the field of medicine devoted to the care of pregnant women.

heart tones: heartbeats.

Heplock (Heparin lock): a hollow needle with a little lock device that is inserted into a vein so as to allow an IV to be plugged into it. This device is sometimes put into a woman's hand or arm during early labor so that hospital personnel have access to a vein in the event that some kind of fluid or medicine is later needed.

hysterectomy: surgical removal of the uterus done through an incision in the abdominal wall or through the vagina.

hysterosalpingogram: usually used in the diagnosis of infertility, this is an X-ray of the uterus and fallopian tubes after dye has been used to outline the uterus and fallopian tubes.

internal monitor (*see* fetal monitors).

intubate: to insert a tube into a body opening, usually through the mouth or nose into the throat, so that oxygen or anesthetic gas can be administered.

IUGR (intrauterine growth retardation): a condition whereby the fetus is not growing as rapidly as expected.

IV (*short for* intravenous): a small catheter inserted into a vein so that medicine or fluids can be administered directly into the bloodstream.

jaundice: a condition whereby a baby's skin develops a yellowish tinge due to the presence of too much bilirubin in the baby's bloodstream.

labor: the process of childbirth. There are three stages of labor: During the first, the uterus contracts and the cervix dilates and effaces; during the second, the baby is expelled or delivered; and during the third, the afterbirth, or placenta, is delivered.

labor-delivery room: a room designed so that a woman can both labor and deliver her baby in one room.

LaLeche League: an international organization whose mission is to promote breast-feeding. There are local chapters that hold support meetings in cities throughout the United States.

Lamaze method of natural childbirth: a method of natural childbirth developed by Fredrick Lamaze, in which the laboring mother uses relaxation techniques and finds an external focal point to concentrate on so that she can control pain.

lysine: an amino acid, sold usually in health food stores, that is used to prevent an outbreak of genital herpes.

meconium: a newborn baby's first bowel movements. It is usually considered best when a newborn has its first bowel movement after birth, but sometimes this can occur in utero, and health care professionals sometimes see it as a red flag for possible complications.

midwife (midwives, *plural*): a person specially trained to help women during pregnancy and birth. Some midwives have medical degrees (such as certified nurse-midwives, who have RN degrees and sometimes graduate level medical degrees), and some are "lay" midwives, who have received less formal medical training and usually have no degrees. Midwives are not doctors and typically will only accept patients who expect to have normal pregnancies.

mucus plug: a "plug" of mucus that accumulates in the closed cervix during pregnancy and that helps protect the fetus from infection. (*See* bloody show.)

neonatologist: a physician who specializes in the treatment of the medical problems associated with newborns and developing babies.

nipple stimulation: the manual stimulation of a woman's nipples that triggers or enhances uterine contractions by releasing hormones.

Nubain: A semisynthetic narcotic used frequently during labor to help dull a woman's awareness of pain.

nurse-midwife: usually a certified nurse midwife (CNW) who has a minimum of a RN or registered nursing degree, and sometimes a graduate-level degree in midwifery or nursing. (*See* midwife.)

OB/GYN (obstetrician/gynecologist): a physician trained as both an obstetrician and a gynecologist.

OR (operating room): a room designed and equipped for surgical procedures.

ovarian cyst: a fluid-filled, closed sac embedded in a woman's ovaries.

ovaries: the two small organs of a woman's reproductive system that contain ova or eggs.

Pergonal: a fertility drug used to help women conceive.

perineal massage: a manual massage of the perineum that relaxes it to help facilitate delivery. Many people believe that massaging or stretching the perineum helps to prevent tearing or the need for an episiotomy during delivery.

perineal stretching: a manual stretching of the perineum that increases the elasticity of the perineum and helps facilitate delivery. (*See* perineal massage.)

perinatal care: care given to women and infants a few months prior to and after birth.

perineum: the area between a woman's vagina and anus.

Pitocin: the synthetic equivalent of oxytocin, the hormone responsible for contractions during labor. Pitocin is sometimes given to women through an IV drip in order to speed up labor.

PKU (phenylketonuria): this is an inherited disease that can be checked for at birth by a simple blood test. Although rare, this disease can result in mental retardation if left untreated.

placenta: the organ to which a developing fetus is connected by the umbilical cord. It is attached to the inner wall of the uterus and nourishes the fetus. (*See* afterbirth.)

placenta abruptio: a condition where the placenta detaches (usually partially) from the inner wall of the uterus.

placenta eating: the eating of the placenta or afterbirth. Many cultures around the world endorse the eating of the placenta as they believe that it contains hormones and nutrients beneficial to the new mother; also, it is sometimes considered symbolically meaningful. Because of the controversial nature of this practice, placenta eating is not a widespread or generally accepted custom in America; nonetheless, it is occasionally practiced, though infrequently discussed.

placenta previa: a condition during pregnancy when the placenta attaches to the uterus in such a way as to completely or partially block the cervix and thereby block the opening to the birth canal.

postpartum blues: sometimes described as like "bad PMS," this form of mild depression typically will affect a new mother within two days after birth. It is widespread and statistics indicate that it affects about 85 percent of new mothers. With support from family and friends, postpartum blues usually pass within a two-week period. (*See* postpartum depression.)

postpartum depression: a more serious form of after-birth depression that usually sets in about two to four weeks after delivery. Without proper attention this form of depression can debilitate the mother and her ability to care for her newborn. A more serious illness, postpartum psychosis, can sometimes develop from this depression; this illness is very severe and can cause some sufferers to abuse their babies or commit suicide or infanticide.

preeclampsia (*sometimes called* toxemia): a treatable condition during pregnancy whereby the mother suffers from hypertension, swelling, and protein in the urine; also, there is reduced blood flow and nourishment for the fetus.

premature atrial contractions: a heartbeat initiated early in the heartbeat sequence, resulting in a skipped beat.

premature labor: when an expectant mother begins to experience labor (has contractions and her cervix begins to dilate and efface) before the 37th week of her pregnancy.

prenatal: a term that refers to the period before birth.

preterm bleeding: vaginal bleeding that occurs before an expectant mother is "at term" or at the 37th week of her pregnancy.

preterm labor (*see* premature labor).

RN (registered nurse): a nurse who has completed a four-year nursing degree at an accredited college nursing program.

section (*see* cesarean section).

sonogram: an image made from ultrasound (soundwave) technology.

speculum: a device used to open up a woman's vagina so that she can be medically examined there.

222   Glossary

spina bifida: a birth defect of the spine, relatively uncommon, that can be tested for during pregnancy.

spinal anesthesia: anesthesia administered through a needle or catheter directly into the spinal canal.

stripping membranes: separating the amniotic membrane from the inner surface of the cervix. This can stimulate labor in first pregnancies.

subcorianic hemorrhage: bleeding beneath the bag of waters.

superovulation: a condition where a woman given fertility drugs will pass two, three, or more eggs down her fallopian tubes in order to enhance fertilization and pregnancy.

surrogate: a woman who carries a baby for another couple. Sometimes the biological father's sperm will be artificially inseminated into the surrogate mother; sometimes the biological mother's eggs are extracted, fertilized, and planted into the surrogate mother with often no biological relationship between the surrogate mother and the adopting parents.

Terbutaline: an antiasthmatic drug that is also prescribed to help control and stop contractions.

toxemia (*see* preeclampsia).

transverse: the term used to describe the position of the baby when it lies sideways across the uterus.

transition: a period during labor marked by frequent and intense contractions and a cervical dilation of six to nine centimeters. The period of transition comes directly before delivery.

trimester: one of the three periods of pregnancy, each lasting three months.

ultrasound: a procedure that uses high-frequency soundwaves in order to produce images or pictures of internal organs. This procedure is often used to check on fetal wellness and development. (*See* sonogram.)

umbilical cord (*or* cord): the cordlike structure that attaches the fetus to the placenta. Its function is to carry blood and oxygen to the fetus, and carry waste products away.

uterus (womb): the organ within a woman's body in which the fetus grows.

vaginal birth: any birth in which the infant is delivered through the mother's vagina.

V-BAC (vaginal birth after cesarean section): a vaginal birth that occurs after the mother has had an earlier baby delivered by C-section.

waters: amniotic fluid.

water breaking: the rupturing of the amniotic sac, usually at the onset of labor or during labor.

RESOURCES

Childbirth and Labor

Academy of Certified Childbirth Educators
2001 E. Prairie Circle, Suite 1
Olathe, KS 66062
800/444-8223
913/782-5116

American Academy of Husband-Coached
Childbirth (The Bradley Method of Natural Childbirth)
PO Box 5224
Sherman Oaks, CA 91413-5224
800/422-4784 (800-4-A-Birth)

American College of Nurse-Midwives
1522 K Street NW, Suite 1120
Washington, DC 20005
202/347-5445

American College of Obstetricians and
Gynecologists
409 12 Street NW
Washington, DC 20024
202/638-5577

Association of Labor Assistants and
Childbirth Educators (ALACE)
PO Box 382724
Cambridge, MA 02238
888/222-5223

CDC National AIDS Hotline
800/342-2437

Cesarean/Support Education and Concern
(C/SEC)
22 Forest Road
Framingham, MA 01701
508/877-8266

Doulas of North America (DONA)
1100 23rd Avenue E
Seattle, WA 98112
206/324-5440
FAX: 206/325-0472

Informed Homebirth and Parenting
PO Box 1733
Fair Oaks, CA 95628
916/961-6923

International Childbirth Education
Association (ICEA)
PO Box 20048
Minneapolis, MN 55420
612/854-8660

Lamaze International
1200 19th Street NW, Suite 300
Washington, DC 20036
800/368-4404

Lesbian Services Program of Whitman-
Walker Clinic
1407 S Street, NW
Washington, DC 20009
202/939-7875

March of Dimes Birth Defects Foundation
1275 Mamaroneck Avenue
White Plains, NY 10605
800/MODIMES

Midwives Alliance of North America
1411 North Main
Newton, KS 67114
888/923-6262

National Association for Parents and
Professionals for Safe Alternatives
in Childbirth (NAPSAC)
Route 1, Box 646
Marble Hill, MO 63764
573/238-2010

National Association of Childbearing
Centers
3123 Gottschall Road
Perkiomenville, PA 18074
215/234-8068

National Down Syndrome Society
666 Broadway
New York, NY 100012
800/221-4602
212/460-9330

Breast-feeding Support and Information

LaLeche League International, Inc.
Box 1209
9616 Minneapolis Avenue
Franklin Park, IL 60131
800/LA LECHE
708/455-7730

Grief and Loss

Bereavement Services RTS
1910 South Avenue
LaCrosse, WI 54601
800/362-9567, ext. 4747
608/791-4747

Pregnancy and Infant Loss Center
1421 E. Wayzata Boulevard
Suite 30
Wayzata, MN 55391
612/473-9372

Sudden Infant Death Syndrome (SIDS)
Alliance
10500 Little Patuxent Parkway
Columbia, MD 21044
800/638-SIDS

Multiple Births

Center for Study of Multiple Births
333 E. Superior St., Rm. 464
Chicago, IL 60611
312/266-9093

National Organization of Mothers of Twins
Clubs, Inc.
800/243-2276

Twins, the Magazine for Parents of
Multiples
5350 S. Roslyn Street, Suite 400
Englewood, CO 80111
800/328-3211

Twin Services
PO Box 10066
Berkeley, CA 94709
510/524-0863

FURTHER READING

American College of Obstetricians and Gynecologists. *Planning for Pregnancy, Birth, and Beyond*. Dutton, 1995.

American Medical Women's Association Staff. *The AMWA Guide to Pregnancy and Childbirth*. Dell, 1996.

Arms, S. *Immaculate Deception II: A Fresh Look at Childbirth*. Celestial Arts, 1994.

Benson, M. D. *Pregnancy Myths: An Obstetrician Demystifies Pregnancy from Conception to Birth*. Marlowe, 1998.

Bovo, M. J. *The Family Pregnancy: A Revolutionary Holistic and Medical Guide to Maternity*. Fine, 1994.

Bradley, R. A. *Husband-Coached Childbirth*, rev. ed. Bantam, 1996.

Brown, D. *Mama's Little Baby: The Black Woman's Guide to Pregnancy, Childbirth, and Baby's First Year*. Dutton, 1997.

Cohen, N. W., and L. J. Estner. *Silent Knife: Cesarean Prevention and Vaginal Birth after Cesarean*. Bergin and Garvey, 1983.

Cole, R. L. *The Gentle Greeting: An Obstetrician's Guide to Planning a Loving Pregnancy and Birth Experience*. Sourcebooks, 1998.

Curtis, G. *Your Pregnancy: Questions and Answers*. Fisher, 1995.

Dalton, K. *Depression after Childbirth: How to Recognize, Treat, and Prevent Postnatal Depression*. Oxford University Press, 1997.

Davis, E. *Heart and Hands: A Midwife's Guide to Pregnancy and Birth*, rev. ed. Celestial Arts, 1997.

De Crespigny, L., and R. Dredge. *Which Tests for Your Unborn Baby?* Oxford University Press, 1991.

Dick-Read, G. *Childbirth without Fear*, rev. ed. HarperCollins, 1984.

Evans, N. *The A to Z of Pregnancy and Childbirth: A Concise Encyclopedia*. Hunter House, 1994.

Flamm, B. *Birth after Cesarean: The Medical Facts*. Fireside, 1992.

Flatto, E. W. *Home Birth: Step-by-Step Instructions for Natural and Emergency Childbirth*. Plymouth Press, 1998.

Gaskin, I. M. *Spiritual Midwifery*, rev. ed. Book Publishing Co., 1990.

Gillespie, C. *Your Pregnancy Month by Month.* HarperCollins, 1998.

Goldberg, L. *Pregnancy to Parenthood: Your Personal Step-by-Step Journey through the Childbirth Experience.* Avery, 1998.

Griesemer, L. M. *Unassisted Homebirth: An Act of Love.* Terra, 1998.

Harper, B. *Gentle Birth Choices.* Inner Traditions International, 1994.

Herman, B., and S. Perry. *The Twelve-Month Pregnancy.* Lowell House, 1997.

Howell-White, S. *Birth Alternatives: How Women Select Childbirth Care.* Greenwood, 1999.

Hutcherson, H. *Having Your Baby: A Guide for African-American Women.* Ballantine, 1997.

Jackson, D. *With Child: Wisdom and Traditions for Pregnancy, Birth and Motherhood.* Chronicle, 1999.

Johnson, J., and M. Odent. *We Are All Water Babies.* Celestial Arts, 1995.

Johnson, R. V. *Mayo Clinic Complete Book of Pregnancy and Baby's First Year.* Morrow, 1994.

Jones, C. *Mind over Labor.* Viking Penguin, 1988.

Kalegis, M. M. *Giving Birth.* Sugarday, 1997.

Karmel, M. *Thank You, Dr. Lamaze.* HarperCollins, 1983.

Kaufman, E. *Vaginal Birth after Cesarean: The Smart Woman's Guide to VBAC.* Hunter House, 1996.

Keough, C. *New Baby Book.* Better Homes and Gardens, 1998.

Kitzinger, S. *The Complete Book of Pregnancy and Childbirth,* rev. ed. Knopf, 1997.

————. *Your Baby, Your Way: Making Pregnancy Decisions and Birth Plans.* Pantheon, 1987.

Kitzinger, S., and L. Nilsson. *Being Born.* Dorling Kindersley, 1989.

Kitzinger, S., and P. Simkin. *Episiotomy and the Second Stage of Labor,* 2d ed. Pennypress, 1986.

Klaus, M. H., J. Kennel, and P. H. Klaus. *Mothering the Mother: How a Doula Can Help You Have a Shorter, Easier, Healthier Birth.* Addison Wesley, 1985.

Kleuger-Bell, K. *Unspeakable Losses: Understanding the Experience of Pregnancy Loss, Miscarriage and Abortion.* Norton, 1998.

Korte, D., and R. Scaer. *A Good Birth, A Safe Birth,* rev. ed. Harvard Common, 1992.

LaLeche League International. *The Womanly Art of Breastfeeding,* rev. ed. NAO Dutton, 1997.

Lamaze, F. *Painless Childbirth.* Pocket Books, 1983.

Leboyer, F. *Birth without Violence: The Book that Revolutionized the Way We Bring Our Children into the World,* rev. ed. Inner Traditions, 1995.

Lichy, R. *The Waterbirth Handbook: The Gentle Art of Water-Birthing.* ACCESS Publishers Network, 1993.

Lindsey, J. W., and J. Brunelli. *Your Pregnancy and Newborn Journey: A Guide for Pregnant Teens.* Morning Glory, 1998.

Lee, S. *The NAPSAC Directory of Alternative Birth Services.* NAPSAC Reproductions, 1998.

Lees, C., K. Reynolds, and G. McCartan. *Pregnancy and Birth: Your Questions Answered.* D. K. Publishing, 1997.

Marti, J. *Holistic Pregnancy and Childbirth.* Wiley, 1999.

Matthews, A. M. *Excited, Exhausted, Expecting: The Emotional Life of Mothers-to-Be.* Berkeley Publishing Group, 1995.

McCartney, M. *The Midwife's Pregnancy and Childbirth Book: Having Your Baby Your Way.* Holt, 1995.

McCutcheon, S. *Natural Childbirth the Bradley Way.* Penguin, 1996.